C'MON THE

Wrexham FC Yearbook 2007-08

ICH DIEN

1873 1873

WREXHAM F.C.

Edited by Peter Jones and Richard Owen

Designed by Richard Owen Statistics by Peter Jones
Photographs by the Evening Leader

We would like to thank the following people for their contributions to this project:

Kevin Baugh, Bruce Clapton, Steve Cooper, Mark Currie, Dave Davies, Gareth M.Davies, Sandra Edwards, Les Evans, Steve Evans, Arfon Griffiths MBE, David Griffiths, Rob Griffiths, John Humphries, Barry Jones, Bryn Jones, Gavin Jones, Lindsay Jones, Colm O'Callaghan, Geraint Parry, Dave Preece, Gary Pritchard, Richard Purton, Paul Sleeman, Mark Williams, Richard Williams, Martin Wright & Rob Wynne.

Wrexham Supporters Trust

Produced by Wrexham Supporters' Trust Sponsored by the Evening Leader

Subscribers

A warm thank you goes out to the following pre-subscribers without whom this book would never have been possible.

Frank Czulowski	Wrexham	Roger Lloyd	Worthing
The Twigg Family	Chirk	Bruce & Ben Clapton	Cefn-Y-Bedd
Alan Constantine,	Wrecsam	Richard Evans	Derby
Howard Austin	Acrefair	Rae Benjamin	Bradford, Canada
Owen Preece	Wrexham	Mark Williams	Wrexham
Darren Morris	Morda	Clare Chiddicks	Winsford
Steve Edwards	Nantwich	David Preece	Bolton
Jim & Fran	Ynys Mon Reds	Kevin Salisbury	Chatham, Kent
Phil 'Flinty' Formstone	Gresford	Steven David Hughes	Oswestry
Lindsey Charles	Rhosllanerchrugog	Stephen Parrott	London
Ian Beckett	Malpas	Ray Williams & Family	Guilsfield, Powys
Mike Garrigan	Rhos Reds	Wrexham County Borough Council Credit Union Limited	
Nigel Evans	Malpas	Gareth Ellis	Bromborough
Vic Ellson	Neston	Dyfan Wyn Owen	Trefynwy
Simon & Owain Roberts	Welshpool	Peter Williams	Wirral
Darrel Thorold	Hope	Philip L. Thomas	Wrexham
Paul Davies	Wrexham	Stuart P. Thomas	Wrexham
Andy Kelsall	Johnstown	Gary Coombes	St.Martin's
Morgan Owain Denby	Hope	Martin & Denise Jones	Llay
Richard Purton	Wrexham	Terry Purton	Wrexham
Andrew Maggs & Naomi Davies	Brynteg	Robert & Haydn Taylor	Wrexham
Robert Geraint Lloyd	Borras Park Reds	Paul Matthias	Gwersyllt
Robert Gareth Lloyd	Borras Park Reds	Mervyn H. Davies	Glossop, Derbyshire
Libby Lloyd	Borras Park Reds	Phil Egan	Warrington
Aled Huw Lloyd	Borras Park Reds	Tony Graham	Wrexham
Eifion Pugh	Higher Kinnerton	Simon Summers	Whitchurch
David Roberts	Birmingham	Rob Wynne	Rhos Reds
Gwenda Miller	Wrexham	Rhos & District Reds	
Nathan Davies	Highland Reds	Louise Roberts	Wrexham
Euryn Davies	Wrexham	Adrian Roberts	London
Neil Thomas	Wrexham	Keith 'Fuzzy' Jones	Wrexham
Phil Jones	Southampton Reds	Ivor Hewitt	Buckley
Alan Hinton	Ellesmere	Mark Drury	Dudleston Heath
Graham Hinton	Ellesmere	Dave Roberts	Manchester
Fiona Pountney	Wrexham	Mark Harber	Wrexham
Kathryn & Iwan Jones	Rugby	Marc Jones	Wrecsam
Brian Davies	Shrewsbury	Ian Parry	Leicester
Hywel, Lucy & Glyn Roberts	Edenbridge, Kent	Patrick J. Davies	Oswestry
Lorcan Adrian	Whitchurch	Mark Griffiths	Wrexham
Glyn Davies	Wrexham	Dyfan Jones	Bwlchgwyn
Rob Davies	Mold	Tracie Griffiths	Wrexham
Rob Clark	Wrexham Supporters' Association	Wrexham Supporters' Association	
John Humphreys	Shropshire Reds	Peter Beatty	Wrexham
Rob Griffiths	Northwich	Andrew "Biscuit" Davies	Gwersyllt
Steve Robinson	Acrefair	Deuddegfed Dyn - Twelfth Man	
William, James and Alistair Coleman	Cambridge	Griff	Cefn Mawr Reds
Ian and Tomos Roberts	Kings of the Kop!	Tom and Heledd Stanford	Wrecsam
George Stewart	Gresford Dragons	Tom Matischock	Gresford Dragons
Vince Whelan	Gresford Dragons	Dyfan Jones	Wrexham
Paul Williams	Gresford Dragons	Gavin Pugh	Porthmadog
Michael Collins	Kinnerton		

First published in Great Britain in 2007 by:
Wrexham Football Supporters' Society Limited, PO Box 2200, Wrexham, LL12 9WG.

Printed and bound in Great Britain in 2007 by:
Blueprint, 47 Carlton Crescent, Gwaun Miskin, Pontypridd, CF38 2RS.

Copyright 2007 Wrexham Football Supporters' Society Limited.

ISBN: 978-0-9554179-1-7

Contents

Back row L-R: Conal Murtagh, Andy Fleming, Neil Taylor, Anthony Williams, Michael Jones, Gareth Evans, Levi Mackin, Jamie Reed.

Third row L-R: Andy OBoyle (Head of Sports Science), Brian Prandle (Chief Scout), Danny Williams, Mike Williams, Richard Hope, Shaun Pejic, Chris Llewellyn, Steve Evans, Josh Johnson, Matt Done, Mark Morris (Goalkeeping Coach), Mel Pejic (Physio).

Second row L-R: Michael Proctor, Juan Ugarte, Neil Roberts, Brian Carey (Manager), Steve Weaver (First Team coach), Marc Williams, Mark Jones, Effion Williams.

Front row L-R: Ryan Valentine, Matt Crowell, Mike Carvill, Wes Baines, Simon Spender, Alex Darlington.

Brian Carey

Welcome along to a new season and the 2007/08 edition of the Wrexham Supporters' Trust Wrexham FC Yearbook. Like last year's production, this has been a real labour of love for all those involved in producing it and congratulations to them on such a fine effort. This is my first full season as manager of the club and following a baptism of fire, I had the chance to take a step back over the summer months and assess the direction I see will move this team forward.

You will have seen and heard me quoted after the Boston United match, saying that I wanted our survival to be the springboard to future success and that we must not allow the club to slip into such dire circumstances again - well, three months later and I feel no different as we prepare for the coming campaign.

There have been a few departures from the playing staff, but I really felt that we needed to bring in more new faces to supplement what was already a decent squad. Competition for places has been a primary concern and although we will alter things as we go along, I hope that is just what we have achieved during the close season. With the introduction of four more senior players, two of whom helped us in the final weeks of last year, there has been a major boost in lifting the level of experience available to the squad.

The younger lads will be able to look up to these players and draw on their experiences with other teams. As they have all arrived from clubs who have done well in recent years - they therefore have that winning mentality about them, which is just what I want to instil throughout the squad. While I don't want to dwell on the past, the knowledge gained from surviving and turning around our fortunes last year, will, I hope, give the players who came through it, an inner strength and determination not to see things repeated.

The future is now with us and after a very productive pre-season, and we have to thank both Liverpool and Blackburn Rovers for agreeing to travel to the Racecourse for games, as well as Seamus Heath and Andy Hall for working so hard on our tour to Northern Ireland, we can now get down to the real work of improving the club's performances on the pitch. The backroom staff who are working with me, have not stopped over the summer, and we have done our best to make sure that the team is as prepared as we can make it for the coming nine months.

I know that expectations are high and we will do our best to fulfil those hopes, but it will not always be easy and your continued support will mean a great deal to us. The backing we have also received from our sponsors has been vital, with Leasedirect in particular stepping forward and signing up for an extended contract when other companies might have been tempted to shy away.

Finally, I must give thanks to everyone who rallied round the club during its hour of need. The numbers who passed through the turnstiles over the last two months to offer their support was staggering and showed just what this team means to the people of North Wales and further a field. The increase in Season Ticket sales for this year has backed up that support and means we have a solid base on which to take the club on.

I often think back to the reception that we got at the end of the Notts County game at Easter, after conceding that last minute own goal to slip to yet another defeat, but the fans stayed with us and I certainly drew strength from the belief that you showed in us. Let's all now work towards lifting this team once again and seeing where we can take it in the season ahead.

Who's who ?

CONTACT
Wrexham Football Club (2006) Ltd
The Racecourse Ground, Wrexham, LL11 2AN

TELEPHONE
Match & Ticket sales 01978 262129 Ext 1
Catering, Hospitality & Functions 01978
262129 Club Shop 01978 262129 Ext 2
Commercial & Sponsorship Department 01978
262129 Ext 3 Football in the Community 01978
358545 Collier's Park Training Ground 01978
853223

WEBSITE AND EMAIL
Website www.wrexhamafc.premiumtv.co.uk
Enquiries info@wrexhamfc.tv
Sponsorship sponsorship@wrexhamfc.tv
Racecourse Lotto lotto@wrexhamfc.tv

CLUB OFFICIALS
Chairman Neville Dickens, Vice Chairman Geoff
Moss, Chief Executive Anthony Fairclough,
President Arfon Griffiths MBE, Vice-Presidents
Dave Bennett, Malcolm K. Davies, Dave Griffiths,
John Marek & Wrexham Supporters' Trust.

BEHIND THE TEAM
Manager Brian Carey, First Team Coach Steve
Weaver, Coach Roy Evans, Head
Physiotherapist Mel Pejic, Head of Sports
Science Andy O'Boyle, Reserve Team Manager
Joey Jones, Reserve Team Coach George
McGowan, Reserve Team Physiotherapist Mike
Williams, Goalkeeping Coach Mark Morris, Chief
Scout Brian Prandle, Chief Scout (9-16yrs) John
Rearden, Centre of Excellence Head of Youth
Steve Cooper, Centre of Excellence Manager
Andy Davies, Centre of Excellence Recruitment
Officer Stuart Webber, Centre of Excellence
Physiotherapist Richie Buchanan Centre of
Excellence Physiotherapist Ritson Lloyd,
Centre of Excellence Physiotherapist Jen
Taylor Club Doctors Malcolm Greensmith, Hywel
Hughes, Keith Park, Groundsman Johnny
Edwards

THE ADMINISTRATION STAFF
Club Secretary Geraint Parry, Commercial
Manager Phill Sadler, Safety Officer Colin
Edwards, Function & Catering Manager Graham
Rushton, Accounts Manager John Coats,
Accounts Assistant, Sue Edwards, Ticket
Sales Gill Dugan, Administration Marjorie Pike,
Centre of Excellence Administrator Tricia
Deary-Furber, Club Shop Sales Dave McGuire

Trust President Arfon Griffiths' message
Llythyr Arlywydd grwp ymddiried, Arfon Griffiths

Following the success of last year's yearbook, I am pleased that the Trust is continuing to produce an annual that is a must for all Wrexham fans. A lot of work has gone into this to make it the fascinating read that it is, and once again I wish them every success with it.

Since the last yearbook, a lot has happened. The club have come out of administration thanks to the hard work put in by Neville Dickens and Geoff Moss, but even they didn't foresee or plan for the season that we had to endure. Following the uncertainty that we have all had to suffer the previous three years, everyone was

Yn dilyn llwyddiant blwyddiadur llynedd, dwi'n hapus fod y grwp ymddiried cefnogwyr yn parhau yn flynyddol sydd yn angenrheidiol i gefnogwyr Wrecsam. Cymerodd llawer o ymdrech i wnued y llyfr yn ddarlleniad mor gyffrous, ac unwaith eto hofwn ddymuno pob llwyddiant efo'r llyfr.

Ers y blwyddiadur diwethaf, mae llawer wedi newid. Mae'r clwb wedi dod allan o weinyddiaeth diolch i waith caled gan Neville Dickens a Geoff Moss, ond ni ddychmygodd na chynlluniodd un or ddau yna hyd yn oed gweddill y fath dymor/season a wynebodd y clwb. Yn dilyn anghysurdeb y tair blwyddyn

expecting a rosy future overnight when we came out of administration, but it doesn't work like that, and we all have to be patient has the rebuilding programme, both on and off the pitch, takes shape.

I know one thing; I don't know if my heart would bear another season on the field like we have just had! It certainly made everyone sit up and realise what being a Football League club means, but what was good to see were how the crowds came flooding back to give their support when it seemed we were on our way out. I just hope those same people come back again this season and the team give them the right reasons to cheer; that's being a promotion winning side.

Off the field, I have witnessed the Trust work hard to continue in its aims of buying equity in the Football Club, and to gain Board Representation; I do feel that both of these will happen, but when? Well that remains to be seen, but once the plans for the development are out of the way, we can all focus on taking Wrexham forward and upwards.

It's very noticeable the changes, and improvements that have been made in and around the ground over the summer. Chief Executive Anthony Fairclough is doing an excellent job behind the scenes in bringing further investment into the club, whilst also improving the facilities that have been neglected over the past few years.

Following the Trust's AGM, it was good to see that they will also be able to help out with projects surrounding the club; and helping the club itself. Encouraging more people to come along on match day is imperative, especially the younger element, they are the fans of the future, and it's great to see the Junior Dragons working hard to encourage young fans to

diwethaf lle dioddefwyd yr holl bobl a oedd yn rhan or clwb, roedd pawb yn disgwyl dyfodol gwell ac effeithiol dros nos ond dydy pethau ddim yn gweithio felly, ac rydym i gyd yn gorfod bod yn amyneddgar drwy gydol y broses ailsefydlu, ar y cae ac oddiar y cae.

Dwi'n ymwybodol o un peth yn bendant, dydw i ddim yn gwybod os gall fy nghalon dioddef gweld tymor/season fel yr un diwethaf eto! Achosodd y tymor ar bawb gan wneud iddynt sylweddoli pwysigrwydd bod yn rhan or cynghrair pel droed, ond beth oedd yn werth gweld oedd cynydd y gynulleidfa wrth ir clwb neshau tuag at y diwedd. Dwi'n gobeithio gallai'r un gynulleidfa ddychwelyd y tymor yma a gall y chwaraewyr rhoi rheswm gwahanol iddynt gysuro, sef bod yn dim llwyddianus.

Oddiar y cae rwyf wedi bod yn dyst ar y grwp ymddiried yn gweithion galed iawn yn enwedig gan barhau i brynnu ecwiti yn y clwb pel droed, ac i gael cynrychioliad y bwrdd. Credaf fod y ddau beth yma am ddigwydd, pryd? Wel mae hynny'n gwestiwn arall ond unwaith mae planiau datblygu allan or ffordd gallem i gyd ganolbwyntio ar mynd a Wrecsam ymlaen ac i fyny.

Mae'r newidiadau sydd wedi digwydd dros yr Haf y tu allan ac y tu fewn ir clwb yn weladwy iawn. Mae Pennaf gweithredol y clwb sef Anthony Fairclough yn gwneud sywdd gwych mewn dod a buddsoddiadwyr pellaf ir clwb, tra fod ef hefyd yn gwella cyfleusterau'r clwb.

Yn dilyn cyfarfod cyffredinol blynyddol y grwp ymddiried, roedd yn dda gweld fod y grwp yn gallu helpu allan efo prosiectau sy'n amgylchu'r clwb a'r clwb ei hun hefyd. Mae cefnogi mwy o bobl i ymuno yn y gynilleidfa ar dyddiadau'r gemau yn holl bwysig, yn enwedig y cefnogwyr ifanc

come along to games.

The Trust and the other supporters groups have a big part to play in encouraging fans of all ages to come along and support the club, and this is now the time for everyone to be pulling in the same direction.

It's good to see everyone in and around the club are now all working together to take 'Wrexham Higher'. I recently visited the Collier's Park training ground, and what a fantastic set-up there is there. Right up from the under 8's to the first team squad, the whole structure of the club is geared to bring success for Brian Carey at 3pm on a Saturday afternoon. If you have the chance, take some time out and visit the training ground, it really is a wonderful set up.

I really am looking forward to the coming season with confidence. Brian Carey has built a squad that has strength in all positions, and at the very least I would hope we achieve a play-off position, but as last season proved; 'football is a funny old game!' Enjoy the season.

Arfon Griffiths
MBE

sef dyfodol y cefnogwyr. Mae'n dda gweld y rhai profiadol yn perswadio'r ifanc gymeryd rhan.

Mae'r grwp ymdduried cefnogwyr a grwpiau eraill sydd efo cysylltiad efor clwb efo rol enfawr i chwarae mewn cael mwy o gefnogwyr i ddod i gemau a cefnogir clwb.

Mae'n brofiad cael gweld pawb sydd a chysylltiad efor clwb yn gweithio efo'i gilydd i symud y clwb ymlaen. Yn ddiweddar ymwelais efo Collier's Park i weld gosodiad anhygoel yno, or tim dan 8 yr holl ffordd ir tim gyntaf, mae'r clwb i gyd wed'i sefydlu er mwyn helpu'r rheolwr Brian Carey erbyn 3pm Dydd Sadwrn. Os oes gennych chi amser rhydd dwi'n cymeradwyo ymweld ar lleoliad, mae'n werth chweil.

Dwi'n edrych ymlaen tuag at y tymor nesaf efo hyder. Mae Brian Carey wedi sefydlu tim efo cryfderau ym mhob safle ar y cae, ac rwyf yn gobeithio beth bynnag digwyddai cawn lwyddiant tuag at big y cynghair, ond fel profodd tymor diwethaf mae pel droed yn gem bach wirion!! Mwynhewch y tymor.

Arfon Griffiths
MBE

Cymru ar y Cae Ras

Roedd penderfyniad Cymdeithas Bêl-droed Cymru i chwarae'r gemau cyfeillgar diweddar yn erbyn Liechtenstein a Seland Newydd ar Y Cae Ras, Wrecsam yn llwyddiant ysgubol.

Mae'n rhaid i mi gyfaddef fy mod i wedi poeni yn wreiddiol na fyddai cefnogwyr pêl-droed y gogledd yn troi allan ar gyfer dwy gêm ddibwys yn erbyn timau sydd yn isel fannau rhestr detholion Fifa.
Ond nid oedd angen i mi boeni gan fod dros wyth mil o gefnogwyr wedi ymweld â'r Cae Ras ar gyfer y gêm yn erbyn Liechtenstein a dros bum mil ar gyfer ymweliad y Kiwis.

Yn eu mysg roedd yn galonogol iawn gweld cannoedd, os nad miloedd, o blant ysgol yn heidio draw i'r Cae Ras yn eu crysau, sgarffiau a chapiau Cymru.
Y plant yma yw dyfodol pêl-droed Cymru ac roedd yn hyfryd gweld llu o fysys wedi eu parcio tu allan i'r Cae Ras; roedd fel rhestr o drefi a phentrefi'r gogledd wrth i ni gerdded heibio bysys o'r Bala, o Borthmadog, o Lanberis a Llanrhaeadr ac o glybiau pêl-droed Y Felinheli, Y Fali, Llandudno a Llangefni, ac roedd gwrando ar leisiau ifanc llawn cynnwrf yn ddigon i godi calon hyd yn oed y cefnogwr mwyaf sinigaidd.

Mae cyrraedd maes pêl-droed a gweld y llifoleuadau'n goleuo'r strydoedd cyfagos yn un o fy hoff olygfeydd ac mae'n gyrru ias oer i lawr fy nghefn pob tro rwy'n ei brofi. Mae'n amlwg bod y plant ifanc oedd yn cerdded tuag at Y Cae Ras y noson honno'n profi'r un wefr â mi gan i'r sgwr-sio byrlymus ddod yn fwy amlwg wrth i ni ddechrau clywed oglau'r byrgyrs a ch?n poeth yn yr awyr ac wrth i ni glywed lleisi-au'r gwerthwyr sgarffiau, capiau a batho-dynnau yn ceisio'n hannog i brynu eu nwyddau.

Mae'n annhebygol bod nifer fawr o'r plant fu ar Y Cae Ras yn cael cyfle i deithio i Gaerdydd ar gyfer gemau rhyngwladol yn aml a phrofi'r awyrgylch arbennig yma ac o'r herwydd, mae'n bwysig iawn fod Cymdeithas Bêl-droed Cymru yn sylweddoli bod dyletswydd arnynt i genhadu.

Gan fod gemau Cymru yn cael eu darlledu ar deledu lloeren, mae'n bosib fod nifer helaeth o'r plant fu yn Wrecsam yn fwy tebygol o weld gêm ryngwladol Lloegr na Chymru ac os nad ydym am weld cenhedlaeth gyfan o blant sydd yn gwybod mwy am Steven Gerrard neu Rio Ferdinand na Ryan Giggs a Danny Gabbidon mae angen i'r FAW gynnal mwy o gemau ar Y Cae Ras.

Wrth gydio yn ei raglen, ei fyrgyr a'i het a'i sgarff newydd roedd wyneb Ifan, y mab, yn bictiwr. Roedd wedi cynhyrfu'n lân â'r syniad o weld Ryan Giggs a Craig Bellamy yn y cnawd, yn edrych ymlaen yn arw at gael canu'r anthem genedlaethol ac yn wir obeithio gallu dathlu gôl neu ddwy, ac nid fo oedd yr unig un.

Ac ni siomwyd y cefnogwyr yn y gêm yn erbyn Liechtenstein wrth i Gymru sicrhau buddugoliaeth gyfforddus o 4-0 â dwy gôl odidog gan Jason Koumas ac un yr un gan Craig Bellamy a Chris Llewellyn.

Roedd nifer wedi beirniadu'r penderfyniad gan y rheolwr, John Toshack, i drefnu gêm yn erbyn gwrthwynebwyr mor dila, ond roedd Toshack yn mynnu byddai'n baratoad da ar gyfer y gêm â San Marino yng ngemau rhagbrofol Ewro 2008. Mae'n rhaid cyfaddef bod y gêm wedi bod yn well paratoad na'r hyn drefnodd cyn rheolwr Cymru, Bobby Gould, cyn i Gymru herio San Marino yn ôl ym 1996 - bryd hynny collodd Cymru 0-1 yn erbyn Leyton Orient!

Ac er mai gêm gyfartal 2-2 a gafwyd yn erbyn yr All Whites o Seland Newydd, roedd llond bws o chwaraewyr ifanc o'r Fali wrth eu boddau o fod wedi cael gwylio eu harwyr yn y cnawd.

Roedd nifer o'r plant yn gweld gêm bêl-droed byw am y tro cyntaf erioed ac mae nifer ohonyn nhw wedi bod yn holi pa bryd y byddwn ni'n cael mynd yn ôl i'r Cae Ras i wylio gêm arall.
Felly mae'r gemau cyfeillgar yma yn rhoi cyfle i John Toshack weld sut byddai ambell i chwaraewr yn ymdopi ar y lefel rhyngwladol. Cafodd amddiffynnwr canol Wrecsam, Steve Evans, a chwaraewr canol cae Wrecsam, Mark Jones, ennill eu capiau cyntaf dros Gymru yn erbyn Liechtenstein a chafodd Wayne Hennessey a Chris Gunter yr un fraint yn erbyn Seland Newydd.

Ond yn fwy na dim byd arall, roedd yn gyfle i Gymdeithas Bêl-droed Cymru genhadu yng ngogledd Cymru wrth ddiddanu torf nid ansylweddol o gefnogwyr Cymru'r dyfodol.

Gary Pritchard - BBC Radio Cymru

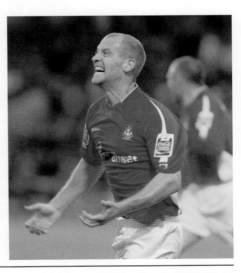

Section 2:
Season Preview 2007/08

Season Preview

Last season League Two was dominated by the sides that were relegated from League One.

Walsall, Hartlepool, Swindon and the MK Dons finished in that order with the Dons missing out on the final automatic play off spot on goal difference from Swindon.

The gulf between the sides last season was so big that MK Dons finished ten points clear of fifth placed Lincoln but lost out in the play off semi-final to Shrewsbury with sixth placed Bristol Rovers seeing off Lincoln to set up the first play off final at the new Wembley Stadium. Bristol Rovers came back from a goal down to defeat Shrewsbury 3-1 in the final to secure the final spot in League One.

At the other end of the table, Torquay were cut thirteen points adrift of safety and Boston joined them in non league football following their defeat to us on the final day of the season.

Ground
Fraser Eagle Stadium

Manager
John Coleman

Last Season
Position: 20th
Points: 50
Home: Lost 3-1
Away: Lost 5-0
Average Att.: 2,260

This Season
Home: Sat 26 Apr
Away: Sat 06 Oct
Title Odds: 50/1

Accrington Stanley

Accrington were threatened with relegation on their return to the Football League last season but managed to achieve safety with one game to spare. We did manage to finish one place above them in the table courtesy of our last day victory over Boston.

Stanley were lucky to escape a points deduction last season after being found guilty of fielding an ineligible player but the Football League decided on a £12,000 fine as suitable punishment.

Top scorer in the league last season was Paul Mullin with fourteen goals and the striker is now in his seventh season with the club.

Accrington faired well at home with ten wins on their own soil but struggled on their travels, recording only three victories.

The bookies are predicting another difficult season for Stanley, making them favourites for the drop but another good home campaign may be enough to steer them to safety.

Barnet

Ground
Underhill

Manager
Paul Fairclough

Last Season
Position: 14th
Points: 59
Home: Drew 1-1
Away: Won 2-1
Average Att.: 2,279

This Season
Home: Sat 20 Oct
Away: Sat 29 Mar
Title Odds: 80/1

Paul Fairclough steered the Bees to a respectable mid table position in the previous campaign which was only their second season back in the Football League.

Their success was built on solid home form and their twelve wins at Underhill helped the Bees to the seventh best home record in League Two last season.

Top priority this season for Paul Fairclough will be to find a goal scorer after Tressor Kandol ended up top goal scorer last season despite joining Leeds United in the January transfer window for £200,000.

The Bees have also submitted £7 million plans to develop their Underhill Stadium to meet Football League Standards. The club had been under threat of expulsion if they do not have 2,000 covered seats by the end of the season.

The development will involve two new stands behind each goal, four new floodlights, disabled facilities and a general improvement in facilities all round the ground.

Bradford City

Bradford's demise from the Premiership to League Two has come in only six seasons.

The sale of striker Dean Windass to Hull in the transfer January window went a long way to condemning Bradford to the basement league and also helped secure Hull's status in the Championship.

Former player Stuart McCall has been appointed as manager for this season and will have a difficult task on his hands following an exodus of players following relegation last season.

Bradford's average attendance was the sixth best in League One and they are looking to average 10,000 fans this campaign after season tickets were slashed to only £138 per person.

Not surprisingly with this support, the bookies have made the Bantams one of the favourites to win the league.

Ground
Intersonic Stadium

Manager
Stuart McCall

Last Season
Position: 22nd(LG1)
Points: 47
Home: N/A
Away: N/A
Average Att.: 8,694

This Season
Home: Tue 12 Feb
Away: Sat 25 Aug
Title Odds: 10/1

Brentford

Brentford finished rock bottom of League One last season after reaching the play offs in their previous two campaigns but failed at the semi-final stage on both occasions.

The Bees have been blighted by off-field financial problems and had to rely on a supporter taking on £3 million of the club's debt to ease their financial burden.

Former England captain Terry Butcher was appointed manager at the end of last season after previously holding managerial positions with Raith Rovers, Motherwell and Sydney following a distinguished playing career.

Like all of the relegated league clubs, Brentford are one of the favourites for promotion this season but Terry Butcher has a lot of team and confidence rebuilding to do after the Bees only recorded eight wins all last season and even finished a point below Rotherham who had suffered a ten point deduction.

Ground
Griffin Park

Manager
Terry Butcher

Last Season
Position: 24th (LG1)
Points: 37
Home: N/A
Away: N/A
Average Att.: 5,600

This Season
Home: Sat 15 Dec
Away: Sat 22 Mar
Title Odds: 16/1

Ground
Gigg Lane

Manager
Chris Casper

Last Season
Position: 21st
Points: 50
Home: Drew 1-1
Away: Lost 1-0
Average Att.: 2,588

This Season
Home: Sat 15 Mar
Away: Tue 04 Dec
Title Odds: 66/1

Bury

The Shakers left it late last year, but not as late as us to secure their league safety after a run of sixteen games without a win left them staring relegation in the face.

Manager Chris Casper offered his resignation last season after fielding an ineligible player in the second round of the FA Cup which led to their disqualification and allowed Chester to progress to round three by default.

Casper signed a two year extension to his contract last year but this was prior to the mid season slump but the bookies fancy another struggle for the Shakers down at the wrong end of the table.

Bury had one of the lowest average attendances last season and with only four wins at Gigg Lane - the lowest in the league - they will have to improve their home form to stay clear of danger. On their travels, Bury had one of the better records and were only one win away from making it into double figures for away victories last time out.

Ground Saunders
Honda Stadium

Manager
Bobby Williamson

Last Season
Position: 18th
Points: 53
Home: Drew 0-0
Away: Won 2-1
Average Att.: 2,473

This Season
Home: Sun 25 Nov
Away: Sun 09 Mar
Title Odds: 25/1

Chester

Like Bury, Chester are one of the favourites for the drop in the eyes of the bookies and new manager Bobby Williamson, who replaced Mark Wright at the end of last season, will have a difficult task ahead of him in his first season in charge.

This is Williamson's first managerial job since 2005 when he parted company with Plymouth after enjoying spells in charge of Kilmarnock and Hibernian. Williamson has appointed Malcolm Thompson as his assistant with the former Rangers coach arriving in time for the new season.

Chester's goal scoring record was not the best last season with only forty goals scored in the league but on the plus side, Chester were strong at the other end of the pitch and only conceded eight more in the league.

Despite our own struggles last season, Chester only managed to finish one place and two points above us in the table and were lucky to have accumulated sufficient points to ensure safety after recording only one win in their last fourteen games of the season.

Chesterfield

Chesterfield finished last season four points adrift of safety and find themselves back in the basement league, ending a six year stay in League One.

Chesterfield started the season on fire but slowly and surely dropped down the league table and this decline cost Roy McFarland his job in March after four years in charge.

Lee Richardson has now taken charge of Chesterfield for the second time with his first stay a caretaker role when ironically Roy McFarland replaced him on a full time basis in May 2003.

Chesterfield will have to improve their scoring record after Caleb Folan ended up top goal scorer with twelve goals - twice the number of his nearest competitor - despite joining Wigan in the January transfer window for half a million pounds.

They ended the season with nine home victories, but their travels cost them dearly, with only three wins all season and none since January.

Ground Recreation
Ground Saltergate

Manager
Lee Richardson

Last Season
Position: 21st (LG1)
Points: 53
Home: N/A
Away: N/A
Average Att.: 4,235

This Season
Home: Tue 02 Oct
Away: Tue 01 Jan
Title Odds: 14/1

Dagenham & Redbridge

Dagenham & Redbridge ran away with the Conference title and ended fourteen points clear of second placed Oxford.

The club was only formed in 1992 following the merger of Redbridge Forest and Dagenham Football Club and finished a respectable third in their first season as a combined club in the Conference.

John Still is in his second spell as manager after initially leaving the club for Peterborough is 1994 only to return ten years later after two spells in charge of Barnet.

Dagenham & Redbridge were controversially denied entry to the league when Boston piped them to the conference title on goal difference in 2002. Boston were later found guilty of financial irregularities but their ten point deduction was carried over to the next season which meant they kept their place in the Football League.

Dagenham & Redbridge suffered more heartbreak the following season when they lost to Doncaster in the play off final but they finally secured their promotion to the Football League in convincing style last season.

Ground
Glyn Hopkin Stadium

Manager
John Still

Last Season
Position: 1st (CON)
Points: 95
Home: N/A
Away: N/A
Average Att.: 1,756

This Season
Home: Mon 24 Mar
Away: Sat 08 Dec
Title Odds: 25/1

Ground
The Darlington Arena

Manager
Dave Penney

Last Season
Position: 11th
Points: 65
Home: Won 1-0
Away: Drew 1-1
Average Att.: 3,819

This Season
Home: Sat 02 Feb
Away: Sat 11 Aug
Title Odds: 10/1

Darlington

We travel to the Quakers for the opening game of the season and come across a familiar face in winger Neil Wainwright who is now starting his seventh season with the north east club.

Last season was a mixed affair for the Quakers as they finished six points and four places from a play-off position but you always felt that they were on the fringe of the play-offs rather than breaking into them.

Manager Dave Penney is starting his first campaign in charge of Darlington after being appointed manager in October 2006 following a successful five year spell in charge of Doncaster.

The Quakers are a good outside bet for promotion this season but will have to improve on their home form if they are going to break away from mid-table and into the promotion chase.

The Quakers have been struggling financially and have asked the Council to back a refinancing plan that involves additional use of their stadium, which includes an indoor ski slope.

Ground
Blundell Park

Manager
Alan Buckley

Last Season
Position: 15th
Points: 59
Home: Won 3-0
Away: Lost 2-1
Average Att.: 4,379

This Season
Home: Fri 22 Feb
Away: Sat 12 Jan
Title Odds: 20/1

Grimsby Town

Grimsby were struggling for most of last season and at one point looked destined for non-league football but a turn around in form from February 2007 onwards resulted in a comfortable mid-table finish for the Mariners.

The start to last season, which included a 3-0 defeat at the Racecourse, was a disaster for the Mariners and they found themselves just one place above the relegation zone when they parted company with Graham Rodger during November but the arrival of Alan Buckley managed to steady the ship.

Alan Buckley is in his third spell in charge of Grimsby and his main priority will be to address the goal scoring problem with three players finishing top scorers during the last campaign with only eight goals each.

The Mariners were not helped with the loss of striker Michael Ready who was blighted by injury last season after recording fourteen goals in the previous campaign when the Mariners lost out in the play off final to Cheltenham.

Hereford United

The Bulls had a respectable return to the Football League last season following a nine year absence in the Conference.

Hereford were on the fringe of the play offs for most of the campaign but a poor end to the season, with only one win in their last thirteen games, resulted in them tailing off to a mid table position.

Hereford struggled for goals last season with only forty five scored in their forty six games. Their top scorer was Alan Connell, with only nine goals in the league, but he has joined Brentford after only one season with the club.

Hereford have a unique set up with experienced manager Graham Turner also doubling up as Club Chairman. Former Wolves manager Turner has been in charge of the Bulls since the start of the 1995 campaign.

It looks to be a new look Bulls side for the new season with manager Turner admitting he is looking to bring in six more players in addition to the three he signed at the beginning of July.

Ground
Edgar Street

Manager
Graham Turner

Last Season
Position: 16th
Points: 55
Home: Won 1-0
Away: Lost 2-0
Average Att.: 3,328

This Season
Home: Sat 01 Sep
Away: Sat 26 Jan
Title Odds: 40/1

Lincoln City

After starting the season with a long trip to Darlington, we also end the season with a long cross country trip to Lincoln.

Lincoln have been the nearly men of the play offs for the last five seasons. Having qualified for the end-of-season knock-out competition since 2003, The Imps have fallen short at the semi-final stage three times and lost twice in the final on the other two occasions.

Last-season it was eventual winners Bristol Rovers who knocked Lincoln out in the semi-finals but Lincoln were looking good for one of the automatic positions until their form dropped off towards the end of the season with only two wins in the last thirteen games.

Our comprehensive away victory at Sincil Bank last season completed the double over The Imps and was crucially the start of our end-of-season run in that went a long way to securing our league safety.

Ground
Sincil Bank

Manager
John Schofield

Last Season
Position: 16th
Points: 55
Home: Won 2-1
Away: Won 3-0
Average Att.: 5,176

This Season
Home: Sat 29 Sep
Away: Sat 03 May
Title Odds: 20/1

Ground
Moss Rose

Manager
Ian Brightwell

Last Season
Position: 22nd
Points: 48
Home: Drew 0-0
Away: Lost 2-0
Average Att.: 2,428

This Season
Home: Sat 05 Apr
Away: Sat 13 Oct
Title Odds: 40/1

Ground
Field Mill

Manager
Billy Dearden

Last Season
Position: 17th
Points: 54
Home: Drew 0-0
Away: Lost 3-0
Average Att.: 3,176

This Season
Home: Sat 01 Mar
Away: Sat 17 Nov
Title Odds: 33/1

Macclesfield Town

Macclesfield were rocked with the news at the end of June 2007 that manager Paul Ince was heading south to join fellow League Two side MK Dons.

Ince completed a remarkable escape for the Silkmen in the last game of the season by steering them to unlikely safety (before Boston were deducted ten points for entering administration).

Ince arrived at Moss Rose in November 2006 with Macclesfield rock bottom, without a win and only five points in the league, but somehow managed to steer Macclesfield to safety.

The Silk Men moved quickly to replace Ince with Ian Brightwell arriving in a matter of days and he was quick to appoint former Scotland international Asa Harford as his assistant.

Brightwell was reserve team manager at Moss Rose and played the last of his 460+ league appearances for the Silkmen in October 2006. He was also caretaker manager before Ince succeeded Brian Horton last season.

Mansfield Town

Last season in the league was rather uninspiring for Mansfield supporters as they were probably the only team that was never in danger of relegation but never looked like pushing for a play off position.

The Stags were not the only team to have a poor end to last season with only one win in their last ten games of an uneventful campaign.

The Stags will have to improve on their ten home wins last season as well picking up more than four victories on their ravels but will have to do so without the services of top scorer Richard Barker.

Barker joined Hartlepool at the beginning of 2007 in a £80,000 transfer but still ended up top scorer with fifteen goals last season.

Barker had registered forty league goals in just over ninety games for the Stags since joining in 2004 and always had the knack of finding the back of the net against us - scoring six times in his last four games - a welcome loss!

Milton Keynes Dons

The most disliked team in the Football League missed out on promotion last season in the play-offs after finishing just a point off the final automatic place.

Shrewsbury then defeated the Dons over two legs in the semi-finals who also had to deal with the loss of manager Malcolm Allen when the former Brentford boss joined Championship side Leicester City in the close season.

The Dons moved into their new 30,000 all-seater stadium for the new campaign with Paul Ince taking over from Malcolm Allen and are second favourites for the title according to the bookies.

The Dons have somehow kept hold of top scorer Izale McLeod throughout the summer despite him attracting a lot of interest after scoring sixty goals in just three seasons with the club.

His striker partner Clive Platt has joined Colchester in a £300,000 move but Ince has brought in the experienced Kevin Gallen as his replacement from QPR on a free transfer.

Ground
stadium:mk

Manager
Paul Ince

Last Season
Position: 4th
Points: 84
Home: Lost 2-1
Away: Lost 2-1
Average Att.: 6,034

This Season
Home: Sat 19 Jan
Away: Sat 16 Feb
Title Odds: 8/1

Morecambe

Former Macclesfield and Northern Ireland manager Sammie McIllroy guided the Shrimps to a memorable conference play off final victory over Exeter to gain promotion to the Football League for the first time in their history.

Their first away league game is also our first home game of the new campaign but Morecambe have lost some key players since their memorable day out at the new Wembley Stadium.

Despite offering Chris Blackburn the best contract in the club's history, the 24-year-old defender has joined League One Swindon Town on a free transfer and a tribunal will have to set the fee for striker Danny Carlton who has joined Carlisle after scoring the winning goal in the play off final.

McIllroy's experience as manager will prove invaluable to the Shrimps this season after previously guiding Macclesfield Town into the Football League and subsequent promotion to the now League One before joining his home country as manager.

Ground
Christie Park

Manager
Sammy McIllroy

Last Season
Position: 3rd (CON)
Points: 81
Home: N/A
Away: N/A
Average Att.: 1,598

This Season
Home: Sat 18 Aug
Away: Tue 29 Jan
Title Odds: 40/1

Ground
Meadow Lane

Manager
Steve Thompson

Last Season
Position: 13th
Points: 62
Home: Lost 1-0
Away: Lost 2-1
Average Att.: 4,974

This Season
Home: Sat 19 Apr
Away: Sat 27 Oct
Title Odds: 20/1

Ground
London Road

Manager
Darren Ferguson

Last Season
Position: 10th
Points: 65
Home: Drew 0-0
Away: Lost 3-0
Average Att.: 4,974

This Season
Home: Sat 5 Jan
Away: Sat 9 Feb
Title Odds: 10/3

Notts County

The Magpies enjoyed their travels last season and ended up with one of the better records away from home.

County will have to address their home form to be contenders for the play offs with only eight victories at Meadow Lane all last season.

Manager Steve Thompson will be looking to build on his first season in charge with the Magpies ranked as an outside bet for promotion.

County have had a busy summer with seven players joining on free transfers with manager Thompson still looking to add to his squad.

The Magpies started off well last season and in much travelled striker Jason Lee, they had an unlikely top goal scorer.

The much maligned striker - 'of pineapple on his head fame' - ended the season with sixteen goals which is a good return for a player now in his thirty-sixth year.

Peterborough United

Darren Ferguson and Kevin Russell make their first return to the Racecourse at the start of the new year and will be expected to be in poll position for promotion by then.

Ferguson has splashed the cash since joining the Posh at the beginning of the year with nine players arriving at London Road with one further player expected to join before the season starts.

Ferguson's first win as manager ironically came against Wrexham when Posh ran out comfortable 3-0 winners at London Road earlier on this year.

Ferguson did manage an upturn in Peterborough's fortunes but they paid for a run of eight straight defeats at the turn of the year and just missed out on the final play off spot by six points.

Ferguson's fiery nature has already transferred to his managerial style when he was charged with using abusive words to a match official in the 1-1 draw at Chester at the end of April!

Rochdale

Rochdale were one of the better footballing sides to the visit the Racecourse last season but their 2-1 win at the Racecourse started a poor run of form that cost manager Steve Parkin his job.

Former Wrexham player Keith Hill, who was Denis Smith's first signing back in 2001, when he joined on loan from Cheltenham, was a surprise choice but his arrival resulted in a noticeable up turn in form for Dale.

Rochdale were struggling one place above the relegation zone midway through the season but a run of thirteen wins out of the last twenty-one games meant Dale missed out on the play offs by just five points.

Rochdale had no problems finding the back of the net last season and finished joint second top scorers in League Two last season with seventy goals. Chris Dagnall ended the season top goal scorer on eighteen and Keith Hill is close to adding to his firepower with the capture of Alan LeFondre from Stockport after the striker scored four times in seven games in a loan deal last season.

Ground
Spotland

Manager
Keith Hill

Last Season
Position: 9th
Points: 66
Home: Lost 2-1
Away: Drew 2-2
Average Att.: 4,974

This Season
Home: Wed 26 Dec
Away: Sat 8 Sep
Title Odds: 20/1

Rotherham United

Despite starting the season on minus ten points, after the Millers entered into a voluntary arrangement with their creditors, Rotherham slowly slid down the table.

In the end, only four victories in their last twenty-six league games left the Millers cut adrift at the bottom of League One but they did manage to finish above Brentford in the final reckoning.

Rotherham parted company with manager Richard Knill in March this year after they went on a run of fourteen games without a win.

Knill was in his second spell in charge of the club and departed Millmoor with Rotherham thirteen points adrift of safety. Mark Robins' appointment failed to turn matters around, although the former Manchester United and Rotherham striker has now been given the job on a full-time basis.

The main priority for Mark Robins will be to find new strikers after the two top scorers from last season have departed the club for pastures new.

Ground
Millmoor

Manager
Mark Robins

Last Season
Position: 23rd (LG1)
Points: 38*
Home / Away: N/A
Average Att.: 4,763
incl. 10 point deduction

This Season
Home: Sat 15 Sep
Away: Sat 22 Dec
Title Odds: 18/1

Ground
The New Meadow

Manager
Gary Peters

Last Season
Position: 7th
Points: 71
Home: Lost 3-1
Away: Won 1-0
Average Att.: 4,730

This Season
Home: Sun 4 Nov
Away: Sun 13 Apr
Title Odds: 20/1

Shrewsbury Town

A good end-of-season run in, except for our victory in our last ever visit to the Gay Meadow, Shrewsbury sneaked into the final play off spot courtesy of a better goal difference than Stockport.

They were still ranked outsiders when paired with MK Dons in the semi-final, but despite seeing off the Dons, the final against Bristol Rovers was a step too far.

Shrewsbury are starting the new campaign in a new 10,000 all-seater stadium but we will have to wait until April 2008 for our first visit to the New Meadow.

Shrewsbury's success last season was built on a solid defence with only a goal a game on average conceded and a run of fourteen games without defeat which propelled them into play off contention.

Danger man Derek Asamoah remains at the club along with top scorer Michael Symes as manager Gary Peters will be looking to build on the success of his fourth season in charge of the Shropshire club.

Ground
Edgeley Park

Manager
Jim Gannon

Last Season
Position: 8th
Points: 71
Home: Lost 1-0
Away: Lost 5-2
Average Att.: 5,514

This Season
Home: Sat 29 Dec
Away: Sat 22 Sep
Title Odds: 16/1

Stockport County

Stockport made Football League history last season after claiming nine straight wins without even conceding a goal.

The floodgate well and truly opened once their goal was finally breached and a disappointing end to the season resulted in The Hatters missing out on the play offs on goal difference.

The record breaking run ended with eleven games still to play, but just two further victories meant that Stockport dropped out of contention for an automatic promotion spot and then missed out on the play offs.

It was still a positive season for The Hatters after struggling at the wrong end of the table in the previous campaign and manager Jim Gannon, assisted by former Wrexham player Peter Ward, will be looking to build on the success of the last campaign.

Stockport will have to address their away form as only seven victories on their travels proved costly in the end after enjoying one of the better home records in the league.

Wycombe Wanderers

Wycombe's two seasons under the stewardship of former Champions League Winner Paul Lambert have followed a similar pattern: a fast start that appeared to drain all their reserves before tailing off disappointingly into mid table as the finishing line approached.

Wycombe have somehow managed to keep hold of Jermaine Easter so far after the Welsh international netted twenty-three times in all competitions last season but they have lost the experience of captain Tommy Mooney who has joined Walsall in the league above.

Despite the partnership of Easter and Mooney netting twenty-nine league goals, the rest of the squad only managed twenty-three between them as the Chairboys finished the season without a win in their final eleven games.

Paul Lambert almost managed to persuade former Celtic team mate Neil Lennon to join Wycombe but the Northern Ireland international opted for Nottingham Forest in League One.

Ground
Adams Park

Manager
Paul Lambert

Last Season
Position: 12th
Points: 62
Home: Lost 2-0
Away: Drew 1-1
Average Att.: 4,983

This Season
Home: Wed 7 Nov
Away: Tue 11 Mar
Title Odds: 16/1

First Team Fixtures 2007/08

Date			Time	H/A	Opponents	Competition
August	Sat	4th	15.00	A	Lincoln City	CCL2
	Tues	14th	19.45	H	Port Vale	CC1
	Sat	18th	15.00	H	Morecambe	CCL2
	Sat	25th	15.00	A	Bradford City	CCL2
	Tues	28th	19.45	H	Aston Villa	CC2
September	Sat	1st	15.00	H	Hereford United	CCL2
	Tues	4th	19.15	H	Macclesfield	JPT1
	Sat	8th	15.00	A	Rochdale	CCL2
	Sat	15th	15.00	H	Rotherham United	CCL2
	Sat	22nd	15.00	A	Stockport County	CCL2
	Sat	29th	15.00	H	Lincoln City	CCL2
October	Tues	2nd	19.45	H	Chesterfield	CCL2
	Sat	6th	15.00	A	Accrington Stanley	CCL2
	Sat	13th	15.00	A	Macclesfield Town	CCL2
	Sat	20th	15.00	H	Barnet	CCL2
	Sat	27th	15.00	A	Notts County	CCL2
November	Sun	4th	12.00	H	Shrewsbury Town	CCL2
	Weds	7th	19.45	H	Wycombe Wanderers	CCL2
	Sat	10th	15.00	TBC	TBC	FAC1
	Sat	17th	15.00	A	Mansfield Town	CCL2
	Sun	25th	12.00	H	Chester City	CCL2
December	Sat	1st	15.00	TBC	TBC	FAC2
	Sat	8th	15.00	A	Dagenham & Redbridge	CCL2
	Sat	15th	15.00	H	Brentford	CCL2
	Sat	22nd	15.00	A	Rotherham United	CCL2
	Weds	26th	15.00	H	Rochdale	CCL2
	Sat	29th	15.00	H	Stockport County	CCL2
January	Tues	1st	15.00	A	Chesterfield	CCL2
	Sat	5th	15.00	H	Peterborough United	CCL2 (FAC3)
	Sat	12th	15.00	A	Grimsby Town	CCL2
	Sat	19th	15.00	H	Milton Keynes Dons	CCL2
	Sat	26th	15.00	A	Hereford United	CCL2 (FAC4)
	Tues	29th	19.45	A	Morecombe	CCL2
February	Sat	2nd	15.00	H	Darlington	CCL2
	Sat	9th	15.00	A	Peterborough United	CCL2
	Tues	12th	19.45	H	Bradford City	CCL2
	Sat	16th	15.00	A	Milton Keynes Dons	CCL2 (FAC5)
	Fri	22nd	19.45	H	Grimsby Town	CCL2
March	Sat	1st	15.00	H	Mansfield Town	CCL2
	Sun	9th	12.00	A	Chester City	CCL2 (FAC6)
	Tues	11th	19.45	A	Wycombe Wanderers	CCL2
	Sat	15th	15.00	H	Bury	CCL2
	Sat	22nd	15.00	A	Brentford	CCL2
	Mon	24th	15.00	H	Dagenham & Redbridge	CCL2
	Sat	29th	15.00	A	Barnet	CCL2
April	Sat	5th	15.00	H	Macclesfield Town	CCL2 (FACSF)
	Sun	13th	12.00	A	Shrewsbury Town	CCL2
	Sat	19th	15.00	H	Notts County	CCL2
	Sat	26th	15.00	H	Accrington Stanley	CCL2
May	Sat	3rd	15.00	A	Lincoln City	CCL2

Key: CC2 = Coca Cola League 2; CC = Carling Cup; JPT = Johnstone's Paint Trophy; FAC = FA Cup.

Reserve & Youth Fixtures

Date		H/A	Opponents
August	22nd	A	Blackpool
	27th	H	Carlisle United *
September	10th	H	Burnley
	18th	A	Manchester City
	24th	H	Preston North End
October	9th	A	Chester City
	22nd	H	Tranmere Rovers
	31st	A	Rochdale
November	7th		FA Youth Cup 1
	12th	H	Bury
	21st		FA Youth Cup 2
	28th	A	Morecombe
December	10th	H	Accrington Stanley
	12th		FA Youth Cup 3
	17th	H	Blackpool
January	9th	A	Carlisle United *
	16th	A	Preston North End *
	21st	H	Chester City
February	6th	A	Tranmere Rovers
	18th	H	Rochdale
	27th	A	Bury *
March	17th	H	Morecombe
	26th	A	Accrington Stanley
April	9th	A	Burnley
	21st	H	Manchester City
	30th		Play-off SF

Date		H/A	Opponents
August	11	A	Macclesfield Town
	18th	H	Tranmere Rovers
	25th		In service training
September	1st	A	Wigan Athletic
	8th	H	Walsall
	15th		
	22nd	H	Port Vale
	29th	A	Stockport County
October	6th	H	Morecombe
	13th	H	Chester City
	20th	A	Wigan Athletic * (NC1)
	27th	H	Wigan Athletic
November	3rd	A	Shrewsbury Town
	10th	H	Stockport County
	17th	A	Port Vale
	24th		NC2
December	1st	A	Chester City
	8th	A	Blackpool
	15th	H	Macclesfield Town
January	5th	A	Walsall
	12th	H	Shrewsbury Town
	19th	A	Tranmere Rovers
	26th	A	Rochdale
February	2nd		
	9th	H	Accrington Stanley
	16th	A	Blackpool
	23rd		NC3
March	1st	H	Burnley
	8th	A	Bury *
	15th	H	Carlisle United
	29th	A	Morecombe
April	5th	H	Oldham Athletic
	19th	A	Preston North End
May	3rd		In service training

*All matches kick-off at 7.00pm apart from those marked * which kick-off at 2.00pm.*

With Liverpool Reserves no longer using our ground, we will bring a number of Pontin's Holidays League games back to Wrexham, with at least the first three home fixtures scheduled for the Racecourse. From October 2007, games will take place at Globe Way, the home of Buckley Town FC.

*Matches marked * kick-off at 10.30am*

Key: NC = North Cup

Anthony Williams (1)

Signed on loan from Carlisle in March 2006 Anthony became a vital part of our league survival fight, making a total of nine appearances (conceding four goals) and looking incredibly safe in the process. A former Welsh Under-21 international, he is a great boost to the squad when he signed a contract this summer. Anthony will hope that now playing for a Welsh club will further enhance his international chances.

Previous clubs:
Blackburn Rovers, QPR (Loan), Macclesfield Town (Loan), Huddersfield Town (Loan), Bristol Rovers (Loan), Gillingham (Loan), Macclesfield Town (Loan), Hartlepool United, Swansea City (Loan), Stockport County (Loan), Grimsby Town, Carlisle United, Bury (Loan).

Position	Goalkeeper
Nationality	Welsh
Birthplace	Maesteg
Date of Birth	20/09/77
Height	6'2" (188cm)
Weight	13st 9lbs (86.34kg)

Wrexham Career Statistics

	League		FA Cup		WPC		Carling		JPT			
	apps	gls	apps	gls	apps	gls	apps	gls	apps	gls	apps	gls
06/07	9	0	-	-	-	-	-	-	-	-	9	0
Total	9	0	-	-	-	-	-	-	-	-	9	0

Simon Spender (2)

Perhaps the biggest beneficiary of the change in management last season, the 21-year-old full back will be hoping to continue his excellent end of season form into the new campaign. Having made a telling contribution to our league safety with a string of assists in the latter stages of the season, manager Brian Carey was quick to tie the youngster down to a new contract. The energetic right back, a Welsh Under-21 International, will be looking to make the position his own this time around.

Previous clubs: None

Position	Defender
Nationality	Welsh
Birthplace	Mold
Date of Birth	15/11/85
Height	5ft 11in (180cm)
Weight	11st 0lbs (69.92kg)

Wrexham Career Statistics

	League		FA Cup		WPC		Carling		JPT			
	apps	gls	apps	gls	apps	gls	apps	gls	apps	gls	apps	gls
03/04	3/3	0	-	-	-	-	-	-	-	-	3/3	0
04/05	9/4	0	2	0	0/1	0	0/2	0	2	0	13/7	0
05/06	15/3	2	1	0	1/2	1	-	-	1	0	17/5	3
06/07	23/2	2	-	-	-	-	1	0	-	-	24/2	2
Total	50/12	4	3	0	1/3	1	1/2	0	3	0	57/17	5

Ryan Valentine (3)

Valentine signed for his hometown club on a free transfer after leaving Darlington in the summer of 2006. In four seasons as a regular in the north east he made 176 appearances, scoring 4 goals. Equally accomplished in either fullback role, the tough tackling defender had a promising first season at the Racecourse last time out. The former Everton youngster impressed Wales coach John Toshack enough in the early part of last season to earn a call up to the squad to face the Czech Republic and Brazil, but has yet to earn a cap. He played a vital part in our survival bid, scoring the crucial penalty in the must win game against Boston United to level the score at 1-1.

Previous Clubs: Everton, Darlington

Wrexham Career Statistics

	League		FA Cup		WPC		Carling		JPT			
	apps	gls	apps	gls	apps	gls	apps	gls	apps	gls	apps	gls
06/07	32/2	2	1	0	1	0	1	0	1	0	36/2	2
Total	32/2	2	1	0	1	0	1	0	1	0	36/2	2

Position	Defender
Nationality	Welsh
Birthplace	Chirk
Date of Birth	19/08/82
Height	5ft 10in (178cm)
Weight	11st 5lbs (72.18kg)

Shaun Pejic (4)

Despite signing for Wrexham back in August 2000, and making over 144 appearances for the club in that time, 'Pej' is still only 24 years old! This stylish defender has much improved over the course of the last few seasons, and was many people's choice to grab the 'Player of the Season' award last year, only to be beaten by fellow centre-half Steve Evans. With more competition in the heart of defence this season, much is expected of Shaun in 2007/08.

Previous clubs: None

Wrexham Career Statistics

	League		FA Cup		WPC		Carling		JPT			
	apps	gls	apps	gls	apps	gls	apps	gls	apps	gls	apps	gls
00/01	1	0	-	-	-	-	-	-	-	-	1	0
01/02	11/1	0	-	-	1	0	-	-	-	-	12/1	0
02/03	23/4	0	1	0	1	1	2	0	2	0	29/4	1
03/04	20/1	1	-	-	-	-	1	0	1	0	22/1	1
04/05	30/5	0	2	0	2	0	2	0	4/1	1	40/6	1
05/06	26	0	-	-	2/1	0	-	-	1	0	29/1	0
06/07	33	0	3	0	1	0	1	0	-	-	38	0
Total	144/11	1	6	0	7/1	1	6	0	8/1	1	171/13	3

Position	Defender
Nationality	Welsh
Birthplace	Hereford
Date of Birth	16/11/82
Height	6ft 0in (183cm)
Weight	12st 2lbs (77.18kg)

Steve James Evans (5)

A towering, uncompromising centre-back, Steve made a remarkable impact in his first season in the Football League. A local lad, he began his career with stints as a trainee at Crewe Alexandra and West Brom, but was not offered professional terms by either club. Seven successful seasons at TNS followed before Denis Smith brought him to the Racecourse last summer. An impressive start to the season caught the eye of Wales manager John Toshack, and he made his international debut in a friendly against Liechtenstein on 14th November 2006. One aspect of his game that Steve will be hoping to improve upon is his disciplinary record, as he served three separate bans last season.

Previous Clubs: Crewe Alexandra, West Bromwich Albion, TNS Llansantffraid, Oswestry Town (Loan)

Position	Defender
Nationality	Welsh
Birthplace	Wrexham
Date of Birth	26/02/79
Height	6ft 5in (195cm)
Weight	13st 10lbs (87.16kg)

Wrexham Career Statistics

	League		FA Cup		WPC		Carling		JPT			
	apps	gls	apps	gls	apps	gls	apps	gls	apps	gls	apps	gls
06/07	34/1	2	3	0	-	-	1	0	1	0	39/1	2
Total	34/1	2	3	0	-	-	1	0	1	0	39/1	2

Richard Paul Hope (5)

A surprising, yet welcome pre-season signing from fellow League Two club, Shrewsbury. Richard began his career with Anthony Williams at Blackburn, where he was a trainee, before going on to play for the likes of Darlington, York, Northampton and Chester. He made 38 league appearances or the 'Wurzels' last season captaining them to the League Two play-off final, where they eventually lost to Bristol Rovers. Will add some height to the back four as Richard measures 6 ft 2, inches and will be a key player in our push for promotion!

Previous Clubs: Blackburn Rovers, Darlington, Northampton Town, York City, Chester City, Shrewsbury Town.

(No appearances for Wrexham FC to date)

Position	Defender
Nationality	English
Birthplace	Stockton-on-Tees
Date of Birth	22/06/78
Height	6ft 2in (188cm)
Weight	12st 6lbs (78.93kg)

Mark Alan Jones (7)

A player who started last season in a blaze of glory, scoring five goals in our first seven matches, and a Welsh cap v. Liechtenstein. 'Jonah' unfortunately picked up an injury just before Christmas that was to hamper him for the rest of the season. Hopefully, having been fully rested, we will be treated to some more typically Jonah-esque goals this season, and who knows, possibly another Welsh call up? Let's hope so. as his midfield trickery often lights up the dullest of games.

Previous Clubs: None

Wrexham Career Statistics

	League		FA Cup		WPC		Carling		JPT			
	apps	gls	apps	gls	apps	gls	apps	gls	apps	gls	apps	gls
02/03	0/1	0	-	-	-	-	-	-	-	-	0/1	0
03/04	0/13	1	-	-	0/1	0	-	-	-	-	0/14	1
04/05	18/9	3	1/1	0	3	1	0/1	0	6/1	1	28/12	5
05/06	42	13	1	0	3	2	1	0	1	2	48	17
06/07	30/1	5	2	1	1	0	2	1	1	0	36/1	7
Total	90/24	22	4/1	1	7/1	3	3/1	1	8/1	3	112/28	30

Position	Midfielder
Nationality	Welsh
Birthplace	Wrexham
Date of Birth	15/08/83
Height	5ft 11in (180cm)
Weight	10st 10lbs (68.1kg)

Daniel Ivor Llewellyn Williams (8)

Wrexham Supporters Trust's player of the season for the last two seasons, Danny is a Wrexham lad who takes great pride in playing for his hometown club. Equally adaptable at centre-half or in midfield, it is likely to be the latter that he operates this season. Started out at Liverpool as a youngster, but never quite made the breakthrough into the first team despite making it to the bench on one occasion. Now in his fourth season back at the club, he scored 4 goals last season, including the fans' goal of the season against local rivals Shrewsbury Town.

Previous Clubs: Liverpool, Doncaster Rovers (Loan), Kidderminster Harriers, Chester City (Loan), Bristol Rovers

Wrexham Career Statistics

	League		FA Cup		WPC		Carling		JPT			
	apps	gls	apps	gls	apps	gls	apps	gls	apps	gls	apps	gls
99/00	24	1	4	1	4/1	0	2	0	1	0	35/1	2
00/01	14/1	2	-	-	4	0	2	0	-	-	20/1	2
04/05	20	0	-	-	2	0	2	0	3/1	1	27/1	1
05/06	45	4	1	0	3/1	0	1	0	1	0	51	4
06/07	40	3	3	1	-	-	2	0	1	0	46	4
Total	143/1	10	8	2	13/2	0	9	0	6/1	1	179/3	13

Position	Midfielder
Nationality	Welsh
Birthplace	Wrexham
Date of Birth	12/07/79
Height	6ft 1in (185cm)
Weight	13st 0lbs (82.63kg)

Neil Wyn Roberts (9)

Club captain Neil spent a frustrating last season watching his teammates from the stands. Injuries meant he made only 17 starting league appearances and scored 4 goals in the process. Highly respected by players and fans alike, Neil gives the club a massive boost by just appearing in the starting line up. He will no doubt be looking to build upon his appearances and goal tally this year. The few goals that 'Robbo' did score last season proved invaluable to secure our league status, as he netted against our rivals Chester and Shrewsbury as well as scoring the only goal against Torquay in a vital home win.

Previous Clubs: Bangor City (Loan), Wigan Athletic, Hull City (Loan), Bradford City (Loan), Doncaster Rovers

Wrexham Career Statistics

	League		FA Cup		WPC		Carling		JPT			
	apps	gls	apps	gls	apps	gls	apps	gls	apps	gls	apps	gls
97/98	29/5	8	3/1	1	6/3	1	-	-	0/1	0	38/10	10
98/99	11/11	3	3	1	3	1	1	1	2/1	2	20/12	8
99/00	18/1	6	5	2	2	1	-	-	-	-	25/1	9
06/07	17/2	3	-	-	-	-	1	0	-	-	18/2	3
Total	75/19	20	11/1	4	11/3	3	2	1	2/2	2	101/25	30

Position Forward
Nationality Welsh
Birthplace Wrexham
Date of Birth 07/04/78
Height 5ft 10in (178cm)
Weight 11st 0lbs (69.92kg)

Michael Anthony Proctor (10)

Michael holds the unfortunate claim to fame of scoring two own goals in one match! He did so for Sunderland against Charlton Athletic in a Premiership match in 2003. Signed permanently this summer on a three year contract from Hartlepool after enjoying a successful loan spell at the Racecourse in the latter stages of last season, during which he scored two vital goals in our successful battle for survival. Described as a 'clever and bright footballer' by manager Brian Carey, he was used last season both on the right flank and up front; expect the same versatiltiy this time around.

Previous Clubs: Sunderland, Hvidore (Loan), Halifax Town (Loan), York City (Loan), Bradford City (Loan), Rotherham United, Swindon Town (Loan), Hartlepool United

Wrexham Career Statistics

	League		FA Cup		WPC		Carling		JPT			
	apps	gls	apps	gls	apps	gls	apps	gls	apps	gls	apps	gls
06/07	9	2	-	-	-	-	-	-	-	-	9	2
Total	9	2	-	-	-	-	-	-	-	-	9	2

Position Forward
Nationality English
Birthplace Sunderland
Date of Birth 03/10/80
Height 5ft 11in (180cm)
Weight 12st 0lbs (76.27)

Christopher Mark Llewellyn (11)

In his second spell with the club having made over 150 appearances for the 'Dragons'. However, last season he took on the nickname of the 'Hokey Cokey Kid' by many people for putting 'two feet in' where he shouldn't! Izzy's class speaks for itself when he's on the pitch. A hugely important player for us last season, chipping in with nine league goals and many more assists. A very versatile squad member who can play up front, or as a wide midfield player. It was strongly rumoured that Izzy was to leave at the end of last season, but lets hope he settles down again, and adds to his Welsh caps.

Previous Clubs: Norwich City, Bristol Rovers (Loan), Hartlepool United.

Wrexham Career Statistics

	League		FA Cup		WPC		Carling		JPT			
	apps	gls	apps	gls	apps	gls	apps	gls	apps	gls	apps	gls
03/04	44	8	1	0	3	1	1	0	1/1	0	52/1	9
04/05	46	7	2	1	1	0	1/1	1	7	3	55/1	12
06/07	39	9	2	0	-	-	2	2	1	0	44	11
Total	129	24	5	1	4	1	4/1	3	9/1	3	151/2	32

Position	Forward
Nationality	Welsh
Birthplace	Merthyr
Date of Birth	29/08/79
Height	5ft 11in (180cm)
Weight	11st 6lbs (72.64kg)

Matthew Thomas Crowell (12)

Matty endured a frustrating season last time round, having been sidelined since suffering a knee injury in the FA Cup defeat to Derby County in January. Bridgend born Crowell joined Wrexham in 2003, having come through the ranks on the south coast with Southampton. He has represented Wales Under-21's numerous times since arriving at the Racecourse, and was in the Wrexham team that lifted the LDV Vans Trophy in 2005. Awarded a six month contract in order to prove his fitness, the tough tackling midfielder will be hoping to show Brian Carey he has a role to play in the coming season.

Previous Clubs: Southampton

Wrexham Career Statistics

	League		FA Cup		WPC		Carling		LDV			
	apps	gls	apps	gls	apps	gls	apps	gls	apps	gls	apps	gls
03/04	9/6	1	-	-	1/1	0	0/1	0	1/1	0	11/9	1
04/05	22/6	0	1	0	2	0	-	-	5/1	0	30/7	0
05/06	26/3	3	-	-	2	0	-	-	-	-	28/3	3
06/07	10/5	0	1	0	-	-	2	0	1	1	14/5	1
Total	67/20	4	2	0	5/1	0	2/1	0	7/2	1	83/24	5

Position	Midfielder
Nationality	Welsh
Birthplace	Bridgend
Date of Birth	03/07/84
Height	5ft 9in (175cm)
Weight	10st 10lbs (68.1kg)

Michael Jones (13)

Young goalkeeper Michael Jones - aka 'Carrots' - is a more than a capable understudy to current club number one goalkeeper Anthony Williams. Having made his debut at just 16, he has been patiently waiting to seize his chance of a first team place, and he will be keen to establish himself this season. Unfortunately for him, his only appearances last season came in the ill-fated 5-2 defeat in the League at Stockport County and in the Welsh Premier Cup defeat at Newport County. Surely out to prove a point this season?

Previous Clubs: None

Position	Goalkeeper
Nationality	English
Birthplace	Liverpool
Date of Birth	03/12/87
Height	6ft 3in (191cm)
Weight	13st 0lbs (82.63kg)

Wrexham Career Statistics

	League		FA Cup		WPC		Carling		JPT			
	apps	gls	apps	gls	apps	gls	apps	gls	apps	gls	apps	gls
04/05	0/1	0	-	-	-	-	-	-	-	-	0/1	0
05/06	6/1	0	-	-	-	-	-	-	-	-	6/1	0
06/07	1	0	-	-	1	0	-	-	-	-	2	0
Total	7/2	0									8/2	0

Eifion Wayn Williams (14)

Another 'Williams' at the club! There was a huge buzz around the town when we found out that we'd secured the signing of North Walian Eifion. Surely it was some sort of late April fool joke that Hartlepool had let him go? He'd only managed to score 53 goals in total for them! Will do us nicely thank you very much, he's always scored goals for whatever club he's been at, and I'm sure we'll be no exception.

Previous Clubs: Caernarvon Town, Barry Town, Torquay United, Hartlepool United

(No appearances for Wrexham FC to date.)

Position	Forward
Nationality	Welsh
Birthplace	Bangor
Date of Birth	15/11/75
Height	5ft 11in (180cm)
Weight	11st 1lbs (70.31kg)

Michael Paul John Williams (15)

Like his younger brother Marc, Mike is a Welsh Under-21 international. Despite having only signed in 2005, he has already made over fifty first team appearances for us. This goes to underline the faith and hope that the management staff have in this young defender, who looks solid defending and quick going forward. Mike is a versatile defender who is equally at home playing at either centre back or at left back.

Previous Clubs: None

Wrexham Career Statistics

	League apps	gls	FA Cup apps	gls	WPC apps	gls	Carling apps	gls	JPT apps	gls	apps	gls
05/06	7/5	0	-	-	1	0	-	-	-	-	8/5	0
06/07	20/11	0	3	0	1	0	2	0	1	0	27/11	0
Total	27/16	0			2	0	2	0	1	0	35/16	0

Position	Defender
Nationality	Welsh
Birthplace	Bangor
Date of Birth	27/10/86
Height	5ft 11in (180cm)
Weight	12st 0lbs (76.27kg)

Josh Johnson (17)

Signed from San Juan Jabloteh in his native Trinidad in August 2006. He made his debut in the 3-0 home win over Grimsby, but his early promise hasn't quite materialised, and he only went on to appear a further nine times, contributing one goal in the process in our 3-1 home defeat to Accrington Stanley. Despite his lack of impact so far, you get the impression that there is an awful lot more to come from this lightning fast winger.

Previous clubs: San Juan Jabloteh

Wrexham Career Statistics

	League apps	gls	FA Cup apps	gls	WPC apps	gls	Carling apps	gls	JPT apps	gls	apps	gls
06/07	10/12	1	1/1	0	-	-	1	0	1	0	13/13	1
Total	10/12	1	1/1	0	-	-	1	0	1	0	13/13	1

Position	Forward
Nationality	Trinidadian
Birthplace	Carenage, Trinidad
Date of Birth	16/04/81
Height	5ft 10in (178cm)
Weight	10st 7lbs (66.67kg)

Levi Mackin (18)

Despite hailing from Chester, Levi has represented Wales at Under-21 level, winning his first cap against Northern Ireland. He is a central midfield player, able to play a holding role or break forwards, who previously helped the youth team capture a league championship. A regular squad player over the last few seasons, his Wrexham career has been somewhat stop-start thus far with injury hampering his progress. He will be hoping to put injuries behind him this coming season, and show just why he is so highly rated by the Wrexham backroom team.

Previous clubs: none

Wrexham Career Statistics

	League apps	League gls	FA Cup apps	FA Cup gls	WPC apps	WPC gls	Carling apps	Carling gls	JPT apps	JPT gls	apps	gls
03/04	1	0	-	-	-	-	-	-	-	-	1	0
04/05	5/5	0	-	-	1	0	0/1	0	-	-	6/6	0
05/06	3/13	0	-	-	0/1	0	0/1	0	0/1	0	3/16	0
06/07	1/6	0	0/1	0	1	0	0/2	0	-	-	2/9	-
Total	10/24	0	0/1	0	2/1	0	0/4	0			12/31	0

Position	Midfielder
Nationality	Welsh
Birthplace	Chester
Date of Birth	04/04/86
Height	6ft 0in (183cm)
Weight	12st 0lbs (76.27kg)

Andy Fleming (19)

Another product of the of youth set up at Wrexham, midfielder Fleming is highly rated by the Racecourse coaching staff and was recently rewarded for his development with a new contract. He made his debut in January of last season as an early substitute in the 1-1 draw at Darlington. It wasn't long before he made an impact after picking up a booking soon after entering the fray! A full debut was soon to follow, in a 0-0 draw against archrivals Chester, a match in which the youngster showed maturity beyond his years. He will be hoping to add to his 2 appearances to date this coming season.

Previous Clubs: None

Wrexham Career Statistics

	League apps	League gls	FA Cup apps	FA Cup gls	WPC apps	WPC gls	Carling apps	Carling gls	JPT apps	JPT gls	apps	gls
06/07	1/1	0	-	-	-	-	-	-	-	-	1/1	0
Total	1/1	0	-	-	-	-	-	-	-	-	1/1	0

Position	Midfielder
Nationality	English
Birthplace	Liverpool
Date of Birth	05/10/87
Height	6ft 0in (183cm)
Weight	11st 5lbs (72.18kg)

Denis Smith - Wrexham Legend. Good luck Brian, the future starts here.

Matty Done (20)

This exciting, pacy winger has a huge future in front of him. Matty seems to be one of those few players who can come on the pitch and change a game. New boss, Brian Carey, took the gamble of resting him at the tail end of last season only to bring him back with devastating effect in the 1-0 win over Bristol Rovers. Another product of the youth system at Wrexham, Matty made his debut for the club back in 2005 against Doncaster in the Coca Cola Cup, although he had to wait until a year later to score his first goal for us in our 3-0 home win over Grimsby last August.

Previous Clubs: None

Wrexham Career Statistics

	League		FA Cup		WPC		Carling		JPT		Total	
	apps	gls	apps	gls	apps	gls	apps	gls	apps	gls	apps	gls
05/06	1/5	0	-		-	-	0/1	0	-	-	1/6	0
06/07	26/7	1	2	0	1	0	1	1	1	0	31/7	2
Total	26/12	1	2	0	1	0	1/1	1	1	0	32/13	2

Position	Forward
Nationality	English
Birthplace	Shrewsbury
Date of Birth	22/06/88
Height	5ft 10in (178cm)
Weight	10st 4lbs (65.32cm)

Marc Williams (21)

Another of the club's Welsh Under-21 internationals, Marc has had a bright start to his career with some energetic performances up front. His non stop running and enthusiasm, not to mention his ability to hold the ball up, has impressed and he was a regular in Brian Careys early team selections. Indeed, he scored the first goal of the Carey era, and the first of his Wrexham career, with a fine header at Swindon. Williams made his Under-21 debut against Northern Ireland in August 2006. In his second game for the squad Williams came off the bench and scored twice in a 3-2 defeat to Israel, before being controversially sent off!

Previous Clubs: None

Wrexham Career Statistics

	League		FA Cup		WPC		Carling		JPT		Total	
	apps	gls	apps	gls	apps	gls	apps	gls	apps	gls	apps	gls
05/06	2/2	0	-		-	-	-		-	-	2/2	0
06/07	11/5	1	0/1	0	-		-		-	-	11/6	1
Total	13/7	1									13/8	1

Position	Forward
Nationality	Welsh
Birthplace	Bangor
Date of Birth	27/07/88
Height	5ft 10in (178cm)
Weight	11st 12lbs (75.29kg)

Connell Murtagh (22)

Former Hearts midfielder Conall Murtagh became Brian Carey's third summer signing after putting pen to paper on a 2-year contract. The Northern Ireland Under-21 international had originally agreed to join Southport after a successful season in the Welsh Premier League with Rhyl, where he was voted in the league managers' team of the season. However, as soon as Wrexham's interest became known the 'Sandgrounders' agreed to tear-up the contract to allow Murtagh to resurrect his professional career. Murtagh still has a year to complete of a biomedical sciences course at Manchester University, which he will do with full support from the 'Dragons'.

Previous Clubs: Hearts, Raith Rovers, Altrincham, Connah's Quay Nomads, Rhyl

(No appearances to date for Wrexham FC)

Position	Midfielder
Nationality	Northern Irish
Birthplace	Belfast
Date of Birth	29/06/85
Height	5ft 11in (180cm)
Weight	11st 7lbs (73.03kg)

Mike Carvill (24)

Michael became Brian Carey's first permanent signing for the club after being released by Charlton Athletic in January 2007. Northern Ireland's record goalscorer at Under-17 level, the 19 year old came through the ranks at the Valley before injury hampered his progress. A versatile performer capable of playing as an out-and-out forward or behind the front two, he scored his first Wrexham goal in the 2-1 defeat to Newport County in the FAW Premier Cup quarter final last season. A lethal finisher at his best, the Belfast-born marksman will be out to prove his worth this season.

Previous Clubs: Charlton Athletic

Position	Forward
Nationality	Northern Irish
Birthplace	Belfast
Date of Birth	03/04/88
Height	5ft 8in (173cm)
Weight	10st 7lbs (66.68kg)

Wrexham Career Statistics

	League		FA Cup		WPC		Carling		JPT			
	apps	gls	apps	gls	apps	gls	apps	gls	apps	gls	apps	gls
06/07	1/6	0	-	-	1	1	-	-	-	-	2/6	1
Total	1/6	0	-	-	1	1	-	-	-	-	2/6	1

Gareth Evans (24)

A promising young centre back, 'Gaz' was initially released prior to last season before funding was found to offer him a new contract. He quickly grabbed his second chance making his debut as a second half substitute in the Carling Cup victory over Sheffield Wednesday, going on to make 14 appearances. Signed by Wrexham from NEWI Cefn Druids, the former Wolverhampton Wanderers youth player was the first player to renew his contract in the summer, penning a new 2-year deal.

Previous Clubs: None

Position	Defender
Nationality	Welsh
Birthplace	Wrexham
Date of Birth	10/01/87
Height	6ft 1in (185cm)
Weight	12st 2lbs (81.64kg)

Wrexham Career Statistics

	League		FA Cup		WPC		Carling		JPT			
	apps	gls	apps	gls	apps	gls	apps	gls	apps	gls	apps	gls
06/07	9/3	0	-	-	-	-	0/2	0	-	-	9/5	0
Total	9/3	0	-	-	-	-	0/2	0	-	-	9/5	0

Jamie Reed (27)

A prolific goalscorer for the reserves who hasn't quite transformed that form to the first team. However, you could argue that he hasn't really been given the chance to prove himself, having made just seven substitute appearances and no starts. Jamie has looked a direct player and physically strong despite only just turning twenty. He almost bagged his first league goal when he went awfully close to scoring twice against Darlington in the dying minutes last season. He will have a lot of competition this season, but may prove valuable for us if he can start scoring first team goals.

Previous Clubs: Glentoran (loan), Colwyn Bay

Position	Forward
Nationality	English
Birthplace	Chester
Date of Birth	13/08/87
Height	6ft 0in (183cm)
Weight	11st 7lbs (73.03kg)

Wrexham Career Statistics

	League		FA Cup		WPC		Carling		JPT			
	apps	gls	apps	gls	apps	gls	apps	gls	apps	gls	apps	gls
04/05	-	-	-	-	0/1	0	-	-	-	-	0/1	0
05/06	0/3	0	-	-	-	-	-	-	-	-	0/3	0
06/07	0/4	0	-	-	0/1	0	-	-	-	-	0/5	0
Total	0/7	0	-	-	0/2	0	-	-	-	-	0/9	0

Juan Ugarte (30)

Probably the most frustrated/frustrating player at the club! Reds fans are already aware of the huge goalscoring talent that is Juan Ugarte from when he first knocked in 22 goals in all competitions in 2004/2005, to when he helped us to lift the LDV Trophy. Juan actually made three substitute appearances last season, although it seems an absolute age since he last started for the club. Will we see him this season? Let's hope so!

Previous Clubs: Real Sociedad, Dorchester Town, Crewe Alexandra

Position	Forward
Nationality	Spanish
Birthplace	San Sebastian, Spain
Date of Birth	07/07/80
Height	5ft 10in (178cm)
Weight	11st 6lbs (72.64)

Wrexham Career Statistics

	League		FA Cup		WPC		Carling		JPT			
	apps	gls	apps	gls	apps	gls	apps	gls	apps	gls	apps	gls
04/05	23/7	17	1/1	0	2	3	-	-	5/1	6	31/9	26
05/06	2	0	-	-	0/1	1	-	-	-	-	2/1	1
06/07	0/2	0	0/1	0	-	-	-	-	-	-	0/3	0
Total	25/9	17	1/2	0	2/1	4	-	-	5/1	6	33/13	27

The First Year Professionals

Name	Wesley Baines
Position	Defender
Nationality	English
Birthplace	Chester
Date of Birth	12/10/88
Height	5ft 11in (180cm)
Weight	11st 3lbs (71.21kg)

Name	Alex Darlington
Position	Forward
Nationality	Welsh
Birthplace	Wrexham
Date of Birth	26/12/88
Height	5ft 10in (178cm)
Weight	11st 0lbs (69.92kg)

Name	Neil Taylor
Position	Defender
Nationality	Welsh
Birthplace	St. Asaph
Date of Birth	07/02/89
Height	5ft 9in (175cm)
Weight	11st 3lbs (71.21kg)

Centre of Excellence 2007/08

After the ups and downs of last season the club in general feels extremely confident of being in a position of progressing, and ensure that we are a big part of the forward strides.

With regard to football development, the coaching of the YT's will be combined this season between Joey Jones and myself, with Joey taking the lead with the reserve team, and myself with the youth team. It's good to know that if a player takes the opportunity to maximise his potential, then his progress will be encouraged, as has been proved with the likes of Marc and Mike Williams, Michael Jones, Jamie Reed, Gareth Evans, Matty Done and Andy Fleming, who have all made their first team debuts in recent years.

The timetable set out for the youth players this season has been set out to ensure a full range of activities that will allow time to be spent on the all important aspects of a players development. Much time will be spent on technical, tactical, physical and social work both individually and as a team.

Coaching Team

Head of Youth Steve Cooper, Centre of Excellence Manager Andy Davies, Head of Recruitment Stuart Webber, Head of Sports Science Andy O'Boyle, Physiotherapists Richie Buchanan & Ritson Lloyd, Administrator Tricia Deary- Furber, Chief Scout John Reardon, Regional Scout Ron Parry, Education & Welfare Jonathan Miller.

Steve Cooper, Head of Youh

Many of the second years gained a lot of experience from last year, playing in both youth and reserve team games. It's important that as a team we couple this experience with enthusiasm from the first years, and work hard to ensure we have a successful season in the Puma Youth Alliance. I for one feel we have enough ability, strength and depth to have a strong push in both the league and cup competitions.

Finally, as a youth department we will be looking to ensure we work hard, enjoy ourselves and stick together in everything we do, there is no reason why we can't reap huge rewards both as a team, and in inspiring individuals.

Our Vision for the Future

Wrexham Football Club is determined to continue to produce youth players that meet the high standards necessary to continue the future development of the Club. We intend to achieve this vision by selecting young footballers from our local community with outstanding football potential. We will always encourage the player's development by providing them with a programme designed for emphasising the full range of personal growth.

Once again we find ourselves raring to go for another season, it only seems like yesterday we were finishing up from last season, but as you know things move quickly in football.

Since the end of last season there has been a change in staff structure, with Steve Weaver moving up to become assistant to Brian Carey, while I have moved into the role of Head of Youth and Andy Davies will be the Centre of Excellence manager, with Stuart Webber overseeing recruitment. Without doubt, the new members bring a wealth of knowledge from previous coaching and playing experience. I am sure this will prove to be a positive move for the youth department at Wrexham.

We have also made vast improvements to the facilities at Collier's Park; with the new 3G-field turf being accompanied by a seated stand area for spectators to use. The centre now has a new office base to the rear of the main building, with changing rooms and toilets. As you will agree Wrexham Football Club continues to improve and enhance its facilities for the benefit of all its players.

As I hope you are now aware the general aims of the centre are to create an environment that caters for all the players needs helping them maximise their potential. Within this the players should enjoy their free time at the club ultimately helping them develop as players and as young men.

Finally, it's important that once again, we all pull together and make sure that we reach our aims for the season helping us to realise the overall aim of Wrexham FC in producing home grown players for the first team.

Steve Cooper
Head of Youth, Wrexham FC

Centre of Excellence Squads 2007-08

Under 9's: Coach Danny Copnall
Llan Ap Gareth, Nathan Brown, Ben Burrows, Owen Lloyd Davies, Owen Goodenough, Ryan Harrington, George Harry, Peter Rhys Jones, Brady McGilloway, Cameron Meadows, Jack Pennington, James Saul, Scott James Towers, Jake Vanschie.

Under 10's: Coach Ian Hughes
Nathan Paul Broadhead, Jack Chambers, Matthew Clewley, Kieran Joseph Evans, Cameron Gardner, Ryan Hughes, Thomas Hughes, Michael McNee, Rakim Yasir Newton, Stephen David Rimmer, Alex Tiernan, Shaun William Trousdale, Thomas Vickers.

Under 11's: Coaches, Mark Cox & Mike Walsh
Danny Burgess, Jonathan Crump, Matthew Dunbabin, Jake Fernandez-Hart, Matthew Graham-Hammons, Connor Hughes (GK), James Jones, Daniel Jones (GK), Jake Phillips, Daniel Reynolds, Ben Richards, Joshua Robertson.

Under 12's: Coach Ben Heath
Thomas Batten, Iwan Cartwright, Oliver Cooke, Ryan Crump (GK), Jordan Evans, Ryan Kershaw, James Littlemore, Jordan Maddock, Danny Myers, Jack Smith, Curtis Strong, Richard Tomassen, Cory Williams, Jordan Williams.

Under 13's: Coach, Kevin Quigley
Thomas Allen-Davies, Adam Bailey, Wesley Bennett, Oliver Bentley, Luke Douglas, Roberts David Evans, Conor Patrick Fay, Tom Freeman, Conner Luke Kendrick, Adam Lee, Gregory Patrick Mills, Kyle Parle, Aled Parry, Jonathan Parry, Kevin David Rawlinson, Jonathan Royle.

Under 14's: Coaches Gus Williams & Neil Roberts
Niam Arsan, George Baxter, Jared Bennett, Chris Boswell, Ryan Edwards. Max Fargin, Naser Farhat. Elliott Hewitt, Kieran Murphy, Nathan Nicholls, Matthew Owen, Christopher Pulford, Matthew Regan, William Roberts, Connor Shutt, Stephen Tomassen

Under 15's: Coaches Tony Merola & Roger Preece
Thomas Boam, Niall Challoner, James Colbeck, George Cowell, Joseph Culshaw, Owen Davies, Stephen Ferrigan, Michael Jones, Iwan lewis, Jon-Paul Molyneux, Louis Moss (GK), Danny Murphy (GK), Max Penk, Liam rice, Conor Swale, Daniel Ward.

Under 16's: Coach Roger Preece
Thomas Bainbridge (GK), Daniel Birks, Ryan Catahan, Leon Clowes, Phillip Davies, Joshua Griffiths, Joseph Imlach, Jordan kane, Joshua Marsh, Edward Moss, Charlie Proctor, Joshua Kyle Rush, Nicholas Rushton, Kieran Smith.

Under-18s Coach Steve Cooper, **Goalkeeping Coaches** Mark Morris, Tom Roberts & Fred Price.

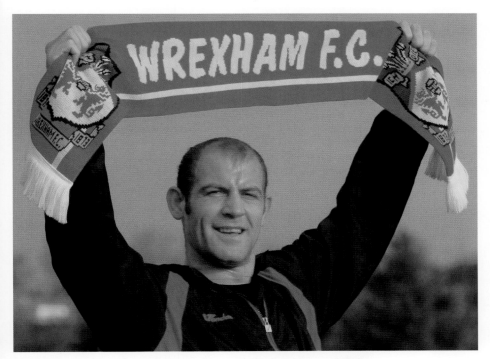

A Football League debut at 27!

The Evening Leader's Richard Williams interviews Steve Evans on his 'Roy of the Rovers' rise to international status.

STEVE EVANS could be forgiven for pinching himself to check what's happened to him over the past twelve months. Having had spells at Crewe Alexandra and West Bromwich Albion as a youngster without securing a professional contract or getting first team experience, at 27 he thought the chance of playing in the Football League was past him.

That was until Wrexham manager Denis Smith stepped in to sign the towering centre-half last summer. "I'd had great times with TNS, but when the chance to join Wrexham came I took it with both hands, and I could never imagine what was to happen to me this time last year - I was just concentrating on doing well for TNS.

Steve had joined League of Wales side TNS, formerly Llansantffraid, for the 1999/2000 season. And of his time with the 'Saints' he said; "I had seven good years at TNS. I was the league's player of the year in 2005, and in the top three for the award the last four seasons I was there. We won the league three times, the Welsh Cup once, and the League Cup. We won just about everything."

Steve soon adapted to the step up, and immediately established himself as a first team regular. He got off to a great start by scoring on his home debut in a 3-0 win over

Grimsby Town. "That was a fantastic feeling, and I couldn't have asked for a better start than to score for my home town club on the Racecourse with my family and friends watching."

Evans' form meant he soon became one of the first names on the team-sheet and he was only absent through suspension having been sent-off three times of the Reds last year! But Evans admitted some aspects of playing in the Football League took getting used to; "I found the fitness and physical demands - week in, week out - more demanding on me at Wrexham. Rather than play just one tough game with TNS every six weeks, there is no easy games in the Football League. It took a while to adapt. At first, I was shattered in the last 15-20 minutes of a match, but I soon got there. Football wise it went well from the start really. I just go out with the right frame of mind and I felt comfortable."

Having established himself as an imposing, uncompromising defender, Evans went on to make 34 league starts and one substitute appearance last season, scoring two goals in the process, but having been used to success at TNS where he had Champions League experience against Liverpool, his first season at Wrexham was all about avoiding relegation to the Conference.

Safety was eventually reached in a nail-biting last day of the season match with Boston United, who dropped into the Conference League. Delighted with how things have developed on a personal note, he is hoping Wrexham can be challenging at the right end of League Two this season.

Steve Evans in training with his new Wales team mates Lewis Nyatanga and Ryan Giggs

"Hopefully everything is going in the right direction here now and I can start winning things with Wrexham. We have got to do a lot better than last season and I am sure we will. We have brought some good players in, and we are optimistic that we can be challenging for promotion. I really enjoyed my first season at Wrexham and in the Football League. I felt I had a good season. I am over the moon with how it went; it could not have gone much better, except my three stupid sending offs. I have to keep it going this season and hopefully reproduce the form from last year."

If Evans does just that, you can expect him to feature in many more Wales squads.

Steve Evans in action against Ireland at Croke Park

Evans' eye-catching performances for Wrexham at the start of last season soon caught the eye of the Welsh team manager John Toshack, who gave him an international debut in last November's friendly against Liechtenstein at The Racecourse.

And winning a first cap for his country - in his home town - meant everything to the former Welsh semi-professional international; "I am just grateful to John Toshack for giving me a chance. I did not expect to get called up. It was a shock but when it came, I thought 'I'm going to take my chance.' Being called up is one thing, but then to be told I was starting was a dream come true. And with the game played at The Racecourse, it was a fantastic feeling. I just tried to do everything right and it went well for me."

Evans now has five full caps to his name and he is grateful to the faith shown in him by Toshack, who knows he can rely on the defender; "I started against Northern Ireland in Belfast and did well. I was proud to be wearing the Wales shirt again," added Evans. "Then came the qualifiers against the Republic of Ireland and San Marino in March. I was not expecting to start, but John Toshack picked me - I was chuffed to bits. If he thinks I am good enough then there is nothing to worry about. And I feel I have done well in the games I have played for Wales. I came on as a substitute for the second half in the New Zealand game, but it was still an honour to be involved. And obviously it made it that extra bit special playing for my country at The Racecourse. "I was on the bench for the qualifier against the Czech Republic, and although I never got on, I am chuffed to be part of it. Hopefully it continues."

Along with his five Welsh caps, Steve gained further confirmation that he is now an established Football League player when the fans voted him as the club's player of the season - not bad for a first full season in the Football League. "It's been a fantastic year from a personal point of view - absolutely brilliant," said Evans. "Getting the chance to play for my hometown club was a dream, and getting called up for Wales was a huge honour." Long may it continue…

Section 3:
The History of Wrexham FC

A Tribute to Denis Smith
Wrexham FC Manager (2000-2007)

DENIS SMITH hit the ground running on the Monday in October 2001 when he was unveiled as the new manager of Wrexham and watched the club's reserve team in action that evening at Preston North End.

The young Dragons shipped seven goals in a frankly awful Deepdale performance and Smith was particularly scathing in his assessment of one Racecourse young-ster on show. "He'll never be a footballer as long as he's got a hole in his ****," he told me afterwards in the car park.

He didn't mean it, of course, instead making it his business to work with the player concerned, who has since gone on to carve out a very respectable career in the

game and is now closing in on 200 Football League appearances.

But that was Smith all over, viewing the defeat as a personal insult even though he barely knew the names of the players he had inherited from his predecessor, Brian Flynn.

On another, much later, occasion at Torquay United, Smith had arranged to spend the rest of the weekend with wife Kate at their daughter's home in Cornwall.

The home side won 1-0 and before Smith emerged from the dressing room, she said: "It's okay for you, you've only got to spend five minutes with him, we've got to put up with him for at least an hour in the car."

Put simply, he hated losing football matches, no matter what the circumstances, and he didn't much care for anyone who did not share that attitude. It was a philosophy instilled in him as he grew up in the less than salubrious district of Mere in the Potteries where he soon learned to stick up for himself and his working class family.

Luckier than most of his contemporaries in that his talent enabled him to live the dream of every back-street football-mad youngster, he rarely took his gift for granted and never gave less than 100% every time he turned out for his hometown club.

His loyalty and service to Stoke City earned him legendary status and if he was occasionally guilty of reminding people of that, he nevertheless always recognised how privileged he was to be able to pursue the career of his dreams.

Denis Smith guided Wrexham Football Club through the difficult times under Mark Guterman

As a result, he had little patience with those who didn't share his values - old-fashioned though they seem nowadays - and no sympathy whatsoever for anyone he suspected of merely going through the motions to pick up a substantial pay packet.

Those principles provoked conflict - and a subsequent parting of the ways - with a handful of Wrexham players during Smith's time at the Racecourse, but they proved crucial to the club's survival under the woeful chairmanship of Mark Guterman.

Guterman's financial mismanagement and the complete absence of a long-term strategy - for reasons that were to become all too clear - effectively sabotaged the manager's efforts to preserve and improve his 2003 promotion-winning squad, first choice strikers Andy Morrell and Lee Trundle both out of contract and moving away during the summer.

The 45 league goals they had jointly contributed were sorely missed the following season as Wrexham scored a total of just 49, yet remained in contention for the League One play-offs until the final 10 matches of the campaign.

What made the team's performance all the more creditable was that behind the scenes the very fabric of the club was being ripped apart - unpaid wages, phones being cut off and unpaid bills resulting in no heating or hot water at the training ground.

It was no mean feat that Smith maintained morale in coping with the sort of problems he had never experienced before during a long management career, but despite the club's financial woes he approached the 2004-5 season with a degree of optimism, having signed Andy Holt during the summer and with newly-installed chairman Alex Hamilton at least ensuring that players were being paid and day-to-day expenses being met in a hand to mouth existence.

A 14-point haul from the opening eight games augured well, even without World Cup injury victim Carlos Edwards, but Wrexham's form faltered when goalkeeper Andy Dibble missed 10 matches at the time off-field events were coming to a head.

Smith signed unknown striker Juan Ugarte, who made his debut from the bench in a 5-1 defeat at Luton - the first of four straight league defeats - and the Spanish import was still without a league goal in his ninth appearance at Scunthorpe on the day the club was put into administration.

The automatic 10-point deduction not only saw Wrexham drop from 16th to 22nd in the table, but it also infuriated Smith, who felt after fighting for more than 12 months with one arm tied behind his back that the offending limb had now been cut off.

For all the bravado and public persona that followed the Dragons boss was offended by the sanction, which he habitually blamed for all the subsequent below-par performances that were to follow.

The New Year return by Edwards and the signing of loan goalkeeper Ben Foster from

Stoke City did little to improve the club's League One fortunes and for every super show from Ugarte, who netted four goals at Chesterfield and five at Hartlepool, there were the 4-0 defeats at Sheffield Wednesday and the 5-1 Racecourse hammering by Tranmere Rovers.

Thankfully Wrexham were more Jekyll than Hyde in the LDV Vans Trophy competition and it was a proud moment for Smith when the club secured their first major Football League knock out honour on a never-to-be forgotten afternoon at the Millennium Stadium.

But memorable as the victory was - and equally vital in terms of providing the cash to keep the club afloat - Smith would have swapped it all for League One survival because he knew better than most that relegation would take him back to where he had started the job four years previously.

The season just gone is well documented elsewhere in this publication, but no-one, hand on heart, can guess what the outcome would have been had Smith not been shown the Racecourse door in January.

What is beyond dispute, however, was the dignified manner with which he accepted the decision and his subsequent generosity in making himself available for advice and counsel whenever it was requested by his successor Brian Carey.

One wonders what different future might have been in store for both Wrexham and Smith had the likes of Guterman, Rhodes and Hamilton displayed the same measure of integrity in their dealings with him.

Denis Smith and Kevin Russell formed a formidable partnership

Racecourse Nights To Remember

This year Wrexham's Racecourse Ground celebrated 130 years as the World's oldest international football venue. Wales' first ever-international match took place on the Racecourse on 5th March 1877 when Scotland won 2-0. Including that game, 92 full international matches have now been played on the ground, and here we look back on one of those 'Racecourse Nights to Remember'.

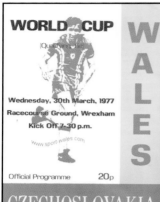

Wales: (Coach: Mike Smith)
Dai Davies (Everton), Rod Thomas (Derby County), Joey Jones (Liverpool), John Mahoney (Stoke City), Leighton Phillips (Aston Villa), Ian Evans (Crystal Palace), Peter Sayer (Cardiff City), Brian Flynn (Burnley), Terry Yorath (Coventry City), Nick Deacy (PSV Eindhoven), *Leighton James (Derby County) replaced by sub Mickey Thomas (Wrexham)*

Czechoslovakia: (Coach: Vaclav Jezek), Alexander Vencel (Slovan Bratislava), Karol Dobias (Spartak Trnava), Ladislav Jurkemik (Inter Bratislava), Pavel Biros (Slavia Prague), Jan Pivarnik (Slovan Bratislava), Koloman Gogh (Slovan Bratislava), *Jozef Moder (Locomotive Kosice) replaced by sub Miroslav Gajdusek (Dukla Prague)*, Antonin Panenka (Bohemians Prague), Jaroslav Pollak (VSS Kosice), Marian Masny (Slovan Bratislava), Zdenek Nehoda (Dukla Prague).

Referee: Mr A. Da Silva Garrido (Portugal)

Wales 3 Czechoslovakia 0
World Cup Qualifier Group Seven: 30th March 1977

Wales had been drawn in a three team-qualifying group with Scotland and Czechoslovakia for the 1978 World Cup, which meant playing just four games. As usual it was a tough group for Wales, and having lost their opening game 1-0 to the Scots at Hampden Park, they needed to win this game to keep their hopes alive.

Yet another memorable night for the Welsh team at the Racecourse saw a partisan crowd of 18,022 willing Mike Smith's side on to a rousing performance that saw Leighton James have without doubt his finest game for his country, despite having been restored to the team at the eleventh hour when injury to others had dishevelled the original squad.

The Welsh started sharper and more direct in attack, quick to challenge at the back, as they gradually overwhelmed the Czechs. It was along the wings where Wales gave the Czechs much to worry about, with James having the skill to lure and unsettle his opponents. Peter Sayer, too, was lively enough to trouble the Czechs, and both were involved in the goal that set Wales on course in the 27th minute.

James, toppled by a challenge from two opponents on the left, accepted a short free-kick from Flynn, and he placed his cross low towards the near post; Sayer reached for it and Vencel, who expected him to make contact, moved to his right to cover; both missed the ball, with the goalkeeper going one way, and the ball passing him on the other side to bounce gently into the goal amid jubilation from the home crowd.

To that point Vencel hadn't been tested, although Wales had won four corners. A curling free-kick by Panenka thudded into Davies' chest, and a quickly taken shot by Nehoda passed a foot or so wide of the post. Pollak worked hard in midfield, but the Czechs could not sustain possession, though one of Masny's corners just sailed over the bar with Davies beaten, before he then did well to turn away Jurkemik's splendid shot from 25-yards.

The second half saw the crowd's noise level raised in a bid to stir the Welsh team on, while the Czech's clearly needed to improve their work rate. They replaced the ineffective Moder with Gajdusek, but the Welshmen had their tails up; the backs were steadfast, and Brian Flynn, the smallest player on the field grew in stature as the match evolved, with nippy interceptions and perceptive use of the ball.

A moment of doubt finally put the match firmly in Wales' grasp, James, now out on the right wing, pushed a pass forward for John Mahoney to chase; the Czechs hesitated, apparently anticipating offside, but Mahoney ran on, put his pass into the jaws of the goal, where Sayer just failed to control it, but the ball ran on to Nick Deacy who steered it into the goal in the 65th minute.

The Racecourse Roar was now in full voice, urging Wales on. With 'Hymns and Arias' bellowing around the ground, the Welsh were not going to allow an advantage like this to slip away, and with fifteen minutes left they claimed a third goal. Flynn nipped back to win the ball with a tackle in his own half and sped away with it up the left flank; he spotted James streaking through the remnants of the Czech's defence and guided an accurate pass into his path. James took it forward a yard or two and tucked it away to set off wild scenes of joy.

It was a stirring performance against the odds, and amid scenes of wild celebrations, but later came cautious judgment from Welsh team manager Mike Smith: "We have two hard matches to play yet before we can start thinking about Argentina."

Despite calls to play the Scottish game at the Racecourse fortress, they fell on deaf ears as the Welsh FA decided to play the game in England at Anfield in a bid to bring in much needed revenue, but how it cost us dear as we well know...

The Welsh team line-up left to right; Terry Yorath, Rod Thomas, Dai Davies, Nick Deacy, John Mahoney, Brian Flynn, Joey Jones, Leighton James, Leighton Phillips, Ian Evans & Peter Sayer.

Wrexham FC: Third Division Champions 1977-78

The 30th Anniversary of Wrexham Football Club's Third Division Championship side: Wrexham's greatest!

This season Wrexham Football Club celebrates the 30th Anniversary of what was the most memorable season in the club's history - 1977/78. It was a season that saw Wrexham win the Third Division championship in style, and here Peter Jones looks back on that unforgettable campaign with the manager of that time, Arfon Griffiths.

With the 1976/77 season almost at a close, John Neal's side needed just three points from their last five games to win promotion. Arfon explained: "We won one of those points in a scoreless draw at home to the league leaders Brighton & Hove Albion, but I was injured in that game, which meant I missed the last four games, with what I think was a pulled muscle. We then lost both home and away to our rivals Crystal Palace, while drawing with Oxford in-between. It meant we had to win our last game of the season at home to the champions Mansfield Town.

Wrexham FC 1977/78 Third Division Championship winning side:

Back Row: (L-R) John Lyons, Dixie McNeil, Mel Sutton, Tony Larkin.

Middle Row: (L-R) Bobby Shinton, Wayne Cegielski, John Roberts, Alan Hill, Dai Davies, Eddie Niedzwiecki, Steve Kenworthy, Les Cartwright & George Showell (Physio).

Front Row: (L-R) Alan Dwyer, Stuart Lee, Mickey Thomas, Arfon Griffiths (Manager), Gareth Davies (Captain), Graham Whittle, Mike Williams & Mickey Evans.

Arfon Griffiths' analysis of the 1977-78 team:

Dai Davies: "What can I say about Dai? A very good organizer, he tells players what to do, and with his experience, along with Dixie, was a good addition to the squad, which strengthened us enough to go that one step further than the previous season.

Eddie Niedzwiecki: "A young lad at the time, who came in and did more than was asked of him. He learned a lot from Dai, and came of age in the game against Swindon. It was a shame his career ended so early."

Alan Hill: "Quiet, but effective, consistently steady. Never let the side down."

Mickey Evans: "Could play in a number of positions. The best defender we had. Great at nullifying a marked opponent."

Alan Dwyer: "He didn't know how good he was. Should have without doubt played at a higher level. Quick going forward, but lacked confidence in his abilities."

Gareth Davies: "A superb reader of the game. The Bobby Moore of the Third Division. A good leader."

John Roberts: "A ready made replacement for Eddie May, and did an equally as good a job. A very good defender who was very good at frightening opponents - which you could do in them days!"

Mickey Thomas: "Had a cockiness about him. A wonderful player, and a never-say-die attitude. He just wouldn't stop running, and one of the main reasons we went up."

Bobby Shinton: "Bought for a bargain £20,000 from Cambridge. Most skilful player we had. He didn't have a lot of pace, but could beat players which took some doing. Could score goals as well."

Mel Sutton: "Did a great job for me as assistant manager, and as a player he made Bobby Shinton the player he was. An excellent pro, one of the fittest at the club."

Dixie McNeil: "The best goalscorer the club have ever had without a doubt. How he didn't play in the First Division is beyond me. Could also give as much as he got from centre halves."

Graham Whittle: "A brilliant striker of the ball. He started off in midfield, but we found he drifted out of the game at times, so put him up front where he scored goals for fun. Great goals they were too, but he could also head a ball well."

Les Cartwright: "Found the club for his style of play, left sided midfield player who could pass people and put in great crossers. Coming to Wrexham rejuvenated his Welsh career."

John Lyons: "A real goal poacher. He didn't get too involved in build-up play, but knew where the goal was."

Wayne Cegielski: "Ideal cover in defence. Always came in and did a good job. A good reliable defender."

Wrexham clinched promotion after a 7-1 win over Rotherham United at the Racecourse

"I was having a fitness test on the morning of the game, when the news broke that Middlesbrough wanted John Neal as their new manager. Not surprisingly the chairman Fred Tomlinson was very upset at the timing of the story, and to make matters worse I failed my fitness test and missed the game. We lost to a last minute Ernie Moss goal to miss out on promotion. It was a disaster. The home dressing room was not a nice place to be. We were gutted to say the least.

"The following morning I spoke to John Neal who asked me if I would go to Middlesbrough with him as his assistant. I told him I would think about it, but the following day I went into training and Mel Sutton said he hoped I wasn't going to, as we had the nucleus of a good team here, and we could do it next season. It was his words, and the fact that I had just moved to a new house that made me decide my future was at Wrexham.

"I was then approached by the chairman, Fred Tomlinson about taking charge, and I had no hesitation in doing so. I had been coach and assistant-manager to John Neal for some time by then, and so I had a very good insight into what was required. I made Mel my assistant, and Mickey Evans player/coach.

"In looking at the team, like Mel, I too felt we were good enough to make a serious challenge, but I knew we needed to have some more experience and depth in the squad, as I felt we never had ready made replacements when injuries occurred the previous season. My first signing was Les Cartwright from Coventry City, but to be honest the deal had already been set up by John Neal. With the tax year ending we knew we had money to spend, and paid £40,000 for him.

"It wasn't long before John Neal came calling, and he wanted Billy Ashcroft. I was willing to listen, if the fee was right. The previous year Bolton had made an offer for Billy, but John turned it down as it wasn't enough. I turned down John's initial offer as I felt it wasn't enough. Billy started the season for us, and it was then that John came back with an improved offer of £120,000, which we accepted."

Those opening games also saw a controversial change in goalkeeper, with Brian Lloyd being dropped for promising youngster Eddie Niedzwiecki. Arfon said of the decision; "That was a tough decision for me. Brian was a very good goalkeeper, but I felt he lacked command and organization of the people in front of him, and I knew Dai Davies, who I had played in front of for Wales was available at Everton.

Brian Lloyd was sold to Chester for £6,000, and Dai was bought for what proved to be a bargain £8,000. A further signing to replace Billy Ashcroft was made in Hereford United striker Dixie McNeil for £60,000. "Both proved great acquisitions for us. Dai told the people in front him what he wanted, and made defenders better players. Hereford wanted £100,000 for Dixie, but we knew they were in financial difficulty at the time and held out. In the end we got yet another bargain. We knew Dixie was a very good player, as he always played well when he played against us, but bigger clubs weren't looking to give him a chance because of his age. He could have played at a higher level no doubt.

"They both made their debuts at home to Swindon, and we recorded only our second win of the season in eight games, with Dixie scoring the first goal in the 2-0 win. People looking back and think it was all rosy that season, but having had over 20,000 for the Mansfield game, the first league game of this season saw only 5,490 turn up. We'd lost almost 15,000 fans over the summer! It wasn't until Boxing Day we had over 10,000 fans, but it never dropped under that figure the rest of the season.

"We made great progress in the League Cup and reached the quarter-finals with wins over Stockport, Charlton, Bristol City, and Swindon before losing 3-1 at home to the European Cup winners, Liverpool, with Kenny Dalglish scoring a hat-trick. In the FA Cup we beat Burton Albion, Preston, Bristol City, Newcastle and Blyth [Spartans] before going out again in the quarter-finals stage to Arsenal.

"We had some great cup games during this period. We didn't care who we played. First Division sides were scared to play us - everything was falling into place. We'd give most teams a game; the players were excellent. As a team we had the right balance on both the right and the left of the field, and we had strength down the middle. However, one of the games that gave us great cause for concern was the FA Cup fifth round home tie with Blyth Spartans. We were saved by the skin of our teeth, and really should have been out. The replay will always live with me. A guy came into the hotel, and told us all the tickets for the stands were sold, and that it would be a sell out. We thought he was exaggerating, but as we drove towards the ground on the team bus, we all thought 'that guy was telling the truth!' The crowds were amazing, almost 43,000 in St.James Park, with many locked out. Thankfully, we overcame Blyth in front of a very partisan home crowd."

For only the second time in the club's history, Wrexham had reached the quarter-final stage of the FA Cup, where they met Arfon's former club Arsenal, who were without doubt fortunate to win 3-2 with even Gunners boss, Terry Neill admitting; 'I will not dispute Wrexham deserved a draw. They played exceptionally well, but I didn't think we played as well as we can. We had a bit of a scare it could have gone either way.'

Of that game Arfon said; "Luck wasn't on our side, but I felt it was a blessing in disguise really as our main priority was promotion. We'd also come to the attention of the national press, and all the euphoria surrounding the cup can side-track you."

The following game saw Wrexham travel to Swindon. "We got over the disappointment of losing in the cup, as we won 2-1, with John Lyons scoring both goals. It was that game that gave me an inkling that it was going to be our season. We played Bury at Gigg Lane shortly after, and I remember we had what I thought was a perfectly good goal disallowed. I was up on my feet ranting and shouting, when the Bury manager, Bob Stokoe, shouted over to me; 'sit down, and don't

Arfon Griffiths, Manager of the Year 1977-1978

worry, your troubles will start in the Second Division next season!' It made me realise how close we really were to going up.

Promotion was clinched in a 7-1 home win over Rotherham; "It was one of those games that everything went in. We had no pressure really, as we had games to spare, but it was a pleasure to see us do it in style. We then went to Hereford to clinch the championship, and what a superb following we had there. The last game of the season saw us play Sheffield Wednesday at Hillsborough, and Jack Charlton had his players line up to see us out. It was a nice gesture. We finished the season by winning the Welsh Cup with a two-legged win over a very good Bangor City side, who were then in the old Northern Premier League.

"Winning the Third Division championship made up for the previous year. It wasn't easy starting off, but we did it with only a squad of 16 to 18 players really, because Stuart Lee, Brian Lloyd and Billy Ashcroft only played a few games at the beginning of the season. One thing that pleased me most, was killing off that old myth, 'they don't want to go up!'

"It is without doubt the best Wrexham side I have ever seen. We played over sixty games that season, but the players knew if they went out of the side, they'd struggle to get their place back in; but as any manager will tell you, 'it's not the team that takes you up, it's the squad'.

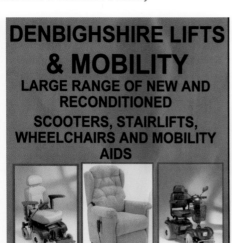

Wrexham Pioneers

In our first yearbook, Wales and Wrexham Football Historian Gareth M. Davies took us back in time to the pioneering days of the game and the early Wrexham players who also wore the Welsh shirt. This time around he continues on the trail taking in the period of the 1880's.

Thomas Burke was a teammate of James Trainer at Wrexham Grosvenor and Wrexham FC. A future Welsh custodian with Bolton Wanderers and Preston North End. Tom was described as a 'capable half-back with a sure kick, who made intelligent use of the ball.' Burke won his first cap for Wales while at Wrexham, but when the club were thrown out of the FA Cup in March 1884 following disturbances against Oswestry, he was recruited by Wrexham Olympic, who were their successor club. He was a painter by profession, and was one of a number of footballers from North East Wales in the 1880's who were to join Newton Heath - predecessors of today's Manchester United, while also taking up employment with the parent Lancashire and Yorkshire Railway Company. Hence the most famous football club in existence owes much to this part of the world, and our 'pioneer players' who played a very important part in their formation!

Burke won eight caps for Wales; three while with Newton Heath, but when moving to the Football Alliance Tom lost his place and returned to his birthplace with Wrexham Victoria, playing alongside fellow Welsh internationals with Wrexham FC connections Job Wilding, Billy Harrison and Harry Trainer. He also won a Welsh Cup winners medal in 1883 for Wrexham against Druids (Ruabon), and was also on the score sheet for Wales in the 8-2 victory over Ireland in Belfast on 11th April 1885.

The next Wrexham FC representative in a Welsh shirt was to be *John Arthur Eyton-Jones*, who won all four of his Welsh caps while at the club. John Arthur began playing football with Wrexham Hare and Hounds FC. Described as 'an athletic player full of dash and enthusiasm, his strongest suit was constructive play, but an erratic shot'. Such was the jargon of the day in the 1880's! Against Ireland in 1883 he was adjudged to 'have speed; is smart on the ball; passes with judgement and appears to be able to stay - an essential quality'. Jones eventually moved to Liverpool to study medicine and joined Bootle FC whilst also in Everton's books as an amateur (at that time the

Robert Davies

Awarded three Welsh caps, whilst playing for Wrexham FC and Wrexham Olympic. Later went on to become a Football Association of Wales referee.

Davies was described as a slightly built individual with much natural ability, which he put to good use in a number of footballing dribbling contests which he won in the 1880's. Known as 'Bob Pugh' to Wrexham people, he later kept the Albion Hotel in Wrexham.

'Toffees' played at Anfield!). He set up his practice back home in Wrexham during 1889, and was later House Surgeon at Liverpool Royal Infirmary. During the 1914-18 war he served as a captain in the R.A.M.C. and 1st Welsh Border Mounted Brigade.

Like Burke, Jones had also moved to Wrexham Olympic in early 1884 from the now disbanded Wrexham FC and was also a team-mate in the 1883 Welsh Cup winning side of the latter. He was a wing half/forward, however *Robert Davies* who also played in the 1883 Welsh Cup side was primarily just a forward who gained three Welsh caps, two with Wrexham, and the latter with the Olympic side.

He was described as a slightly built individual with much natural ability, which he put to good use in a number of footballing dribbling contests which he won, and were popular competitions in the 1880's. Known as 'Bob Pugh' to Wrexham people he was at one time an FAW referee and later kept the Albion Hotel in Wrexham.

Yet another of Wrexham's 1883 Welsh Cup winning side (and he wont be the last in this section!) to be capped by Wales was *Walter Davies* who won his only international appearance in a 6-0 thrashing of Ireland at the Racecourse on 9th February 1884.

He had joined up with his hometown in late 1882 after starting up with the junior club Wrexham Victoria. A well built full back his defensive qualities saw him signed up by Derby County in November 1884 during their pre Football League days, but later returned to Wrexham in 1886 with another junior club to join Wrexham Gymnasium.

No doubt that *Herbert Sissons* has one of the highest ratios of international goals per game for Wales on record, notching up four in his three games, including a hat trick on his debut against Ireland in 1885. The centre forward with the 'Olympic' side at the time learnt his football at Grove Park Grammar School and later appeared for the works XI at his father's Cambrian brewery. Bert was a noted goalscorer and much valued by Wrexham and its successor Wrexham Olympic. He also took over as treasurer of the FAW for twelve months until leaving Wrexham in 1886 at 24 to study medicine. Sadly, while undertaking his studies in Hackney, London he contracted diphtheria and died aged just 29! Sisson had also represented North Wales and his county Denbighshire, which played regular representative games at that time.

Back to that 1883, and Wrexham's Welsh Cup winning side against Druids, and anoth-

George Thomas
Another member of Wrexham's 1883 Welsh Cup winning side against Druids. Thomas also captained Wrexham Olympic in 1884/85 and was awarded two Welsh caps.

Wrexham-born Thomas was described as a 'tall, well built fullback, strong in the air and an awkward opponent'. He played in two internationals against England and Scotland in March 1885.

er member who was warded Welsh honours in *George Thomas*, a Wrexham born full-back who played in two internationals against England at Blackburn in a 1-1 draw, and on the Racecourse v. the Scots, which ended in a disappointing 1-8 defeat; both in March 1885. He was described as a 'tall, well built fullback, strong in the air and an awkward opponent'.

At club level Thomas formed a fine fullback partnership with Harry Edwards and captained Wrexham Olympic in 1884/85. Earlier with Civil Service (Wrexham) and Wrexham FC, George began to have less time for football in order to concentrate on his mineral water business, and he retired during 1887.

Job Wilding played his first game for Wrexham as a 17 year old against Birmingham Excelsior, and eventually became a regular member of the Olympic outfit (formed in the aftermath of the banning of Wrexham FC). His profile of the time makes interesting reading 'never hurried, invariably acts with discretion and plays an admirable game'. After winning his first six of nine caps at Wrexham, Job moved to Liverpool working for the corporation and playing for Everton and later Bootle FC.

A report of the Everton v Wrexham match at Anfield Road in January 1886 (Six years before Liverpool FC were formed) commented; 'of the Everton players none performed as well as Wilding'. He returned to Wrexham in 1888, and was also with Westminister Rovers: a colliery team. The winger/centre forward notched four goals for Wales, including two in the record 11-0 demolition of Ireland at the Racecourse in March 1888.
A moulder by trade, having served an apprenticeship with an agricultural implement maker, but later worked as an iron founder at Chester. Job was also a Welsh League referee and a one-time assistant trainer to Wrexham FC. Not forgetting either that he was noted as a very fine wicket keeper for Wrexham CC.

Robert Roberts began his football career with Rhostyllen before joining Wrexham Olympic, and was one of their first signings on formation. The fullback played twice against Ireland in 1886 and 1887. The game in the former was won 5-0, at the Racecourse. However, the latter occasion saw Wales on the losing side in Belfast 4-1 and Bob Roberts much to his astonishment had to play the whole game between the sticks as an emergency goalkeeper!

A hard working player and sound defender the Wrexham club captain retired in 1892 and eventually became trainer for many years. He worked in Bersham Colliery as a young man and was a keen territorial.

The elder brother of Robert (above) *William Roberts* unlike him was a forward, accumulating four caps for his country in 1886 and 1887, getting on the score sheet against Ireland, and in the same team as his brother. Described as 'always in the thickest of the fight' and 'tricky and comical, and occasionally brilliant'. He gained all his caps with Wrexham and Wrexham Olympic, and after them joined his brother at Rhostyllen.

Bill worked as a collier and later at a leatherworks, and was the sixth member of the Wrexham team who won the Welsh Cup in 1883 to be capped.

William Roberts

Awarded four caps for Wales between 1886 and 1887 whilst playing for Wrexham and Wrexham Olympic.

Roberts was escribed as 'always in the thickest of the fight' and 'tricky and comical, and occasionally brilliant'. He later joined his brother, Robert Roberts, at Rhostyllen. Bill worked as a collier and later at a leatherworks, and was the sixth member of the Wrexham team who won the Welsh Cup in 1883 to be capped.

Interesting to note that Wrexham's home games in the third and fourth round of the above competition were played at Rhosddu Recreation Ground, which was used around this time due to the Racecourse Landlords - The Cricket Club - upping the rent by £10!!

Mold born *Samuel Jones* won caps for Wales while with Wrexham in 1887 and Chester in 1890.

A tall rangy full-back, Sam was a tireless worker with a powerful kick. Although never a first choice for his country he remained 'on the fringe' for a number of seasons, even after returning to junior football with Caergwrle. His three-season stint with the Olympic from 1884-87 was followed by a five-year affair with Chester, including when they became founder members of the combination league in 1890. Jones began work as a coal miner in his early teens and this continued up to his retirement. In his spare time he was a member of the territorial army and a keen bandsman.

Alfred Owen Davies gained nine caps in all and one of this was with Wrexham against Scotland in 1889 at the Racecourse in a 0-0 draw.

In the book 'Association Football' published in 1900 the following description is fascinating; 'a terrible fellow he was to opposing forwards, dashing almost to recklessness, a very strong and heavy charger, a splendid header and a clever kick. His weak points were an inability to combine with the rest if the defence'.

A native of Barmouth, the full-back started playing football seriously while studying medicine at Edinburgh. He qualified in 1886 and for a spell assisted the London Swifts before moving to Wrexham.

An amateur, Davies played for Wrexham and Druids, finding time to start a job at Overton in 1889 and to instigate the founding of the Welsh League in March 1890. After a spell with Crewe, he returned to Wales in1892 and became a GP in Machynlleth, and was later medical officer and coroner for the town.

A breeder of horses and keen amateur actor, Alfred Owen was an uncle by marriage to England fullbacks AM and PM Walters, and was the first Welshman to appear in the Welsh, Scottish, and English FA Cup competitions.

A player who now appears in other reference books as T.Carty was *Thomas Patrick McCarthy* who won his only Welsh cap with Wrexham against Ireland on 27th April 1889 in Belfast.

One of two brothers who both played for Wrexham and Chester, but with very different styles: Tom was a cool and stylish defender while brother Ted had a bad reputation as a 'rough and often violent player'. Tom had learned the game with Wrexham Excelsior, but first attracted attention when in the Wrexham side that lost 1-3 to the London Swifts in the 1888/89 FA Cup.

When taking up employment in Chester he joined the local club, however he broke his leg in an FA Cup tie at Lincoln in January 1890. The injury in effect ended a very promising career, which could have finished up in the newly formed 'Football League'! A printer by trade Tom McCarthy worked for several years at the office of Chester Chronicle.

Samuel Gladstone Gillam succeeded Alf Pugh as Wrexham Olympics custodian, and in 1889 the two figured in an unusual substitution incident! James Trainer who had been selected in goal was not released by Preston to face Scotland. However, the selectors were not informed until just before the kick-off. Gillam was quickly sent for, while Pugh stood in for him for the first half hour of the match at Wrexham. Perhaps a case of the first substitution in reverse!!

Sam had first caught the eye of the selectors when representing Denbighshire against Walsall in 1887, and the following year turned out for Bolton against Everton and Preston. Described thus 'Defended his charge in marvellous fashion, accounting for shot after shot in a style that brought forth hearty cheers.'

Gillam who had previously played for Wrexham Lever, Olympic and later Wrexham FC, also turned out for Shrewsbury and Chirk, but in 1890 moved to London and was captain of London Welsh FC for three years.

In the 1920's he was vice-president of London Welsh and made the following comment on his first international:

"We drew without any goals being scored, and when we assembled at the Wynnstay Arms (Wrexham) in the evening to dine together, there was a heated argument as to whether Scotland had actually scored a goal with a shot which I had tipped over the bar; there were no nets in those days, anyway the Scots took it badly and swore that I had swindled them out of a win".

Next year we will look at the Wrexham Welsh internationals that appeared for God's country leading up to the end of the 19th Century.

Gareth M. Davies.

Wrexham FC Hall of Fame

Tommy Bamford

Wrexham Supporters' Association honours the legends of the club through its Hall of Fame. The Hall of Fame was launched on September 20th, 2003 when twenty of Wrexham FC's all-time greats were inducted as its inaugural members on a very special evening at The Racecourse. Five new names have been added to the Hall of Fame each year since 2003, to further recognise the achievements of the club's greatest servants. To date the Supporters' Association has inducted forty three members.

Entry is not restricted to players; anyone who has made a great contribution to the club - in any capacity - from administrator to manager to supporter, can be considered. Wrexham have always relied on the Herculean efforts of individuals whose loyalty and desire to see the club succeed enable it to out-perform larger, more illustrious opponents. Membership of the Hall of Fame provokes great debate amongst supporters who are unanimous in their support for some legends and split in their support for others!

There were many difficult decisions to be made as the list of legends was whittled down to an initial twenty names in 2002, as many difficult issues had to be considered. How do you compare performances across eras when standards differed so widely? How can a player's entire career be assessed, when slumps of form are measured against the good times? How many non-players should be included? Should a short, spectacular spell at The Racecourse be recognised as much as a long, steady period of service to the club?

There was certainly a lively debate when the original twenty names were decided upon by a committee of supporters with over one hundred years experience of watching Wrexham FC! This expert committee has now been expanded further to include representatives from Wrexham Supporters' Trust and the Buckley Reds in order to widen the appeal of the Hall of Fame and to make it truly representative of the supporters' movement.

The new committee will be meeting very soon to agree the next group of legends to be inaugurated into the Hall of Fame in 2007. A very special award ceremony will be held on October 19th in the new Bamford suite of the refurbished Centenary Club to induct the new members and to reflect on the achievements of the forty three members already inducted. All members of the Hall of Fame and the families of those legends who have sadly passed away will be invited to the event.

All supporters are invited to attend this prestigious event to celebrate the achievements of the true legends of Wrexham FC. Please see Wrexham Supporters' Association website: **http://www.wrexhamdragons.co.uk**, Wrexham FC's official website and the match programme for further details of how to purchase tickets closer to the date.

Founding member of the Hall of Fame, Gary Bennett, with Wrexham legend Billy Ashcroft.

Gareth Davies

Ron Hewitt

Ken Barnes

Mickey Thomas

Wrexham FC Hall of Fame

2002 Award
Tommy Bamford (1929 - 1934)
Albert Kinsey (1966 - 1973)
Gary Bennett (1992 - 1995 & 1997)
Cliff Lloyd (1937 - 1939)
Horace Blew (1897-1911, 1913-1927 & 1932-1936)
Eddie May (1968 - 1976)
Dai Davies (1977 - 1981 & 1985-1986)
Dixie McNeil (1978 - 1982 & 1985 - 1990)
Gareth Davies (1967 - 1982)
Aly McGowan (1953 - 1965)
Alan Fox (1954 - 1964)
John Neal (1967 - 1977)
Arfon Griffiths (1959 - 1961 & 1962 - 1981)
Ted Robinson (1894 - 1943)
Pryce Griffiths (1984 - 1986 & 1988 - 2003)
George Showell (1966 - 1991)
Alf Jones (1923 - 1936)
Mel Sutton (1972 - 1982)
Joey Jones (1971 - 1975, 1978 - 1982 & 1987 to present)
Billy Tunnicliffe (1947 - 1953)

2003 Award
Billy Ashcroft (1970 - 1977)
Mickey Evans (1966 - 1979)
Brian Lloyd (1971 - 1977)
Kevin Russell (1987 - 1989 & 1995 - 2007)
Graham Whittle (1972 - 1982)

2004 Award
Ken Barnes 1961 - 1965)
Karl Connolly (1991 - 2000)
Tommy Bannan (1951 - 1955 & 1957 - 1959)
Tommy Matthias (1912 - 1928)
Bobby Shinton (1976 - 1980)
Ron Chaloner (Special Award)

2005 Award
Phil Hardy (1990 - 2001)
Ron Hewitt (1951 - 1957 & 1959 - 1960)
Sammy McMillan (1963 - 1967)
Denis Smith (2001 - 2007)
Mickey Thomas (1971 - 1978 & 1991 - 1993)
Carroll Clark (Special Award)

2006 Award
Brian Carey (1991 - 1992 & 1996 to present)
Johnny Edwards (1965 - 1980 & 1992 to present)
Brian Flynn (1988 - 2001)
Bert Goode (1910-1911, 1913-1922 & 1923-1926)
Mike Williams (1984 - 1991)
Wrexham Supporters Trust (Special Award)

Where are they now?

It's always nice to keep in touch with old friends. So we thought we'd track down some former Wrexham players to see what they're doing now. Former reds are found all over the world from the League of Ireland to the Singapore J-League to the Major Soccer League in America!

Name	Current Team	League (Position)
Danny Allsopp	Melbourne Victoria	Hyundai A League (Australia)
Matt Baker	MK Dons	League Two
Scott Barron	Millwall	League One
Steve Basham	Exeter City	Blue Square Conference Premier
Phil Bater	Clevedon Town	Southern League Premier Division (Manager)
David Bayliss	Barrow	Blue Square Conference North
Dan Bennett	Singapore Armed Forces Football Club (SAFFC) Singapore J-League	
Dean Bennett	Chester City	League Two
Michael Blackwood	Kidderminster Harriers	Blue Square Conference Premier
Emad Bouanane	Barnt Green Spartak	Midland Combination League
Jon Bowden	Luton Town	Championship (Physio)
Deryn Brace	Carmarthen Town	League of Wales (Player/Manager)
Dave Brammer	Millwall	League One
Mark Cartwright	Colwyn Bay	Unibond First Division South (Director)
Karl Connolly	Prescot Cables	Unibond Premier League
Terry Cooke	Colorado Rapids (USA)	Major Soccer League
Tom Craddock	Middlesbrough	Premier League
Malcolm Crosby	Middlesbrough	Premier League (Reserve Team Coach)
Terry Darracott	Blackburn Rovers	Premier League (Scout)
Kevin Dearden	Millwall	League One (Goalkeeping Coach)
Matt Derbyshire	Blackburn Rovers	Premier League
Andy Dibble	Peterborough United	League Two (Goalkeeping Coach)
Carlos Edwards	Sunderland	Premier League
Jake Edwards	Burton Albion	Blue Square Conference Premier
Paul Edwards	Port Vale	League One
Stuart Elliott	York City	Blue Square Conference Premier
Mark Evans	Caernarvon Town	League of Wales
Craig Faulconbridge	Wingate & Finchley	Isthmian League Division One North
Brian Flynn	Wales Under-21 manager	
Ben Foster	Manchester United	Premier League
Robbie Foy	Scunthorpe United	Championship
Steve Futcher	Airbus UK	League of Wales
Rob Garrett	Stoke City	Championship
Robin Gibson	Droylsden	Blue Square Conference Premier
Carl Griffiths	Maldon Town	Isthmian League Division One (North)
Kevin Hannon	Warrington Town	Unibond League Division One (South)
Jimmy Harvey	Forest Green Rovers	Blue Square Conference Premier (Manager)
Seamus Heath	Northern Ireland Youth Development Officer	
Keith Hill	Rochdale	League Two (Manager)
Shaun Holmes	Finn Harps	League of Ireland
Andy Holt	Northampton Town	League One
George Horan	Rhyl	League of Wales
Bryan Hughes	Hull City	Championship
Tony Humes	Ipswich Town	Championship (Academy Manager)
Simon Hunt	Southampton	Championship (Assistant Manager)
Barry Hunter	Blackburn Rovers	Scout
Clayton Ince	Walsall	League One
Michael Ingham	Hereford United	League Two
Jason Jarrett	Preston North End	Championship
Lee Jones	NEWI Cefn Druids	League of Wales (Joint Manager)

Name	Current Club	League (Position)
James Kelly	Rhyl	League of Wales
Chris Killen	Celtic	Scottish Premier League
Craig Knight	Mynydd Isa	Cymru Alliance League
Dennis Lawrence	Swansea City	League One
Stuart Lee	FC Seattle Storm (USA)	Director of Coaching
Paul Linwood	Chester City	League Two
David Lowe	Wigan Athletic	Premier League (Head of Youth Development)
Andy Marriott	Exeter City	Blue Square Premier (Conference National)
John McAliskey	Mansfield Town	League Two
Lee McEvilly	Accrington Stanley	League Two
Mark McGregor	Port Vale	League One
Jim McNulty	Macclesfield Town	League Two
Craig Madden	Stockport County	League Two (Youth Team Manager)
Paul Mitchell	MK Dons	League Two
Maheta Molango	Unattached at time of print	
Adrian Moody	Rhyl	League of Wales
Craig Morgan	Peterborough United	League Two
Andy Morrell	Blackpool	Championship
Jon Newby	Morecambe	League Two
Eddie Niedzwiecki	Blackburn Rovers	Premier League (First Team Coach)
Armand One	Turun Palloseura	Finland Premier League
Gareth Owen	Airbus UK	Welsh Premier League (Player/Manager)
Waynne Phillips	NEWI Cefn Druids	Welsh Premier League (Joint Manager)
Andy Preece	Worcester City	Conference South (Player/Manager)
Roger Preece	GAP Queen's Park	Cymru Alliance League (Player/Coach)
Paul Raynor	Crawley Town	Blue Square Conference Premier (Assistant Manager)
Kevin Reeves	Swansea City	League One (Chief Scout)
Paul Roberts	Bangor City	League of Wales
Steve Roberts	Doncaster Rovers	League One
Lee Roche	Unattached at time of print	
Kristian Rogers	Port Talbot Town	League of Wales
Marius Rovde	Hamarkameratene	Norwegian First Division
John Ruddy	Everton	Premier League
Mike Salmon	Arsenal	Premier League (Reserve Team Coach)
Hector Sam	Notts County	League Two
Cherno Samba	Plymouth Argyle	Championship
Mark Sertori	Bolton Wanderers	Premier League (Club Masseur)
Kevin Sharp	Northwich Victoria	Blue Square Conference Premier (player/coach)
Matt Shaw	Unattached at time of print	
Ron Sinclair	Stoke City	Championship (Assistant Academy Director)
Alex Smith	Southport	Blue Square Conference North
Kevin Smith	On trial with Lincoln City at time of print	
David Sweet	Mynydd Isa	Cymru Alliance League
Mark Taylor	Newcastle United	Premier League (Physio)
Andy Thomas	Airbus UK	League of Wales
Lee Trundle	Bristol City	Championship
Xavi Valero	Liverpool	Premier League (Goalkeeping Coach)
John Vaughan	Huddersfield Town	League One (Goalkeeping Coach)
Neil Wainwright	Darlington	League Two
Richard Walker	Port Vale	League One
David Walsh	Mynydd Isa	Cymru Alliance League
Jon Walters	Ipswich Town	Championship
Peter Ward	Stockport County	League Two (Assistant Manager)
Paul Warhurst	Northwich Victoria	Blue Square Conference Premier
David Warren	Waterford	League of Ireland
Paul Whitfield	Rhyl	League of Wales
Sam Williams	Aston Villa	Premier League
Mark Wilson	Doncaster Rovers	League One
Tommy Wright	Ballymena United	Irish League (Manager)

Obituaries

The Wrexham players pay tribute to Don Weston

Jimmy McGill (1939-2006)

Former full-back Jimmy McGill passed away at the end of October 2006 in Chester aged 67. Born in Belshill, Lanarkshire on 2nd October 1939, he took up football whilst at Union Street Primary and Larkhall Academy schools in his native Glasgow. It was whilst playing schoolboy football that he was chosen to play for his County along with future Scottish internationals Joe Baker and Sammy Reid, but he missed out when he was laid up with tonsillitis, much to Jimmy's annoyance.

He moved on to junior football with Larkhall Thistle, and at 15 joined Partick Thistle, whilst taking up work as an apprentice joiner, which he combined with playing football. Despite winning three reserve league titles with the 'Jags', he failed to make the break-through into the first team and in May 1959 moved south of the border to join Oldham Athletic when offered the chance.

He made his Football League debut in the opening match of the 1959/60 season, a 2-0 win over Bradford Park Avenue. He went on to miss just eight games all season, but asked for a transfer following the departure of manager Norman Dodgin. He switched to Crewe Alexandra the following summer, leaving Boundary Park by 'mutual consent' following unfounded allegations of match rigging.

Jimmy spent over two seasons at Gresty Road, which included playing in a memorable

2-1 FA Cup win at Stamford Bridge against Chelsea, before moving to Chester in October 1962 having made 81 league appearances for the 'Railwaymen'.

He made his debut for Chester in a 2-0 home win over Bradford City at half-back - a position he occupied for most of his time at Sealand Road. He made a total of 32 league appearances for the 'Cestrians' before Wrexham boss Ken Barnes signed the tough tackling Scot in October 1963 to replace the injured Aly McGowan, and made his debut in a 2-0 defeat at Bournemouth.

However, after six matches Reg Holland replaced him, but he returned in March to put in some spirited performances in the red shirt, which led to Bournemouth making an offer of £4,000 for him, but he turned the move down as he was now playing regular first team football. It was a decision that he was later to regret as once Barnes was replaced as manager, Jimmy again lost his place in the side to Reg Holland, and he was eventually released at the end of the season.

Having made a total of 20 appearances in a Wrexham shirt Jimmy left the Racecourse to join Cheshire League side MacclesfieldTown, but by October he was on the move again to take up an offer of a trial and a return to league football with - Bournemouth! However, Jimmy failed to make an appearance at Dean Court and after a month he returned to Moss Rose, but a knee injury he had received when with Crewe flared up again, and he failed to make another appearance for the 'Silkmen', leaving in the summer of 1965.

Jimmy did play football again, for Bangor City, and in the Welsh League (North) for Porthmadog before finally hanging up his boots.

Having settled in the Chester area, Jimmy returned to his trade as a joiner, starting up his own building business until he was forced to retire in 1991 because of severe arthritis. However, it did not keep him away from his other love - Greyhound racing, having become an owner and trainer, a sport that he thoroughly enjoyed after his football career.

Wrexham Career Statistics

Position:	Defender
Birthplace:	Belshill, Lanarkshire
Birthdate:	02/10/39
Appearances:	20
Goals:	0
Also represented:	Partick Thistle, Oldham Athletic, Crewe Alexandra, Chester City, Macclesfield Town, Bournemouth, Bangor City, Porthmadog.

Appearances and Goals

	League		FA Cup		League Cup		Welsh Cup		Total	
	apps	gls	apps	gls	apps	gls	apps	gls	apps	gls
06/07	17	0	3	0	-	-	-	-	20	0
Total	17	0	3	0	-	-	-	-	20	0

John Schofield 1931 - 2006

Wrexham Career Statistics

Position: Goalkeeper
Birthplace: Atherton
Birthdate: 08/02/31
Appearances: 52
Goals: 0
Also represented: Grendon United, Nuneaton Borough,
                         Birminham City, Cork City, Bromsgrove
                         Rovers, Tamworth.

Appearances and Goals

	League		FA Cup		League Cup		Welsh Cup		Total	
	apps	gls	apps	gls	apps	gls	apps	gls	apps	gls
66/67	46	0	2	0	1	0	6	0	55	0
67/68	6	0	-	-	1	0	-	-	7	0
Total	52	0	2	0	2	0	6	0	62	0

A highly respected goalkeeper at the Racecourse Johnny Schofield passed away on 1st November 2006, at the age of 75, having fought against illness during the months leading up to his death. 'Big hearted and brave' - Johnny survived a pit explosion (at Baddesley Colliery in November 1957) and a fractured skull (playing for BirminghamCity against Manchester United in 1960) and still came up smiling.

Born on 8th February 1931, Johnny began playing football for his hometown club Atherstone, while also appearing for Ansley Hall Colliery. This was followed by a spell with Grendon United before signing amateur forms with Nuneaton Borough, where he was spotted playing for their reserve side by Birmingham City who invited him for trials, from which a part-time contract followed in February 1950, at the age of 19, as he continued to work in the mines.

He spent most of his time at St.Andrews to the great Gil Merrick, but did make his first team debut in October 1952 in a Second Division match at Bury. Over the next five seasons, Johnny continued to deputise for Merrick, and was restricted to just a handful of appearances, but he always acknowledged how much he learned from the 'master'. However, the 1954/55 season saw him brilliantly perform in the 'Blues' run-in which led to the Second Division championship.

Two years later in November 1957, Johnny survived a pit explosion that left him in hospital for three weeks, and in his own words; 'Bloody lucky to be alive!' It was following the accident that he left the mining industry altogether to become a full-time professional at St.Andrews, his patience eventually paying off as he became a regular at St. Andrew's at the start of the 1959/60 season and he was part of the side that did so well in the pioneering years of European football, reaching the finals of the Inter Cities Fairs Cup in both 1960 and 1961.

He helped the Blues lift their only major silverware to date, when he kept a fantastic clean sheet in the second leg of the League Cup Final of 1963 at Villa Park, using his superb reflexes and command in the air to almost single-handedly keep Aston Villa at bay.

After 212 league games for the Blues, he joined Wrexham in 1966, at a time when the club was rebuilding having applied for re-election for the first and only time the year before. The 1966/67 season saw Johnny play in every game, helping the 'Robins' reach the Welsh Cup Final, where they lost 4-3 on aggregate to Cardiff City. Despite only spending a relatively short time at the Racecourse, Johnny was regarded by many fans of that era as one of the best goalkeepers to have pulled on the 'keeper's shirt for Wrexham because of his all-round ability.

After less than two years with us, he joined Cork City for a short spell, before spending six years turning out in non-league football with Bromsgrove Rovers and Tamworth amongst others, including a spell in management at his hometown club Atherstone United. After his playing days were over he ran an off-licence in Atherstone for many years, but his love of football and Birmingham City saw him become a regular at St. Andrew's for many years. In fact, Johnny played an integral part in helping to set up the Blues Historical Society and their ex-Players' Association.

Don Weston 1936 - 2007

Don Weston was a 'gem of a find' when spotted playing whilst serving his National Service in the army at Kinmel Bay camp near Rhyl in the late 1950s. Sadly, Don passed away earlier this year in Mansfield, Nottinghamshire, on 20th January 2007. He was 70.

Born at New Houghton in Derbyshire on 6th March 1936, he went on to represent East Derbyshire schoolboys, but upon leaving school he took up employment in a local coal mine, but continued to play football for his local side, Pleasley Imps. It was whilst with them he turned out for Leeds United as an amateur, but he turned down the offer of becoming professional with them on 'personal grounds'.

Shortly after, and as with many players of his era, Don was called up for his National

Wrexham Career Statistics

Position: Forward
Birthplace: New Houghton, Derbyshire
Birthdate: 06/03/36
Appearances: 96
Goals: 49
Also represented: Birmingham City, Rotherham United,
                  Leeds United, Huddersfield Town,
                  Chester City, Altrincham, Bethesda Town.

Appearances and Goals

	League		FA Cup		League Cup		Welsh Cup		Total	
	apps	gls	apps	gls	apps	gls	apps	gls	apps	gls
58/59	17	8	-	-	-	-	3	4	20	12
59/60	25	13	3	3	-	-	-	-	28	16
66/67	13	6	-	-	-	-	4	1	17	7
67/68	29	13	1	1	-	-	1	0	31	14
Total	84	40	4	4	-	-	8	5	96	49

Service serving with the 31st Training Regiment Royal Artillery, with whom he was stationed at Kinmel Bay camp near Rhyl. It was while excelling in military competition that he was recommended to local Football League side Wrexham, and he took up the offer of a trial, which led to him signing amateur forms in May 1958.

He then went on to make his Football League debut in the opening match of the 1958/59 season, a 1-0 defeat at Swindon Town, but he scored on his home debut a 3-2 win over Notts County. He went on to score 12 goals in 20 games that season, while still serving in the army, though he once broke out of barracks, which earned him 14 days confinement to barracks!

Don soon began attracting the attention of other clubs, which was due to his 'devastating burst of speed, while his shooting power was sensational, and he had a turn of the foot like nobody's business'. Twenty-eight goals in 48 games for Wrexham were enough to persuade Birmingham City to part with a £12,000 transfer fee to secure his services in January 1960.

He made his debut for the 'Blues' in a 2-1 defeat at Manchester United, but he struggled to score goals for his new club, and eleven months later was sold to Rotherham United for £10,000 having scored just three goals in 23 league games. With the 'Millers' he played in the first ever League Cup final, where they lost 3-2 on aggregate to Aston Villa. Thereafter the pacy marksman continued to perform creditably for Rotherham, scoring 21 goals in 76 league games, which was enough to persuade Don Revie to pay £18,000 for his services in December 1962 - the club he'd had the chance to sign for earlier in his career!

Having been bought to fill a gap left by the departed hero John Charles, Weston might have been on a hiding to nothing, but he slotted in smoothly in central attack alongside another recent purchase Jim Storrie, and his cause was enhanced immeasurably by a début hat-trick at home to Stoke City.

Weston missed only seven games in the Second Division title campaign which followed, but although Revie kept faith with him at first, as Leeds made a rousing return to the First Division in 1964/65, he receded to the fringe of the team following the purchase of the England centre-forward Alan Peacock, and was disappointed to be left out of the side that reached the 1965 FA Cup final. He was to go back further down the pecking order when youngster Peter Lorimer's talents began to emerge, and in October 1965, with his 30th birthday approaching, Weston, having scored 24 goals in 68 league games, left Elland Road to move to Huddersfield Town.

He made his debut for the 'Terriers' in a scoreless draw with his former club Rotherham United, but featured only intermittently for the Second Division promotion hopefuls, netting seven goals in 22 league games before taking up an offer from Jack Rowley to rejoin Wrexham, now in Division Four, in December 1966. Much to the delight of the Wrexham faithful, but not as fast as he was first time round, he still went on to score another 21 goals in 48 games for the 'Robins', not a bad average in what was a mediocre side at that time. He eventually left the Racecourse in the summer of 1968 for a brief spell with Chester before dropping into non-league football with

Cheshire league side Altrincham and Welsh League (North) side Bethesda Athletic.

Having hung up his boots he returned to Derbyshire in the village of Pleasley, near Mansfield and took up employment as a car salesman, before going on to run his own car sales business. Don was also no mean cricketer, turning out for his birthplace New Houghton (Mansfield) and also enjoying bowls.

Barry Smith   1934 - 2007

FORMER Wrexham striker Barry Smith died, aged 72 while on a cruise in New Zealand in March 2007. Born in South Kirkby on 15th March 1934, Barry had played his early football for St. Walburga's school, where he was chosen to represent Bradford schoolboys. He later turned out for Bradford United in the West Riding youth league from where he signed for Bradford Park Avenue and playing in their Northern Intermediate League side.

He was later released by the Park Avenue club, from where he joined Farsley Celtic. It was while playing Yorkshire League football for them that he was spotted by Leeds United, and at the age of 17 he gave up his apprenticeship as a plumber to sign professional forms in October 1951. He made progress in the reserves at Elland Road, before finally making his Football League debut for them, and scoring in a 2-0 home win over Fulham. He made just one more appearance for Leeds, a 1-0 home defeat to Leicester shortly after his debut, but in May 1951 he was called up for his National Service.

Serving in the Royal Artillery, he was based mainly near Oswestry, which limited his appearances and his progress. Following his demobilisation he had little opportunity to prove himself, and in May 1955 he joined Third Division North side Bradford Park Avenue. Barry did well in two seasons he spent with Bradford Park Avenue, scoring 38 league goals in 64 appearances, but despite his excellent strike rate, he was allowed to join Wrexham in the summer of 1957.

He spent one season at the Racecourse, rattling in an impressive 15 goals in 22 games, but with both Tommy Bannan and Bernard Evans challenging for a striking

Wrexham Career Statistics

Position:	Centre-Forward
Birthplace:	South Kirkby
Birthdate:	15/03/34
Appearances:	22
Goals:	15
Also represented:	Bradford Park Avenue, Stockport County, Oxford United, Oldham Athletic, Bangor City, Accrington Stanley.

Appearances and Goals

	League		FA Cup		League Cup		Welsh Cup		Total	
	apps	gls	apps	gls	apps	gls	apps	gls	apps	gls
57/58	18	10	1	0	-	-	3	5	22	15
Total	18	10	1	0	-	-	3	5	22	15

role, Barry found it difficult to sustain a regular first team place. During his time in North Wales, he was described as being a 'very well built centre-forward, who can also play on the left-wing'.

Despite his goal ratio, Barry was allowed to leave in the close season of 1958 to join Stockport County. He was to spend just one season at Edgeley Park where he scored five goals in 17 league games before going on his travels again, this time to join the progressive Headington United (later renamed Oxford United) for a season. In August 1960, he returned to the Football League with Oldham Athletic, though his stay was short, as he made just one appearance for the 'Latics' - a 1-1 home draw with Gillingham.

By December he had joined Cheshire League side Bangor City, but returned to League football with Southport in the summer of 1961. However, he failed to make a first team appearance for the 'Sandgrounders' and by October he had been transferred to Accrington Stanley, where he made three appearances, but they were later scratched from the record books when the club resigned from the Football League in March 1962.

Barry then drifted into non-league circles, before settling back in his native Bradford where he became a successful businessman.

Glyn Williams 1922 - 2007

During the past season Wrexham FC learned of the passing away of Glyn Williams, who proudly played for his hometown club during the late 1940s. Glyn was visiting a relative in the South of England when he passed away on 8th March 2007. He was 84.

Born on 15th June 1922, Glyn had first played football in the 1930s for the Wrexham County School for Boys, later to become Grove Park. He also excelled at rugby during this period, but it was football that he took up playing regularly in the local 'Chums League' for Rhosddu and Hightown FC.

His football career was put on hold during World War Two, and in 1942 he was called

Wrexham Career Statistics

Position:	Defender
Nationality:	Welsh
Birthplace:	Wrexham
Birthdate:	15/06/22
Appearances:	4
Goals:	0
Also Represented:	Pwllheli, Flint Town United, Bethesda Athletic

Appearances and Goals

	League		FA Cup		League Cup		Welsh Cup		Total	
	apps	gls	apps	gls	apps	gls	apps	gls	apps	gls
48/49	4	0	-	-	-	-	-	-	4	0
Total	4	0	-	-	-	-	-	-	4	0

up for the Royal Air Force, but failed his medical to become a pilot because of what was described as 'unsafe for a pilot colour vision'. Instead, he worked on ground service, serving in India, where he played football for his station team that won the Delhi Area Cup in 1945!

Following the end of the conflict, Glyn returned home and was invited by manager Tom Williams and secretary Cliff Lloyd to play for the Wrexham 'A' and reserve teams. He signed amateur forms for the club, and following some impressive performances for the reserves he was given his Football League debut in April 1949, when he replaced Eddie Tunney at right-back in a 2-0 home win over Rochdale. Glyn kept his place for the following three games, but Tunney returned to the side for the last game of the season.

That summer, Glyn enrolled at Teachers Training College, where he went on to qualify, but by November of that year, new manager Les McDowall, informed Glyn that he would be released. He then signed for Welsh League (North) side Pwllheli, but his first season with them was difficult as he had been given his first teaching appointment in Rowley Regis in the West Midlands, but in 1950 he returned to Wrexham where he took up an appointment at the Victoria Secondary Modern School.

Playing under the former Welsh international TG Jones at Pwllheli, Glyn won the Welsh League (North) title twice in 1950 & 1951, as well as representing the North Wales Coast FA against the Scottish Junior League. He left Pwllheli in the summer of 1952 to join Flint Town United, and it was here he enjoyed the best spell of his football career, as he helped Flint to win the Welsh Cup in 1954 with a 2-0 win over Chester on the Wrexham Racecourse in front of a crowd of almost 16,000. He also won the Welsh League (North) title three times in 1955, 1956 and 1957, before joining Bethesda Athletic in the close season of 1959, where he brought down his football career in fine style by winning the North Wales Coast FA Challenge Cup in 1961.

In 1960, Glyn moved to the newly opened Bryn Offa school, after the Victoria school had closed. He remained teaching at Bryn Offa until 1982 when he retired. For many of those years, he was connected to Wrexham Athletics Club, serving as Chairman, later becoming a vice-president of both Wrexham and Clwyd AAA's. He lived in Pentre Broughton, Wrexham, and throughout his retirement he was an active member of the Wrexham Hospital League of Friends, which summed Glyn up, as he liked nothing better than helping others.

BEGBIES TRAYNOR
CORPORATE RESCUE & RECOVERY

Proud to be associated with Wrexham Football Club

1 Winckley Court, Chapel Street, Preston PR1 8BU
Telephone: 01772 202000   Fax: 01772 200099

Section 4:
Wrexham's Supporters' Groups

Wrexham Supporters' Trust

Wrexham Supporters' Trust, PO Box 2200, Wrexham, LL11 9WG.
Telephone: 07981 151958
Website: http://www.wst.org.uk
Email: wst@wst.org.uk

A new phase

It wasn't just Wrexham Football Club that began 2006/07 marching into unknown territory, as the Trust itself also had to begin its transition into the next new phase of its development. From its inauspicious beginnings as a conduit for the 'Beer-A-Week' fund, through its time as the guiding force in the fight to save the club, the Trust is again now adapting to a new role within the exciting new era at Wrexham FC.

Trust Aims

Progress on some of the Trust aims has been disappointingly slow this year, in particular those that apply to the Trust's intrinsic relationship with the club both now and in the future. With the redevelopment still ongoing, the issues of supporter board representation, and equity have been put somewhat on the back burner as the club co-owners, somewhat understandably, seek to retain control whilst they still have such significant personal liabilities within the club.

However, once the redevelopment is underway and the last financially restrictive ties to the old days of administration are finally severed, we look forward to making good progress on both these objectives.

It has not all been disappointing though, as we have managed to not only reach our Target 250 amount, but at our AGM in June 2007, the board were able to ring fence a massive £300,000 for the purchase of equity in Wrexham Football Club, to thereby ensure that the clubs supporters will always have a voice.

Events

We have put on a number of extremely successful events the past year. Of particular note was the 'Sweet' concert at the William Aston Hall, where the 70's glam-rockers thrilled the near sell-out crowd with their past hits. Culminating with an impromptu cover version of 'Wrexham Is The Name' ensuring that Andy Scott and the rest of the band served up a truly 'blockbuster' evening for those in attendance.

The Trust organised the annual Player of the Season Dinner, which was again a huge success, as was the club Open Day. Other events in the past year included a Mickey Thomas Q & A, Race Nights, Christmas Party, Quiz's, Poker Night, balloon race and Programme Fair etc; and we are already working hard on next years calendar.

Junior Dragons

2006/07 saw us take over and re-vamp the Junior Dragons. As the fans of the future the Trust recognises the vital role our young fans have to offer. With a re-launch in early Spring 2006, it's new format proved to be a massive success and membership soon soared to over 600 as the junior member of the Wrexham supporting fraternity took their opportunity to be a part of their club.

Looking Ahead

Overall an extremely busy year for Trust members, but one that has shown fantastic commitment from all involved. It is testament to all that hard work and energy that Wrexham Supporters Trust is held in such high regard by Supporters Direct, and is often held as an example for other Trusts to follow.

However, this does not mean the Trust should, or indeed will be, resting on its laurels. Currently the Trust is acting as the catalyst bringing all supporters groups together to co-ordinate their activities and act in a unified direction for the good of the football club. With the continued formation of new local supporters groups, in Rhos and Mold, and more generic groups such as the Deuddegfed Dyn (Twelfth Man) the whole supporters' movement at Wrexham is certainly making great strides going forward.

The Trust will continue to work with the club to build on the solid relationship now in place between the supporters and the club, and through this demonstrates the vital and invaluable role that the supporters have to play in the club's successful future.

Following the recent dark days of uncertainty and worry, there now looks to be exciting times ahead for Wrexham Football Club. With a seemingly very bright future laid out ahead, the Trust aims to play a major part in ensuring that these opportunities afforded our club are not only grasped firmly, but fully embraced to ensure that history is never repeated. If you are not a member of the Trust then we would encourage you to join us; by doing this and working together, we can all move forward to take 'Wrexham Higher'.

wrexham dragons.co.uk

Wrexham FC Supporters' Association - Founded 1926

Wrexham Supporters' Association

Wrexham Supporters' Association, The Turf, Mold Road, Wrexham
Telephone: 01978 266602
Website: http://www.wrexhamdragons.co.uk
Email: rowen@wrexhamdragons.co.uk

The History of Supporters' Clubs in Wrexham

Wrexham AFC Supporters' Club (as it was then known) was born in August 1926 at the Black Lion pub in Wrexham. The driving force behind Wrexham AFC's first supporters' club was Jack Williams who was born in Summerhill in 1898. Jack saw his first Wrexham match in 1910, a Birmingham League encounter with Hednesford Town and was inspired to form a supporters' club. He was a man of great vision who recognised the importance of fans working together and with Tom Hodgson of Northampton Town, formulated the idea of the National Federation of Football Supporters' Clubs, which was inaugurated in 1927.

Wrexham Supporters' Association, as we are now known, owes a great debt to its founder Jack Williams. In recognition of his achievements we named our Player of the Season award after him. The Jack Williams Player of the Season was first awarded to goalkeeper Brian Lloyd at the end of the 1975/76 and has been awarded every year since by the Supporters' Association on behalf of Wrexham Football Club. We make this prestigious award, which is recognized by the club

and players alike, before the last home game of each season and again at Wrexham Supporters' Trust annual award ceremony. A full list of the awards can be found on page 103 of this yearbook.

Our role within Wrexham Football Club
People often ask us what we have done for Wrexham Football Club and how they can become members. Over the years the Association helped to fund and build the old stand on the Kop and ran the Centre Spot club shop in the old Mold Road stand and the official Away Travel Scheme. In recent years we have purchased equipment for Johnny Edwards to keep the Racecourse pitch in tip-top condition and last season purchased an ultrasound machine for Mel Pejic. While the club was in financial trouble we paid for loan players, scouts and day-to-day bills that were not getting paid.

We had over 2,500 members at the height of our success, although recently our membership numbers have fallen. To boost membership and to give all fans an opportunity to join a supporters' club - regardless of income - we have decided

President	Alan Fox
Vice Presidents	John Neal, Ena Williams, Phil Davies
Chairman	Carroll Clark
Secretary	Richard Owen
Treasurer	Carroll Clark
Committee Members	Rob Clarke, Dave Bennett, Phil Davies, Gareth Griffiths, Dave Price.
Meeting Venue	The Turf Hotel, The Racecourse
Membership Cost	Free!
Meeting Frequency	Monthly

to offer free membership during the 2007/08. At the recent Open Day we signed up over 100 new members, a reflection of how popular this new offer is. All fans traveling on official away travel buses will automatically be signed up to our free membership scheme, providing them with free insurance should an away match be cancelled within 6 hours of kick-off.

Looking to the future

Last season three stalwarts of Wrexham Supporters' Association - Ray Clarke, Phil Davies and Dave Davies - retired. During the past ten years Phil, who formerly ran the Racecourse catering, raised almost £100,000 from the 50/50 competition. Dave was the mastermind behind the Centre Spot and the Hall of Fame, and developed the Junior Reds club (jointly with Phil and Ray) at a time when clubs did not recognise the importance of younger fans. Phil has now passed over the running of the 50/50 competition to Kevin Hughes, while Dave and Ray are looking forward to spending more time with their families.

We would like to thank Ray, Phil and Dave for their significant contribution to the Association and the football club over the years. As a result the Association is now looking for new blood to take us forward into an exciting new era. If you are already a member and would like to join our committee then please come along to our AGM in October.

We will be writing to all members two weeks before the AGM to ask for nominations and will publish the date in the local press and on our website. Alternatively, if you would like to simply find out what we do then please come along to one of our bi-monthly public meetings in our new home, the Turf, following our AGM. All members are welcome to attend the AGM and new members are welcome to join at our forthcoming public meetings.

Hall of Fame

We also intend to develop a permanent Hall of Fame display in the Turf so that all fans can join us in celebrating the legends of Wrexham FC. A full history of the Hall of Fame and its members can be found on page 66 of this yearbook and on our website, Wrexham Dragons: http://www.wrexhamdragons.co.uk.

Shropshire Reds

Shropshire Reds, PO BOX 547, Shrewsbury, Shropshire, SY3 8YY
Website: http://www.shropshirereds.co.uk
Email: shreds@wafc123.freeserve.co.uk

Like everyone else with Wrexham Football Club in their hearts the Shropshire Reds have endured a pretty miserable time since the publication of the last Year Book.

In addition to all the sleepless nights brought on by the tumble down the League table we've also had to battle against a general discontent on the terraces that has resulted in dwindling attendances at our meetings. Attempts to arrest this slump have hardly been helped by a number of enforced last-minute changes to our planned meetings - in short, this has been one of those years where, if things could go wrong, then they very often did!

It's therefore understandable that, for the first (and - I sincerely hope - the last) time in our brief but proud history 2006-07 has seen our membership numbers fail to overtake the previous season's total. Just an unlucky thirteenth year for us? Maybe. Though not normally superstitious, we're keeping our fingers crossed.

And, in the midst of all this turmoil, we had to adjust to life without three of the Club's most passionate figures. Denis, Kevin, and Darren all left the Racecourse just as the drama was beginning to turn itself into a crisis. All three had become good friends of the Shreds over the years, and that the suddenness of their departures left no time for proper farewells only added to our gloom.

Before you reach for the anti-depressants let me assure you that this is not an exclusively miserable tale. We began the campaign in good enough order, kicking off by handing over a meaty £4000.00 to the Trust's Equity Fund, and the boys also enjoyed a pretty solid start on the field - giving us all genuine hope that the dark clouds that had been ever-present over the Racecourse these past few years would finally disperse. There is no need to elaborate upon What Happened Next - suffice it to say that our nerves had been well and truly mangled by the time that the final whistle blew. Never have the Shreds been so aptly named!!

Anthony Fairclough came to town a year ago, and he has been a revelation, quietly setting about the Chief Executive's job he was handed to establish some solid

Chairman	John Humpreys
Secretary	David Mainwaring
Treasurer	Brian Davies
Webmaster	Matt Wedderkopp
Committee Members	Gary Coombes, Mark Drury, Andy Foulks, Dave Jones, Pete Jones, Darren Morris, Richard Watkin.
Meeting Venue	Lion Quays Hotel, Moreton
Membership Cost	£6 Adults, £3 Children £13 Family
Meeting Frequency	Bi-monthly

foundations upon which the Club is to be re-built. We've been very impressed with the progress that has been made since his arrival, and we have a commitment to work closely with him to help create the type of Club that we all want.

Still on the subject of personnel changes a familiar face was ushered into the unfamiliar role of Club Manager. A hugely respected Wrexham legend, Brian Carey has certainly negotiated a very steep learning curve to begin to really make his mark. Such is his reputation that he should be able to rely upon the unconditional support of every single Wrexham fan - and, just like the Football Club, we're also organising ourselves properly, with a growing number of independent supporters' groups rallying the troops around the Club's catchment area. Representatives of all these groups now meet regularly, too, so there is a proper structure gradually taking shape to assist the Club wherever we can. The future is indeed looking so much brighter than it did just a few months ago.

That point is perhaps made most emphatically by the fact that Shaun Pejic went home with our Player of the Year Trophy - some fitting reward at long last for a player whose talents have not always been universally appreciated on the terraces.

If you're reading this then you obviously care about Wrexham Football Club. If you care enough to want to make sure that the agonies of the past few years never return then you need to join one of the supporters' groups. There are now enough of them, with the promise of still more to come, for you to find one close to your home (and heart!). Please, make the effort to sign up. All their details may be found in this Year Book, and your membership subscription will give you a voice as the regeneration of our Club continues.

The Shropshire Reds may be contacted via our website www.shropshirereds.com, or by writing to us at PO Box 547, Shrewsbury, Shropshire, SY3 3YY. Alternatively, if it's the personal touch that you crave, the Chairman and Treasurer may be found in Seats P60 and P61 of the Mold Road Stand on match days.

Let's all do our bit!

Rhos and District Reds

The Coach & Horses Inn, Vinegar Hill, Rhosllanerchrugog, Wrexham, LL14 1EH
Telephone: 01978 841 749 (Ian Phillips, Secretary & Landlord of Coach & Horses)
Website: http://uk.groups.yahoo.com/group/rhosanddistrictreds/
Email: rhosanddistrictreds@yahoogroups.co.uk

Rhos and District Reds are one of the newest supporters' groups. Formed in April 2006, the group has grown steadily and now has over 80 members. The idea to form a group came as a result of a chance discussion on Red Passion regarding a particularly bad snowfall; we realised that even on a small road (blocked in by snow!) there were five people who didn't know any of the others were Wrexham supporters.

Many of us were already members of other supporters groups such as the Shropshire Reds, Buckley & District Reds etc.. and seeing the effort these groups put in and the events they enjoy, made us appreciate the fact that we live right on the doorstep of the club and yet very few of us knew each other and there was nothing in place that celebrated being a 'Jacko' and a Wrexham fan.

The Coach and Horses has become the home to the group and the support provided by the licensees Ian & Lynne Phillips has been crucial in the growth of the group. Our aim is to ensure that all Wrexham supporters in the Rhos,

Penycae, Johnstown, Ruabon and Cefn areas have an opportunity to meet up and help support Wrexham FC. We organise regular meetings and have held very successful Question and Answer sessions with both Mark Jones and Stevie Evans.

Being a Brynteg lad I'm sure Stevie had some preconceptions about the Rhos - probably confirmed when he turned up to find no electricity at the pub or the surrounding area! This was due to a very bad storm rather than electricity not having reached the LL14 postcode yet, but given that Stevie had two massive shiners as a result of the operation on his broken nose, it was probably best that the interview was conducted by candlelight anyway!

We also host events such as quiz nights and BBQ's and take a table at the Supporters Player of the Season Dinner at the Lion Quays. We also organised a number of away travel coaches during the season and due to the success we enjoyed and the positive feedback we received from those who travelled on them, it's something we are looking to build on in the new season.

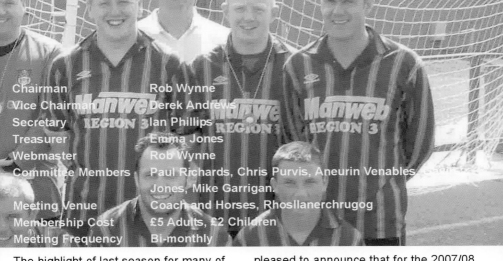

Chairman	Rob Wynne
Vice Chairman	Derek Andrews
Secretary	Ian Phillips
Treasurer	Emma Jones
Webmaster	Rob Wynne
Committee Members	Paul Richards, Chris Purvis, Aneurin Venables, Jones, Mike Garrigan.
Meeting Venue	Coach and Horses, Rhosllanerchrugog
Membership Cost	£5 Adults, £2 Children
Meeting Frequency	Bi-monthly

The highlight of last season for many of the group was winning the Supporters 8 a side tournament held at Colliers Park. It was the first season that we had entered and in fairness we fully expected to get a bit of a thrashing given that the majority of our players were over forty and we'd never even had a kick-about together before! However, the old lads at the back did a fantastic job with some no-nonsense defending, allowing the (slightly) younger midfield and strikers to score some quality goals. Winning the cup was swiftly followed by the crucial win over Boston and it's fair to say that the celebrations that day were legendary! - Many a tale will be told in years to come of everyone drinking beer from the cup and taking it on a tour of all the pubs in Rhos!

Looking ahead to the new season, we fully support the 'Take Wrexham Higher' campaign as we recognise that it's essential that the club continues to grow its support base and increases its turnover in order to compete at the top of the division. All money that is raised by the Rhos & District Reds is used to put on new events for our members and to help support Wrexham FC financially. We are pleased to announce that for the 2007/08 season we will be the official sponsors of Mark Jones' shirt and we hope that is the first of many future contributions. Our aims for 2007/08 are to continue to increase our membership levels, run regular away travel from the Coach & Horses, put on more quality events for our members, host a Christmas 'do' for Wrexham fans, match ball sponsorship and of course, retain our title as Champions of the Supporters 8 a side tournament!

Join us!
New members are always welcome and you can either join on the night of an event, download a Membership form from our website or pick one up from the Coach & Horses.

Rhos Reds: Winners of the Wrexham Supporters 8-a-side Competition 2007

Back Row: (L-R) Chris Purvis, Ian Phillips, Ian Williams, Aneurin Venables, Martin Touhey, Gareth Williams, Paul Richards (Manager), Liam Goode

Front Row: (L-R) Rhys Powell, Derek Andrews, Mark Jones, Rob Wynne, Jamie Richards.

Buckley & District Reds

Buckley and District Reds, PO BOX 182, Buckley, CH7 9BR
Telephone: 07783430301
Website: www.buckleyreds.co.uk
Email: admin@buckleyreds.co.uk

The Buckley & District Reds were formed in January 2006 when 29 people attended the very first meeting which was held at the Hope & Anchor pub in Buckley. By June 2007 we had reached 110 members, with members from as far afield as London & Glasgow!

Aims and Objectives
The club was formed with the following aims in mind:-

1. To bring fans from the Flintshire area & beyond together to raise funds for the benefit of WREXHAM (A) FC
2. Give fans a feeling of involvement in the future of WREXHAM (A)FC
3. To interact with other fans groups
4. Work with other fans groups & WST for the benefit of WREXHAM (A)FC
5. To encourage increased support for WREXHAM (A)FC in the area
6. To promote a friendly atmosphere and to have fun at our fund raising events

Sadly in August 2006 Paul Antrobus, our founding member passed away aged 42, we have raised over £ 1,500 for the Macmillan Nurse charity in his memory,

which the Welsh FA kindly allowed us to have a bucket collection at the New Zealand game in May which raised £500 for the charity.

Since we formed we have sponsored Danny Williams for 2006/07 season, donated £300 to the Centre of Excellence at Colliers Park, donated £100 towards the Junior Dragons Christmas party, taken out a loan note with the WST for £500 towards buying equity in the football club & taken part in the 'Be A Red for a Day' initiative which put £500 into the football club.

The Wrexham FC supporters Player of the Season awards dinner was once again well attended by our members, Dave Watson was the guest speaker, and Willie Miller the comedian, and a thoroughly good day was had by all. If you missed out this year, then make sure your there next year!

For the 2007/8 season we are already committed to sponsoring Danny & Anthony Williams, donating £100 towards the Junior Dragons Christmas party & donated £100 towards equipment for the

Chairman	Bryn Jones
Secretary	Tony Williams
Treasurer	Dave Kelsall
Webmaster	Stuart Cooper
Committee Members	Stuart Cooper, Chris Haynes, Daz Jones, Andy Kelsall
Meeting Venue	Buckley Cricket Club
Membership Cost	£5 Adults, £1 Under 16s
Meeting Frequency	Monthly

newly formed group 'DEUDDEGFED DYN' the 'TWELFTH MAN'.

We also have our website & message board where our members can discuss anything to do with Buckley & District Reds, Wrexham FC or the Welsh national side. We also won the annual 8 a-side knockout at Colliers Park at the first attempt in 2006, but this year finished 4th and 5th, but not without 'war wounds'. Injuries were sustained to Dave Kelsall (bruised groin) and Steffan Tomos (Kidney damage) with Steffan needing to spend the night in hospital. Fortunately both are well on the mend.

Forthcoming events
One forthcoming event that we would ask all Wrexham fans to support is our Hot Pot Supper with the one and only Mr. Wrexham, Joey Jones. This is to take place at Buckley Cricket Club on Friday 12th October 2007, while just over a week later on Saturday 20th October again at Buckley Cricket Club.

Our aim is to raise funds to benefit Wrexham FC directly or indirectly through WST, but to have some fun in doing so!

Holywell & District Reds

The Holywell & District Reds is another active supporters' group which welcomes any Wrexham fan in their area to join them. Regular meetings are held at the Abbotts Arms, Pen-y-Maes Road, Holywell on Sunday evenings.

The Holywell & District Reds were formed in July 2000 by brothers John & Paul Evans, from the Holywell area. The club was started to bring supporters of Wrexham FC from the Holywell area together to organise home and away travel, but also to raise funds for Wrexham Football Club.

Today the Holywell & District Reds have nearly 50 members. It's just £5 for adults and £3.50 for juniors to join, so if you live in the Holywell area get in touch with Paul Evans at evans-p1@sky.com or Shaun Holden at shaunholden11@aol.com.

Chairman:	Paul Evans
Secretary:	John Evans
Committee:	Barry Davies, Shaun Holden.

Cochion Llundain
19 93
London Reds

London Reds Cochion Llundain

Telephone: Barry Jones on 07973 512258
Website: http://www.londonreds.co.uk

The London Reds

The London Reds Cochion Llundain was formed after the famous promotion game at Northampton way back in 1993. Following the match it was noticeable that many Wrexham fans were travelling south not north on the train. We started talking and in June 1993 the London Reds was formed.

Meeting venues

Our meeting venue has changed in the past year as fewer pubs in central London have upstairs rooms available for hire. The lure of cramming in extra drinkers at the expense of a quiet function room has been too much at two of our favourite haunts. Please check our website or contact Barry Jones for details of our next meeting.

Events

For the fifteenth year in succession we will be running a bus to the last home game of the season - Accrington Stanley. The annual the mid-winter bus trip in January will be to Hereford United. As well as train journeys to home and away games we hope to repeat the highly successful 'an evening with Brian Carey'

before the Dagenham away game. We run a 50/50 draw club, which has a top quarterly prize of over £200 as well as a new badge, polo shirt and ceramic mug.

Sponsorship

This year we are sponsoring new Dragons' striker Eifion Williams. The London Reds flag will be on display at all home and away games this coming season alongside the Deuddegfed Dyn (Twelfth Man) flags.

Membership

Application forms, sponsorship activity, the 50/50 draw and details of trips and meeting places at home and away games are available from our Secretary Barry Jones on 07973 512258 or on our web site: **www.londonreds.co.uk.**
Membership costs just £8 per year.

The Committee

Chairman: Dave Harris
Secretary: Barry Jones
Treasurer: Dave Jones
Webmaster: Stuart Roberts

Manchester Reds

Telephone: 07971843376
Website: www.manchester-reds.com
Email: feed_me_till_i_want_no_more@hotmail.co.uk

Chairman:	Peter Banks
Vice Chairman:	Wayne Price
Secretary:	Mike Hughes

Manchester Reds

The Manchester Reds were founded when it became obvious there was a number of Wrexham fans based in Manchester. A few attempts were made to form the Manchester Reds but it was not until November 1997 that there was enough interest to form as a supporters club.

Since formation The Manchester Reds have contributed over £1,500 to Wrexham FC in the form of sponsorship.
As a supporters club the Manchester Reds main function is to arrange travel to home and away games within the Greater Manchester area and further afield, and also hold meetings which are open to all Wrexham fans.

It costs just £5 for waged fans to join the Manchester Reds, and £1 for unwaged fans. We welcome all Wrexham fans from the Greater Manchester area. So if you already live in Greater Manchester, or you know of Wrexham fans that do, then give us a shout and travel to matches with fellow Reds. Contact the Manchester Reds for more details at:
feed_me_till_i_want_no_more@hotmail.co.uk

Mold & District Reds

Mold & District Reds were formed in May 2007, following lots of local interest in forming a supporters' club. Enzo Merola often ran coaches to away games from Mold, and it was these coach journeys that helped persuade others to form the Mold & District Reds to help generate finances to benefit Wrexham FC.

Following our inaugural meeting in June, we have now formed a committee and we hope to build up our membership base throughout this coming season with events and coach travel. Anyone interested in joining the Mold & District Reds should email: **moldreds@hotmail.co.uk**

Chairperson:	Sandra Edwards
Treasurer:	Paul Bryan
Secretary:	Rita Florio
Committee:	Eddie Pritchard, Glyn Hayes, Rob Hughes, Adam Phillips, Les Buxton, Jeffrey Green

Membership Fees are £10 per adult £5 Junior & OAP £20 per family (2 adults and 3 children).

Junior Dragons

The Junior Dragons Story So Far...

The decision to form a new junior supporters club with the sole purpose of celebrating everything Wrexham FC was an easy decision to make. Over the last 20 or so years there have been many young supporters clubs in many guises, but they have all fallen by the wayside due to numerous reasons.

Wrexham Supporters Trust was handed the role of running the junior supporters club in early Spring 2006; at that time Football In The Community were doing a fine job of running the club (they had in excess of 1000 members!) but were struggling to find the time to run it.

Membership

We decided to launch the 'Junior Dragons' on the Club's Open Day held in July 2006; the thinking behind this was that it was a new era for the Club, and therefore a new era for its young supporters. It proved to be a great success with over 250 young people signing up on the day itself.

We've now passed the 500 members mark and we're steadily cruising towards the 600 mark. Since we started we have given each member a membership card, players photo and put on a very successful Christmas party.

Christmas Party

The party was held at Brymbo Cricket Club on 17th December and we had the honour of having 10 first team players turn up to have photographs with the players, and sign autographs for the members. There was also a special guest appearance by the club's very

Wrexham players attended the Christmas party

own 'Wrex the Dragon' and all guests received a special Wrexham FC Christmas present to take away courtesy of the Buckley and District Reds.

Achievements
So, what else has the Junior Dragons achieved so far? Well, we've started a Junior Supporters Club which can only boost the Club's attendances in years to come and maintain interest in the Club with our younger supporters; given each member a voucher for discount on a shirt; given a photo of their favourite player; and have provided two mascots for the Boston home game. At that game we also presented Steve Evans with the 'Junior Dragons Player of the Season' trophy that was donated to us by Angela Antrobus in memory of her late husband, Paul.

Newsletter
Our second Newsletter was produced bilingually in both Welsh and English and we soon hope to form a committee complete with Chairperson and Secretary etc. to oversee the direction of the Junior Dragons. Hopefully, this committee will be able to reach and influence decisions that not only help the Club in its future but also provide our members with a sense of ownership for their football club.

If anyone reading this would like to help the Junior Dragons at committee level, or would like to help out with sponsorship to oversee the cost of running the club, then please contact a Trust Board member for further details. All in all the Junior Dragons seems to have a long and bright future which can only be a positive thing for Wrexham FC and its young supporters.

Wrex the Dragon made a guest appearance at the Chrismas Party

Evening Leader

For the best coverage of youth football across Wrexham and Flintshire, pick up your **Evening Leader** every Wednesday for our 'Football Crazy' supplement.

This supplement showcases the best of youth football - bursting with pictures, reports and results across the region.

Want to see your team's result in the **Evening Leader**

Call the sports desk today **01352 70776**

www.eveningleader.co.uk

Section 5:
Season Review 2006/07

A Review of the 2006/07 Season

Not even the most chronically pessimistic of you - and there are many - could have foreseen the trouble, strife and sheer anxiety that dominated vast parts of last season.

Given the swagger with which we opened the campaign; excellent at home and away during last August and early September, the implosion away at Accrington five weeks into the season was as surprising as it was shocking. And its hangover was one we struggled to shake for months afterwards.

Was the team that caved in so easily at The Crown Ground in any way related to the one that had humbled Sheffield Wednesday at theirs, and been the last unbeaten team in their division? Indeed, it was our two league performances against Accrington Stanley that framed, in many respects, our entire season. Before we encountered them in early-September we hadn't played them competitively for forty years and, were we not to do so again for another forty it would, in many eyes, be too soon.

Initially, last season saw us return to the more fan-favoured 4-4-2 and, as we took the early part of the programme by storm it looked as if the supporters may have had a point about team formation after all. We also benefited greatly during those heady days from the notable contributions of several locals; - the returning Neil Roberts, Steve Evans and Ryan Valentine adding a touch of the parochial into a squad that had, over previous seasons, includ-

Wrexham lost 5-0 to Accrington Stanley in September 2006

ed far too many mercenaries and half-hearted, jobbing pros among its number.

From very early on though, it was apparent that Roberts, pointedly appointed club captain, was carrying an unequal distribution of workload and responsibility on his shoulders. Although he'd never been a prolific goal-scorer, Denis Smith saw him clearly as the motivator we'd lacked since the retirement of Brian Carey and, whisper it, the talisman we'd missed since the sale of Lee Trundle. From early on, Roberts was more than willing to dig in and set the tone, and we rightly welcomed him like a lost God. But the disproportionate allocation of labour was always likely to come at a cost, and it was no surprise when he finally did his ankle at home to Swindon and earned himself the first of many injuries. And the obligatory month in the sickbay.

That very Swindon game also lulled us too into a mis-leading sense of how good we were. On lush surfaces in the early season, we were playing with a decent spring in the step and an ease on the ball we hadn't seen around these parts in years. And most of those 5,500 leaving The Racecourse that afternoon would have been convinced that the season was going to be a fruitful one. The formation was working, the locals were prominent and had all earned their corn and we'd had a large crowd in. Wrexham, we thought fleetingly, were going up. Or at least going close.

We'd already gone to Sheffield Wednesday in the Carling Cup and beaten them so convincingly that neutrals there on the night would have understandably wondered which of the two teams was the Championship one. Granted, Wednesday at a low ebb and struggling under Sturrock were a side designer-made for us; they granted us the space to spray it around and open them up down the channels, which we did liberally. On a magical night at Hillsborough, we certainly showed what we had in the pack. And were then we were promptly de-railed.

Now, the point has long been made that our teams are at their most vulnerable after they've been at their most unbeatable. And so the absence of the injured Neil Roberts would have triggered the pessimist's alarm ahead of our trip to Accrington, a grim and unwelcoming spot if ever, and certainly no place for the rudderless. But no one could have legislated for what transpired merely three days after our most emphatic league performance in ages. Because if Swindon was already the season's high, what transpired at Stanley will long live as a club low.

So was the five-goal reversal at Accrington a blip? or was it a more accurate reflection of our team's standing within its own league? Well, those in the know reckon that, when a team is 'young' - which we were for large tracts of last season - then it's always prone to the odd pummelling. It happens, and it's just a rung on the learning curve, that's all. Pack it away quickly as merely a bad evening at the office.

And we could have forgiven the display at Accrington and maintained the perspective had we not capitulated in the same manner on the following weekend at Stockport, where we defended like schoolboys who'd been scared into submission by the playground bullies. And while another Carling Cup performance, this time at Birmingham, saw us at least dig in and generate no little spirit, the wheels on the wagon had certainly come loose by the time we'd pulled into Mansfield. After another bad hiding, we just looked like we'd been made-over by Trinny and Susannah into cast-iron relegation candidates.

By now Denis Smith's position, heretofore deemed to have been rock solid, even came under scrutiny, and the three goal defeat at Field Mill kick-started in earnest a change in the prevailing mood. Darren Ferguson, typically, called it like many of us had started to see it, when he claimed that, irrespective of our injuries and the age and size of our squad, we should still have been capable of seeing-off the mid-table fodder.

After the Accrington drubbing, Wrexham then lost 5-2 to Stockport County

But by now we were struggling for air, our cause helped only by the fact that there were, disbelievingly, some teams in the division actually worse than us.

And so 2006 will go down as arguably one of the most horrific years in our proud history. To those sports scientists and anoraks among you, our form last August appears on the performance graph as a remote upward blip on a curve that's been otherwise going progressively downwards for the last sixteen months. A deceptive end-of-year gloss was provided by a rare, unexpected and excellent away win at League One leaders Scunthorpe in the FA Cup, a decent home performance against Lincoln, where we won 2-1 (and where it should have been 5), and by a ten-minute cameo at the end of that game by Lee McEvilly. But this, yet again, was yet another false dawn. An eighteen-month contract signed by Juan Ugarte provided some welcome respite and generated some positive PR spin and an out-pouring of ill-informed hoopla on-line, but then the Basque went to ground indefinitely soon afterwards and hasn't been seen since. His future here, as I type, is as uncertain as its been at any time during his career at Wrexham.

Denis Smith had blown much of his buck and based much of his ambition on Ugarte (and McEvilly), but saw little of consequence from either, bar substantial tabs at the physio's. And so by the time we went down 3-1 at home to Accrington on New Year's Day (when they more or less repeated the September dose), our drift towards the relegation mire and a string of passionless performances meant that the writing was well and truly on the wall and Smith was on borrowed time. It was the infamous political right-winger, Enoch Powell, who once remarked that all political careers end in failure. Denis Smith will vouch that the maxim applies too to football management and, ultimately, he just ran out of runway, as you do. But unlike many others who've gone before him here, he'll be remembered too for the good times - and he enjoyed more

Denis Smith offers Brian Carey some advice

than most do at Wrexham - and for his loyalty in the face of Hamilton and Guterman.

Of course football, like life itself, is an
unemotional and callous beast that waits for
no one man, and our one-time skipper and
defensive lynchpin, Brian Carey, was
instantly installed at the helm, initially on a
caretaker, suck-it-and-see basis. Those
expecting an immediate up-turn in fortunes
were left waiting, however, and life under
the new manager continued in pretty much
the same vein, results-wise at least. While
performances (and the team's general fitness and commitment) improved noticeably,
we continued to be dogged by bad luck,
injuries, suspensions and some of the worst
refereeing performances some of us had
ever witnessed, even at our level.

In Carey's first game in charge, away at
Swindon, we were beaten by a penalty that
the referee later admitted was never a
penalty at all, while at home to Stockport we
were un-done four minutes into added time

Denis Smith was sacked after the FA Cup match
against Derby County

by a header from an off-side position that followed a flick-on from a disputed free-kick.
But Carey has never been one for whingeing, and although acknowledging the ill for-
tune at the time, has been around the game long enough to know that these things
invariably even themselves out over time. But by now most of us were wondering
when, if ever, our luck was going to turn? Because time and patience were starting to
run short.

Soon, Darren Ferguson too was off, the first casualty of the Carey-era. Having been
rested over Christmas, he'd been re-instated into our midfield on New Year's Day but,
on a rain-sodden Racecourse, could hardly move. Carey's decision to drop his long-
time friend and colleague was ultimately made with the best intentions of the team and
the club at heart, but was also a stark statement of intent from the rookie manager.

Ferguson's unveiling as Peterborough boss soon after helped to frame a context for
the decision; ultimately, the home dressing room at The Racecourse can accommo-
date only one strong-willed young manager's voice.

For much of the remainder of the season, Carey was fielding what will be the guts of
this season's reserve side and, lacking experience, guile and clout, it was to be ten
long games before we registered our first win under his stewardship. But when Brian
and his staff faced the music at a London Reds do in early March, the manager was at
pains to assure those gathered in deepest Belgravia. Starting the following day at
Barnet, he predicted a new approach from the players. 'I promise you', he said, 'that

you'll see a new team up there tomorrow. He was emphatic too on one other point. 'We will NOT, I assure you, be relegated'. And, buoyed by BC's rousing words, the special guests left the meeting to a prolonged chorus of 'We Are Staying Up' from the faithful. And on both counts, history now tells us, Carey was true to his word.

Up at Underhill we managed to keep all of our players on the pitch for the duration of the Barnet game and emerged victorious for the first time under the new management, coming behind to win 2-1. The post-Barnet optimism continued on the following Friday night when we hosted Bury, and not even two sending-off's (when it could, and maybe should have been three) and the concession of yet another equalising goal well into added time were going to detract from a notable up-turn in the mood. Those who paid their fivers to get in will certainly remember that bitterly cold night in March, where Wrexham's nine men performed with gusto and application for over an hour, unlucky not to have taken all three points following a stunning 80-yard run-and-shot by one of Carey's on-loan diamonds, Robbie Garrett. The manager, though, may recall the night differently, and the recklessness of some of his senior players - and the impact of the subsequent suspensions - will have registered on his mental hard-drive.

But just when we thought we'd turned the corner, regular service was resumed away at Macclesfield subsequently, where we posted a total no-show that was redolent of the last days of the previous management, and came home with our tails between our legs and languishing. And after we'd gone down at home to Notts County - courtesy of a freakish own-goal in the last minute - then even the most optimistic among us were preparing for life this season in The Conference. To many of us, Satan was simply chasing bad debts run up by Mark Guterman and Alex Hamilton, and this was the definitive payback.

Now, when Simon Spender - a local lad of no little promise and who's form over the final ten games of the season was vital to our eventual survival - spoke to the hacks after the Notts County game, he made the somewhat obvious, if outrageous claim, that were we to win our next five games, then we were safe. He claimed that all five of those games were, indeed, win-able and that furthermore, he expected us to deliver maximum points from them. For a team that, heretofore, would have had difficulty scoring on a night-out with Tony Soprano, this seemed just a little too far-fetched. We dismissed Spender as a fantasist and started to plan instead for mid-week trips to Burton Albion and Aldershot. And then, typical of the club we are, we started to win games. And how. At a remove, I guess the season's undoubted highlight is still proba-bly that final day victory at home to Boston United, a win-or-bust scenario that cli-maxed our best run of form in years.

Winning and Losing Streaks

Double Wins:	2	Bristol Rovers & Lincoln City
Double Defeats:	4	Accrington Stanley, MK Dons, Notts County & Stockport County
Won from behind:	3	Barnet, Boston United (H) & Swindon Town (H),
Lost from in front:	5	Grimsby (A), MK Dons (H&A), Rochdale (H) & Swindon Town (A)

Wrexham fans celebrate Michael Proctor's winning goal against Boston United

Aided in no small part by the canny loan-signings of the aforementioned Garrett, Jeff Whitley, Michael Proctor and goalkeeper Anthony Williams, our end-of-season dividend kicked completely against form and, after winning consecutive games, it seemed as if our luck had changed for the better. After Michael Proctor's late (and richly deserved) winner at Gay Meadow gave us the points against Shrewsbury, it seemed as if we now had the wind at our backs, finally. Apart entirely from the significance of winning a close-fought derby game, that win - on our last ever visit to Gay Meadow - meant we'd won three consecutive league games for the first time since our promotion season in 2002/03.

Going to the then high-flying Lincoln at the start of that run and tearing them asunder was also the first time we'd scored three goals in a single game since our second league fixture against Grimsby, back in August. But its most likely that the three con-secutive clean-sheets that provided the bed-rock for our eventual survival - against Lincoln, Torquay and Shrewsbury - will probably have pleased BC most of all.

In every respect, last season was an excruciating one for everyone associated with our football club, and the post-match celebration on the last day was driven exclusively by a sense of relief that we'd survived and stayed in the league. Brian Carey is intelligent enough to know that we cannot endure another season like it again under his tenure and expect to survive. This club can, and should, be challenging regularly at the other end of the table, and that is the management's stated aim. It's simply not good enough to celebrate raw survival; in fact, to conscientious professionals with ambition it's an

Season Highlights

1 Unbeaten for opening six league games.
2 2-0 win at League One side Scunthorpe in the FA Cup.
3 4-1 win at Championship side Sheffield Wed in Carling Cup
4 League wins at Bristol Rovers, Lincoln & Shrewsbury.
5 Steve Evans, Mark Jones & Chris Llewellyn all winning full Welsh caps against Liechtenstein on the Racecourse.
6 Michael Ingham's Northern Ireland full cap v. Wales.
7 Steve Evans winning further Welsh caps v. N.Ireland (a), Eire (a), San Marino (h), & New Zealand (h).
8 Chris Llewellyn's Welsh cap v. New Zealand (h).
9 Under-21 caps for Mike Williams (Wales), Mike Carvill & Rob Garrett (N.Ireland).
10 Last ever team to win a League game at the Gay Meadow,
11 Shrewsbury before being demolished.
12 The 3-1 win over Boston Utd in the last game of the season in front of the biggest league crowd since 1st March 1980 v Shrewsbury Town.

And the lows...

1 Dismissal of Denis Smith & Kevin Russell in January 2007.
2 5-0 defeat at Accrington & 3-1 home defeat by Accrington.
3 Number of injuries incurred during the first half of the Season.
4 The team performance in the 2-0 defeat at Macclesfield.
5 Simon Spender's unfortunate late own-goal at home to Notts County to lose 1-0.

embarrassment, and the goal from here is to celebrate victory and success.

In many ways, the performance against Boston on the last day represented the entire season in microcosm; - we played in patches, looked vulnerable to the physical stuff and, were our opponents made of sterner stuff; the result could have gone either way. But 2006/07 is over now, and history will recall that we endured. And that annual air of mindless optimism that wafts over every single club in the country during the close season has descended.

God only knows what the next eight months has in store for us, but lets just hope that we've learned enough from the experience last season to never want to flirt with the spectre of non-league again. The arrival of a cluster of seasoned and committed professionals into our ranks is certainly to be welcomed, and the emphasis on physical fitness and sports science can only but aid our ambition.

And if Steve Weaver gets his wish and over-sees a forty-goal turn-around, then who knows where we'll be this time next year? Because in spite of everything we've been through this last six years, both on and off the pitch, the sheer joy of the beautiful game is that it's always okay to dream, no matter what.

Player of the Season

Steve Evans collects the Jack Williams Player of the Season Award from Wrexham Supporters' Association's Dave Bennett.

Young Player of the Season

Matty Done was awarded Wrexham Supporters' Association's Young Player of the Season Award for his outstanding performances on the left wing.

Player of the Year
1975/76 Brian Lloyd
1976/77 Graham Whittle
1977/78 Gareth Davies
1978/79 John Roberts
1979/80 Dixie McNeil
1980/81 Steve Fox
1981/82 Eddie Niedzwiecki
1982/83 Robbie Savage
1983/84 David Gregory
1984/85 Jack Keay
1985/86 Mike Williams
1986/87 Mike Williams
1987/88 Kevin Russell
1988/89 Kevin Russell
1989/90 Nigel Beaumont
1990/91 Mark Morris
1991/92 Andy Thackeray
1992/93 Tony Humes
1993/94 Gary Bennett
1994/95 Gary Bennett
1995/96 Waynne Phillips
1996/97 Andy Marriott
1997/98 Brian Carey
1998/99 Dean Spink
1999/00 Darren Ferguson
2000/01 Mark McGregor
2001/02 Jim Whitley
2002/03 Andy Morrell
2003/04 Dennis Lawrence
2004/05 Andy Holt
2005/06 Danny Williams
2006/07 Steve Evans

Young Player of the Year
1983/84 Shaun Cunnington
1984/85 Andy Edwards
1985/86 Shaun Cunnington
1986/87 Roger Preece
1987/88 Darren Wright
1988/89 Darren Wright
1989/90 Gareth Owen
1990/91 Gareth Owen
1991/92 Phil Hardy
1992/93 Jonathan Cross
1993/94 David Brammer
1994/95 Bryan Hughes
1995/96 Mark McGregor
1996/97 Mark McGregor
1997/98 Neil Roberts
1998/99 Robin Gibson
1999/00 Robin Gibson
2000/01 Lee Roche
2001/02 Shaun Pejic
2002/03 Craig Morgan
2003/04 Craig Morgan
2004/05 Mark Jones
2005/06 Mark Jones
2006/07 Matty Done

Coca Cola League 2 2006/07

FINAL TABLE

		P	W	D	L	F	A	W	D	L	F	A	Pts	
1	Walsall	46	16	4	3	39	13	9	10	4	27	21	89	C
2	Hartlepool	46	14	5	4	34	17	12	5	6	31	23	88	P
3	Swindon	46	15	4	4	34	17	10	6	7	24	21	85	P
4	MK Dons	46	14	4	5	41	26	11	5	7	35	32	84	
5	Lincoln	46	12	4	7	36	28	9	7	7	34	31	74	
6	Bristol Rovers	46	13	5	5	27	14	7	7	9	22	28	72	P
7	Shrewsbury	46	11	7	5	38	23	7	10	6	30	23	71	
8	Stockport	46	14	4	5	41	25	7	4	12	24	29	71	
9	Rochdale	46	9	6	8	33	20	9	6	8	37	30	66	
10	Peterborough	46	10	6	7	48	36	8	5	10	22	25	65	
11	Darlington	46	10	6	7	28	30	7	8	8	24	26	65	
12	Wycombe	46	8	11	4	23	14	8	3	12	29	33	62	
13	Notts County	46	8	6	9	29	25	8	8	7	26	28	62	
14	Barnet	46	12	5	6	35	30	4	6	13	20	40	59	
15	Grimsby	46	11	4	8	33	32	6	4	13	24	41	59	
16	Hereford	46	9	7	7	23	17	5	6	12	22	36	55	
17	Mansfield	46	10	4	9	38	31	4	8	11	20	32	54	
18	Chester	46	7	9	7	23	23	6	5	12	17	25	53	
19	**Wrexham**	**46**	**8**	**8**	**7**	**23**	**21**	**5**	**4**	**14**	**20**	**44**	**51**	
20	Accrington	46	10	6	7	42	33	3	5	15	28	48	50	
21	Bury	46	4	7	12	22	35	9	4	10	24	26	50	
22	Macclesfield	46	8	7	8	36	34	4	5	14	19	43	48	
23	Boston *	46	9	5	9	29	32	3	5	15	22	48	36	R
24	Torquay	46	5	8	10	19	22	2	6	15	17	41	35	R

* Boston United deducted 10 points for entering administration.

Mark Jones celebrates his equaliser for Wrexham as a dejected Tommy Mooney looks on

Coca Cola League 2: August 6th, 2006

Wycombe Wanderers 1   Wrexham 1

Tommy Mooney 6   Mark Jones 32

Referee: Patrick Miller (Bedfordshire)
Attendance (Away): 4,763 (525)

H aving only just come out of administration - and with a squad containing a high percentage of local or Welsh players (including the return of Chris Llewellyn and prodigal son Neil Roberts) - Wrexham's long-suffering fans harboured hopes of a successful season ahead.

But Adams Park has never been a happy hunting ground for Wrexham (just one win in ten previous visits!), and the defensive frailties evident in the 5-0 mauling at Port

Vale in the last friendly game gave cause for concern against Wycombe's dangerous strike force.

And these concerns were quickly justified as a series of mistakes gifted the home side a sixth minute lead. Chris Palmer easily waltzed past Simon Spender to cross for Tommy Mooney, whose poorly struck shot somehow squirmed under the body of Michael Ingham and into the net.

Not the ideal start to the season and, for

most of the first half, it looked like the 'Chairboys' would swarm all over a Wrexham side clearly off the pace in the early exchanges.

But just as the home side had been some-what gifted the opening goal at one end, so a defensive howler gifted the 'Dragons' a 32nd minute equaliser at the other. Keeper Ricardo Batista charged out of his area to clear the ball, but only managed to slice it straight to Mark Jones. Jonah still had plenty to do, but showed the compo-sure required to find the unguarded net from fully forty yards out.

Buoyed by this unexpected windfall the 'Dragons' visibly upped the tempo after the break, and with Darren Ferguson orches-trating things from his central midfield position, and debutant Steve Evans form-ing a strong defensive partnership with World Cup hero Dennis Lawrence, they began to look the side more likely to go on and win the game. Roberts went close with one header, and then strike-partner Llewellyn struck the post with another on 67 minutes.

Back came the home side and Ingham, who responded well after his early error, saved from Kevin Betsy, and Ryan Valentine, another Wrexham debutant,

superbly blocked an effort from Matt Bloomfield.

Then, in the last minute, came the moment when Wrexham thought they'd won the game. Matty Done easily beat his full back down the left, his cross shot was only parried by Batista, and Roberts looked certain to score, but Russell Martin was on hand to clear the Wrexham cap-tain's goal bound shot off the line.

The game ended level, but given that last-gasp chance, 'Dragons' fans still left Adams Park thinking about what might have been!

Wrexham:
01 Michael Ingham, 03 Ryan Valentine ■, 05 Steve Evans, 23 Neil Roberts, 06 Dennis Lawrence, 10 Darren Ferguson, 08 Danny Williams, 07 Mark Jones, 11 Chris Llewellyn, 20 Matt Done ■, 14 Simon Spender.

Subs: 12 Matt Crowell, 13 Michael Jones (GK), 16 Levi Mackin, 24 Gareth Evans, 27 Jamie Reed.

Wycombe:
31 Ricardo Batista, 25 Sam Stockley, 04 Russell Martin, 05 Will Antwi, 06 Mike Williamson, 30 Anthony Grant (69), 03 Chris Palmer, 10 Matt Bloomfield, 07 Kevin Betsy, 16 Tommy Mooney, -9 Jermaine Easter (78)

Subs: 02 Lewis Christon, 08 Stefan Oakes (69), 18 Jonny Dixon (78), 22 Sergio Torres, 32 Jamie Young (GK)

Neil Roberts holds the ball up		
Shots on Goal:	10	9
Shots on Target:	2	3
Shots off Target:	8	6
Possession:	62%	38%
Fouls Conceded:	10	12
Corners:	10	1
Yellow Cards:	0	3?
Red Cards:	0	0

Mark Jones is tackled during Wrexham's opening win in League 2

Coca Cola League 2: August 8th, 2006

Wrexham 3   Grimsby Town 0

Steve Evans 16
Chris Llewellyn 34
Matt Done 68

Referee: Dean Whitehouse (Northamptonshire)
Attendance: 5,180 (219)

Wrexham produced a resounding performance to kick-start their home campaign with a deserved 3-0 victory over Grimsby Town, who had just missed out on promotion by losing their League Two play-off final.

It was difficult to fault the 'Dragons' as they were quickest out of the blocks with Danny Williams and Darren Ferguson pulling the strings in midfield.

The home supporters did not have to wait long for the opening home goal of the campaign. Matty Done forced a corner down the Wrexham left, and Ferguson's set play was only partially cleared for him to collect the loose ball and deliver a deep cross to Steve Evans at the back post. He planted his header into the far corner past the exposed Barnes for his first ever

Football League goal.

The 'Mariners' offered little up front, and the only real scare for Wrexham came when Ingham misjudged the bounce of a through ball, but managed to finger tip it away.

Wrexham continued to look dangerous, and Done made good use of space down the left flank, which led to the second goal when he was allowed too much time. He passed inside to Ferguson, whose measured cross to the edge of the area, saw Chris Llewellyn loop a superb header into the top corner from eighteen yards.

At half-time Ciaran Toner substituted Peter Beagrie, and the ineffective Michael Reddy replaced Peter Bore, which had the desired effect as the 'Mariners' almost caught Wrexham napping from the restart. Good attacking play from Isaiah Rankin was halted by a last ditch challenge from Evans, and the former Arsenal trainee should have done better from a back post header following a deep cross.

Graham Rodger's side offered more up front in the second half, and went close again when Toner fired in a low cross. But Wrexham hit back following good play by Llewellyn, and Done made no mistake with

his finish, bending the ball inside of the near post and giving Barnes no chance.

Ryan Valentine went close to extending the 'Dragons' lead when he curled a shot from the edge of the box, but it went narrowly wide of the far post with Barnes well beaten.

Grimsby's lack of threat was summed up well when substitute Bore failed to connect with a bicycle kick late on. Josh Johnson replaced Mark Jones, but the Wrexham goal never looked in any real danger, and the game ended in a deserved 3-0 home victory.

Wrexham:
01 Michael Ingham, 14 Simon Spender, 05 Steve Evans, 06 Dennis Lawrence, 03 Ryan Valentine, 07 Mark Jones (86), 08 Danny Williams, 10 Darren Ferguson (72), 20 Matt Done, 23 Neil Roberts, 11 Chris Llewellyn

Subs: 12 Matt Crowell (72) ■, 13 Michael Jones (GK), 15 Mike Williams, 17 Josh Johnson (86), 27 Jamie Reed.

Grimsby:
01 Phillip Barnes, 02 John McDermott, 06 Justin Whittle, 05 Ben Futcher, 03 Tom Newey, 07 Isaiah Rankin, 04 Gary Harkins, 08 Paul Bolland, 11 Peter Beagrie (45), 09 Michael Reddy (45), 19 Gary Jones

Subs: 10 Ciaran Toner (45), 14 Terry Barwick, 18 Peter Bore (45), 20 Gary Croft, 22 Danny North.

Steve Evans heads the ball clear

	Wrexham	Grimsby
Shots on Goal:	8	7
Shots on Target:	4	2
Shots off Target:	4	5
Possession:	50%	50%
Fouls Conceded:	12	8
Corners:	5	6
Yellow Cards:	1	0
Red Cards:	0	0

Matt Crowell is challenged by a Peterborough player during a Wrexham attack

Coca Cola League 2: August 12th, 2006

Wrexham 0   Peterborough United 0

Referee: Anthony Taylor (Cheshire)
Attendance: 4,706 (211)

With expectations high after the midweek success over Grimsby, Peterborough showed stubborn resistance, as they held out for a point in an evenly contested contest, as Wrexham remained unbeaten after their first three games of the season.

Darren Ferguson failed to shake off a knock picked up in midweek and the 'Red Dragons' had to manage without the craft of their midfield playmaker.
Both teams won early free kicks in dan-

gerous positions. The first fell to the visitors and Michael Ingham had to dive low to his left to turn the ball away after Jamie Day had successfully bent the ball around the wall. At the other end Mark Jones failed to clear the wall from his free kick after a foul on Llewellyn.

With the 'Posh' having the wind advantage, Wrexham struggled to cope with the high balls, and on a couple of occasions Dennis Lawrence misjudged the flight to allow the Peterborough strikers to get in behind the home defence, with decent chances falling to both Trevor Benjamin and Guy Branston.

The home side put together the best move of the game on the stroke of half time when Danny Williams combined with Mark Jones, but his effort ended disappointingly high over the bar.

Peterborough started the strongest after the break, but missed three clear cut headers as the Wrexham defence looked disorganised, and were fortunate to see the visitors direct their efforts wide of the far post.

A mistake by Branston allowed Llewellyn a clear run on goal, and after advancing into the area, the striker beat keeper Tyler with a right footed shot, but the ball clipped the top of the bar and went behind for a goal kick.

The 'Posh' had the ball in the back of the net through Benjamin, but their celebrations were short lived with the linesman flagging for offside.

Matt Crowell was unlucky with a shot deflected, and Llewellyn fired in the rebound that rebounded to Done whose effort was diverted away by another defender.

Day struck the base of Ingham's post after curling his left footed free kick around the 'Dragons' wall from twenty-five yards. Wrexham were then awarded a free-kick deep in stoppage time for a foul on Josh Johnson, but Crowell's effort was blocked by the defensive wall.

In the end a draw was a fair result, but with the number of good chances that had gone begging, especially in the second half, it was Keith Alexander who was by far the happier of the two managers.

Wrexham:
01 Michael Ingham, 14 Simon Spender (59), 05 Steve Evans, 06 Dennis Lawrence, 03 Ryan Valentine ■, 07 Mark Jones, 08 Danny Williams (59), 12 Matt Crowell, 20 Matt Done (77), 23 Neil Roberts, 11 Chris Llewellyn.

Subs: 13 Michael Jones (GK), 15 Mike Williams (59), 16 Levi Mackin (59), 17 Josh Johnson (77), 18 Jon Newby.

Peterborough:
01 Mark Tyler, 07 Adam Newton, 06 Christopher Plummer ■, 04 Mark Arber, 05 Guy Branston ■, 17 Jamie Day (77), 02 Dean Holden, 08 Richard Butcher, 16 Danny Crow (55), 10 Trevor Benjamin, 20 Simon Yeo

Subs:
03 Jude Stirling (77), 09 Justin Richards (55), 12 Mark Bailey, 14 Paul Carden, 18 Shane Huke.

Chris Llewellyn leads the attack.

Shots on Goal:	11	5
Shots on Target:	4	2
Shots off Target	7	3
Possession:	52%	48%
Fouls Conceded:	13	15
Corners:	5	3
Yellow Cards:	1	2
Red Cards:	0	0

Neil Roberts celebrates Wrexham's opening goal in front of ecstatic fans

Coca Cola League 2: August 20th, 2006

Chester City 1

Jamie Hand 81

Wrexham 2

Neil Roberts 42 (pen)
Mark Jones 52

Referee: Uriah Rennie (Sheffield)
Attendance (Away): 4,206 (1,650)

They say that revenge is sweet. So when it comes against your biggest rivals then it must be even sweeter - and yes, it sure was!

Having been on the wrong end of a ridiculous penalty decision during a 2-1 defeat at the Deva Stadium last term, it was pure music to the ears to hear both Chester boss Mark Wright and their fans moaning about the performance of referee Uriah Rennie.

But, quite frankly, who cares what they think? All that matters is that the Dragons continued their unbeaten start to the season, won the game, and restored bragging rights back to normality!

The midweek departure of Dennis Lawrence to Swansea City - coming so soon before the 'derby' - certainly raised a few eyebrows, and Wrexham fans made the short journey over the border with more trepidation than may have been the case otherwise.

Chester just about edged the opening stages as Wrexham struggled to impose any authority on the proceedings. But on 25 minutes came the incident that changed the course of the game. Michael Ingham collected the ball on the edge of his area, and was clattered by Ricky Ravenhill's reckless follow-through. Despite claims that Ingham was outside the box Mr Rennie awarded Wrexham the free kick and showed Ravenhill the red card much to the delight of the Red Army behind the goal.

With Chester having to shuffle their pack, the 'Dragons' finally began to exert themselves on the game, and took the lead three minutes before the break. Matty Done was bearing down on goal when he was crudely brought down from behind by Stephen Vaughan giving the referee no option than to point to the spot. Neil Roberts stepped forward and sent Jon Danby the wrong way, before running the length of the pitch to celebrate!

Twice Chester could have levelled early in the second period, but the 'Dragons' responded and doubled the advantage on

52 minutes when Mark Jones latched onto Steve Evans' pass and lobbed the ball over the advancing Danby. Brilliant!

Game over? Not yet! Wrexham appeared to ease off, and Chester began to look the more likely side to score. The 77th minute dismissal of Evans, having been booked a second time for a shirt pull near the corner flag, gave Chester renewed hope, and so did Jamie Hand when Jamie Hand hit home a low 20-yard drive, but Wrexham held on, and the celebrations continued long and hard!

Chester:
12 John Danby, 19 Paul Linwood, 18 Ashley Westwood (45), 21 David Artell, 17 Laurence Wilson, 19 Ricky Ravenhill ■, 07 James Hand, 20 Roberto Martinez, 04 Stephen Vaughan, 14 Jon Walters (75), 09 Gregg Blundell (75).

Subs: 02 Simon Marples (45), 10 Drewe Broughton (75), 27 Chris Holroyd (75), 32 Paul Rutherford, 33 Philip Palethorpe (GK).

Wrexham:
01 Michael Ingham, 14 Simon Spender (77), 05 Steve Evans ■■, 04 Shaun Pejic , 03 Ryan Valentine ■, 07 Mark Jones, 08 Danny Williams, 12 Matt Crowell, 20 Matt Done (65), 11 Chris Llewellyn, 23 Neil Roberts

Subs: 13 Michael Jones (GK), 15 Mike Williams (77), 16 Levi Mackin, 17 Josh Johnson, 18 Jon Newby (65).

Neil Roberts converts his penalty

Shots on Goal:	9	9
Shots on Target:	6	3
Shots off Target	3	6
Possession:	48%	52%
Fouls Conceded:	12	13
Corners:	10	5
Yellow Cards:	0	2
Red Cards:	1	1

Neil Roberts opens the scoring for Wrexham in the Coca Cola Cup

Coca Cola League Cup Round 1: August 23rd, 2006

Sheffield Wednesday 1   Wrexham 4

Glenn Whelan 79

Neil Roberts 33
Chris Llewellyn 39
Matt Done 63
Mark Jones 84

Referee: Neil Swarbrick (Lancashire)
Attendance (Away): 8,047 (283)

Wrexham turned in a scintillating display at Hillsborough to book a place in the second round and maintain their unbeaten start to the campaign.

The Championship side were quite simply blown away, and the final scoreline, one-sided as it undoubtedly sounds, still flattered Wednesday more than it did Wrexham; though you won't find many Wrexham fans complaining too much about that!

With Steve Evans out suspended after his red card at Chester, in came 19 year-old Mike Williams for his first start of the season, and produced a cracking performance for one so young. Wednesday had their moments, and put the young Wrexham back line (Ryan Valentine the oldest at 24) under a lot of pressure. But they stood firm, refusing to give up any ground, and the attack responded with a display that Wednesday couldn't live with.

Wrexham started brightly, Chris Llewellyn should have done better than direct a free header wide, before the home side began to ask a few questions of their own, with Michael Ingham made a superb full-length save to turn away a Chris Brunt 25-yarder.

It was something against of the run of play when Wrexham opened the scoring in the 33rd minute. Matty Done crossed from the left, Mark Jones' headed across goal, and Neil Roberts controlled the ball on his chest and fired a half volley across Chris Adamson and into the far corner of the net.

Six minutes later it was 2-0. Lee Bullen's poorly directed pass was easily cut out by Llewellyn near the halfway line on the right, and the on-form striker surged forward into the box, cut back inside onto his left foot, and beat Adamson effortlessly.

Done should have made it 3-0 before the break, but finally netted the third goal on 63 minutes when Llewellyn did well on the right. He fed Jones, and the defence failed to deal with his cross, the young

winger gleefully hammering the loose ball home from close range.

Wednesday reduced the deficit with a stunning Glenn Whelan shot from 20 yards on 79 minutes, and briefly the home side sensed a comeback, and it took a cracking save by Ingham to maintain the Dragons' two-goal lead.

But any nerves were dispelled six minutes from time when Llewellyn fed Jones again, and the midfielder coolly curled the ball beyond Adamson into the bottom corner of the net, and cap a stunning all-round Wrexham performance.

Sheffield Wednesday:
22 Chris Adamson, 20 Frank Simek, 21 Madjid Bougherra, 02 Lee Bullen ▪, 14 John Hills, 04 Kenny Lunt, 06 Glenn Whelan, 33 Sean McAllister (67), 11 Chris Brunt, 32 Tommy Spurr, 27 Luke Boden (75),

Subs: 23 Rory McArdle (67), 28 Dave McClements, 29 Richard O'Donnell (GK), 34 Matt Bowman (75), 35 Liam McMenamin.

Wrexham:
01 Michael Ingham, 14 Simon Spender (90), 15 Mike Williams, 04 Shaun Pejic (87), 03 Ryan Valentine, 07 Mark Jones, 08 Danny Williams, 12 Matt Crowell (74), 20 Matt Done, 23 Neil Roberts, 11 Chris Llewellyn.

Subs:13 Michael Jones (GK), 02 Lee Roche (87), 16 Levi Mackin (74), 18 Jon Newby, 24 Gareth Evans (90)

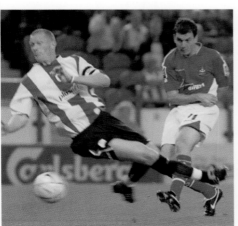

Chris Llewellyn shoots for goal.		
Shots on Goal:	7	6
Shots on Target:	2	4
Shots off Target	5	2
Possession:	57%	43%
Fouls Conceded:	10	6
Corners:	8	2
Yellow Cards:	1	0
Red Cards:	0	0

Mark Jones opens the scoring in typical style

Coca Cola Football League 2: August 26th, 2006

Wrexham 1   Barnet 1

Mark Jones 15   Tresor Kandol 62

Referee: Andy Woolmer (Northamptonshire)
Attendance (Away): 3,403 (189)

A point a piece was probably a fair result as both teams enjoyed periods of dominance, in what was an ill-tempered game that lacked any rhythm.

Wrexham started brightly, and led when Mark Jones fired in a left footer from the edge of the box following good work from Chris Llewellyn. His low shot escaped the dive of Lee Harrison to hit the bottom corner of the net. As the 'Dragons' stepped up the pace, Done's left wing cross

almost caught out Harrison again, who had to back pedal to tip the ball behind for a corner.

Barnet's best attack of the first half ended with Mike Ingham pulling off a superb save that even drew applause from the Barnet keeper. Guiliano Grazioli delivered a cross to the near post, and his strike partner Tresor Kandol arrived first to flick the ball goal wards, but Ingham somehow managed to claw it onto the far post. The second half started in similar fashion with both teams canceling each other out. Barnet improved as the game went on, and their equaliser came just after the hour mark. Matt Crowell lost his footing in midfield as the visitors broke down the right wing. Barry Cogan whipped the ball in across the six-yard box for Kandol to head home from close range at the far post.

The 'Bees' were unlucky not to take the lead four minutes later when Cogan linked up with Jason Puncheon to delightfully lift the ball over the Wrexham defence to pick out Kandol, who once again was unmarked at the back post. This time his header struck the woodwork and the home defence cleared the danger.

With Wrexham now under the cosh, Pejic conceded a needless corner. Grazioli thought he had scored the winner as he swept the ball home after Ingham had dropped the corner, but luckily for him a very generous refereeing decision chalked the goal off for an infringement on the 'Dragons' keeper.

Denis Smith introduced three substitutes with a quarter of an hour left. This meant a tactical switch with Valentine moving to

right back and Llewellyn dropping into left midfield. It took Wrexham a while to adjust and they had to defend desperately from a Barnet corner clearing in a goal-mouth scramble.

Jon Newby almost marked his debut with a goal, Harrison turning his right foot shot over for a corner. Llewellyn then went close for the home side and Nick Bailey for the visitors as both sides pushed for the winner. Despite four minutes added time, the game petered out into a draw.

Wrexham:
01 Michael Ingham, 14 Simon Spender (76), 05 Steve Evans, 04 Shaun Pejic, 03 Ryan Valentine, 07 Mark Jones, 08 Danny Williams (76) ■, 12 Matt Crowell, 20 Matt Done (76), 23 Neil Roberts ■, 11 Chris Llewellyn ■.

Subs: 13 Michael Jones (GK), 15 Mike Williams (76), 16 Levi Mackin (76), 17 Josh Johnson, 18 Jon Newby (76).

Barnet:
18 Lee Harrison, 04 Ian Hendon (45), 06 Anthony Charles ■, 03 Simon King, 05 Adam Gross ■, 23 Barry Cogan, 02 Nick Bailey, 08 Dean Sinclair, 20 Jason Puncheon, 09 Giuliano Grazioli (77), 10 Tresor Kandol ■.

Subs: 01 Ross Flitney (GK), 07 Liam Hatch, 12 Jason Norville (77), 15 Andy Hessenthaler, 16 Paul Warhurst (45) ■.

Steve Evans foils a Barnet attack.

Shots on Goal:	5	5
Shots on Target:	2	2
Shots off Target:	3	3
Possession:	48%	52%
Fouls Conceded:	13	16
Corners:	4	8
Yellow Cards:	3	4
Red Cards:	0	0

Ryan Valentine converts his penalty to put Wrexham on equal terms

Coca Cola League 2: September 9th, 2006

Wrexham 2   Swindon Town 1

Ryan Valentine 68 (p)   Paul Evans 28
Mark Jones 69

Referee: Scott Mathieson (Stockport)
Attendance (Away): 5,257 (717)

Despite losing influential skipper Neil Roberts after just five minutes with a leg injury sustained in the warm up, Wrexham put on a superb display to end the league leaders 100% record.

In the early stages, Darren Ferguson and Danny Williams dominated the midfield and used the wide players, Mark Jones and Matty Done, to good effect. The latter finding plenty of space down the left wing and causing problems to the visitors

defence all afternoon.

Against the run of play, a foul by Williams on Curtis Weston resulted in the opening goal of the game. From the resultant free kick, Paul Evans cleverly curled the ball into the top left corner from all of 35-yards, as Ingham positioned himself in anticipation of a cross to the back post.

Wrexham should have equalised just before the interval. Jones took down a high ball with his first touch, and delivered a cross to the unmarked Jon Newby, but he glanced the ball narrowly wide of the far post.

Swindon had the ball in the net again before the break, but this time the Wrexham offside trap denied Christian Roberts as he slotted the ball past Ingham.

The 'Dragons' made a positive start to the second half, and once again Done caused problems down the left flank. Mark Jones, Steve Evans, Danny Williams and Chris Llewellyn all went close, such was Wrexham's dominance.

Just as the home crowd was beginning to wonder if Denis Smith's men would ever manage to score, the game was turned on its head within the space of two minutes.

Llewellyn latched on to a superb Ferguson through ball, but Peter Brezovan brought him down. Ryan Valentine took the penalty and sent Brezovan the wrong way.

The home side took a deserved lead when a neat pass from Chris Llewellyn set Mark Jones in on goal and, although he did not make the best of contact, he still managed to beat Brezovan with a shot inside the far post to give Wrexham the lead.

With 20 minutes remaining, Denis Wise introduced an unfit looking Paul Ince for his Swindon debut, but the only notable contribution from the former England player was to over hit a pass, and to sky a shot into the Kop, much to the amusement of the home fans.

Wrexham played out the final three minutes of injury time without any scares, and were justly rewarded with three points to keep their unbeaten start to the season in tact, and end Swindon's.

Wrexham:
01 Michael Ingham, 02 Lee Roche ■, 05 Steve Evans, 04 Shaun Pejic, 03 Ryan Valentine, 07 Mark Jones, 08 Danny Williams ■, 10 Darren Ferguson (87), 20 Matt Done, 23 Neil Roberts (6), 11 Chris Llewellyn.

Subs: 12 Matt Crowell (87), 13 Michael Jones (GK), 15 Mike Williams, 17 Josh Johnson, 18 Jon Newby (6).

Swindon:
01 Peter Brezovan ■, 02 Jack Smith, 06 Ady Williams, 15 Andrew Nicholas, 17 Charlie Comyn-Platt, 12 Ricky Shakes (73), 23 Curtis Weston (72), 18 Paul Evans, 08 Aaron Brown (61) ■, 09 Christian Roberts, 10 Lee Peacock ■.

Subs: 03 Jamie Vincent, 04 Paul Ince (72), 28 Andy Caton (61), 16 Fola Onibuje (20), 20 Royce Brownlie (73).

Matty Done races down the left wing.

	Wrexham	Swindon
Shots on Goal:	14	7
Shots on Target:	4	3
Shots off Target:	10	4
Possession:	46%	54%
Fouls Conceded:	6	19
Corners:	11	1
Yellow Cards:	2	3
Red Cards:	0	0

A dejected Denis Smith looks on as Rooster can't believe the score

Coca Cola League 2: September 13th, 2006

Accrington Stanley 5   Wrexham 0

Paul Mullin 41
Ian Craney 49
Gary Roberts 52, 67
Peter Cavanagh 55

Referee: Clive Oliver (Northumberland)
Attendance (Away): 2,689 (799)

The wheels came off the Wrexham bandwagon in dramatic, and totally unexpected, fashion at a gloomy Fraser Eagle Stadium.

It's probably an understatement to say that Stanley's floodlights aren't exactly the best in the League, but at least the lack of light that they dispersed over the pitch meant that the large travelling contingent didn't have the best view of the Dragons' dismal display!

But whilst it would be unfair to play down the home side's performance - after all they did win 5-0 - I don't think it would be totally unfair to claim that the margin of victory had more to do with Wrexham's defensive misgivings than it did anything special from Stanley. For the manner in which most of the goals were conceded was simply comical!

However, there was little in the early stages to suggest what was going to unfold over the course of the evening as Wrexham, missing injured club captain Neil Roberts, started the better of the two sides. Unfortunately this early promise soon faded, the pacy home side began to ask most of the questions, and suddenly the hitherto solid Wrexham back line started to look all over the place.

It was therefore no surprise when the home side opened the scoring on 41 minutes when Michael Ingham could only parry a 25-yard Gary Roberts shot, and Paul Mullin reacted quickest to net the rebound.

Any hopes of a comeback were well and truly dented within the opening ten minutes of the second half as Accrington found the net another three times! Ian Craney's 49th minute corner was inexplicably left by Simon Spender at the near post, and the ball curled directly into the net for the home side's second.

Shaun Pejic then failed to deal with a long punt forward by Ian Dunbavin, and Roberts gleefully snapped up the opportunity to make it 3-0. And with Ingham standing by a post whilst lining up his wall at an Accrington free kick, Peter Cavanagh took

it quickly and curled the ball into the other, unguarded, side of the goal to make it 4-0.

The rout was completed on 67 minutes when the impressive Roberts easily skipped around Ingham before slotting the ball into the empty net with nonchalant ease.

Wrexham were woeful, and the fans let them know exactly what they thought in no uncertain terms. "I'm not stunned, I'm angry and embarrassed", said boss Denis Smith after the game.

Accrington:
25 Ian Dunbavin, 02 Peter Cavanagh ■, 04 Robbie Williams, 12 Phil Edwards, 03 Leam Richardson, 07 Sean Doherty (78), 08 Ian Craney, 06 Andrew Proctor, 17 Andy Todd (76), 11 Gary Roberts, 10 Paul Mullin (79)

Subs: 09 Andrew Mangan (78), 14 Romuald Boco (76), 16 Julien N'da, 18 David Brown (79), 23 Francois Dubourdeau (GK).

Wrexham:
01 Michael Ingham, 14 Simon Spender (59), 04 Shaun Pejic, 05 Steve Evans, 03 Ryan Valentine ■, 07 Mark Jones, 08 Danny Williams, 10 Darren Ferguson, 20 Matt Done (45), 18 Jon Newby (59), 11 Chris Llewellyn ■.

Subs: 12 Matt Crowell, 13 Michael Jones (GK), 15 Mike Williams (59), 17 Josh Johnson (45), 21 Marc Williams (59).

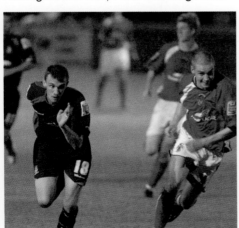

Jon Newby chases the ball.

Shots on Goal:	7	13
Shots on Target:	9	3
Shots off Target	3	6
Possession:	45%	55%
Fouls Conceded:	9	12
Corners:	4	7
Yellow Cards:	1	2
Red Cards:	0	0

Mark Robinson places his penalty past Michael Jones to open the scoring

Coca Cola League 2: September 16th, 2006

Stockport County 5   Wrexham 2

Adam Le Fondre 24, 54, 85, 87   Danny Williams 43, 61
Mark Robinson 23 (pen)

Referee: Ray Olivier (West Midlands)
Attendance (Away): 4,884 (879)

Maybe Accrington wasn't just a blip after all! As at Accrington in midweek, Wrexham were **made to pay for several calamitous defensive moments that 'County' were quick to punish.**

Even so, Wrexham still only trailed 3-2 going into the last six minutes, until two late Adam Le Fondre goals brought his personal tally for the afternoon to four, and left the 'Dragons' having conceded ten goals in the space of just three days -

against two sides near the bottom of the League.

Michael Jones, Gareth Evans and Marc Williams made their first outings of the current campaign. Unfortunately it proved a little too much for the latter two, with Evans being caught in possession and conceding the penalty that led to County's first goal on 23 minutes, and Williams being substituted as early as the 31st minute. This was particularly harsh on the young striker, the decision seeming to have more to do with the inadequacies of those behind him rather than his own performance.

Mark Robinson confidently scored from the 23rd minute spot kick to give County the lead, and almost immediately Jones, admittedly under pressure, failed to deal with Ryan Valentine's poorly executed back pass, and Le Fondre nipped in for one of the easiest goals he'll ever score.

Not only was Denis Smith forced to ring the changes early on due to the poor start, but a head injury to Valentine meant he had to leave the field and be replaced by Simon Spender.

Spender immediately denied Glenn Murray a third goal, before Wrexham grabbed themselves a lifeline just before the break when Danny Williams unleashed a stunning shot from at least 30 yards out that flew past John Ruddy and into the top corner.

However, County regained their two-goal cushion on 54 minutes when more uncertain defending allowed Le Fondre to hook home from close range. But the home side never really kicked on following their third goal, and Ruddy did well to keep out

a well-struck Matty Crowell effort. And County's failure to kill the game off kept Wrexham's hopes alive, especially when Danny Williams was first to a long Mike Williams throw to steer the ball past Ruddy on the hour mark.

Williams went close to completing a hat-trick, and Mark Jones saw an on-target effort blocked. But there was to be no dramatic comeback, and Le Fondre pounced with two goals in three minutes to complete a miserable afternoon for the visitors.

Stockport:
29 John Ruddy, 06 Ashley Williams, 16 Gareth Owen, 05 Michael Raynes ■, 11 Mark Robinson, 26 David Poole (67), 20 Jason Taylor, 07 Keith Briggs, 19 Michael Malcolm (81), 14 Adam Le Fondre, 21 Glenn Murray (69).

Subs: 04 Tony Dinning, 09 Tesfaye Bramble (69), 22 Tim Deasy (GK), 24 Adam Griffin (67), 31 Adam Proudlock (81).

Wrexham:
13 Michael Jones, 03 Ryan Valentine (38), 05 Steve Evans, 24 Gareth Evans, 15 Mike Williams, 07 Mark Jones, 10 Darren Ferguson ■, 08 Danny Williams ■, 11 Chris Llewellyn, 17 Jon Newby (61), 21 Marc Williams (31).

Subs: 12 Matt Crowell (31), 14 Simon Spender (38), 17 Josh Johnson 27 Jamie Reed (61), 31 Vinnie Whelan (GK).

Matty Done shakes off a tackle

	Stockport	Wrexham
Shots on Goal:	13	13
Shots on Target:	7	9
Shots off Target:	6	4
Possession:	59%	41%
Fouls Conceded:	10	11
Corners:	12	2
Yellow Cards:	1	2
Red Cards:	0	0

Lee Roche congratulations Chris Llewellyn on Wrexham's opening goal

Coca Cola League Cup Round 2: September 19th, 2006

Birmingham City 4   Wrexham 1

Cameron Jerome 41   Chris Llewellyn 29
Gary McSheffrey 102, 113
Nicklas Bendtner 117

Referee: Paul Armstrong (Berkshire)
Attendance (Away): 10,491(1,000+)

Just what you want when you've conceded ten goals in the space of seven days is a trip to St. Andrews to face a Birmingham City side that was playing in the Premiership only a few months previous.

However, such is the beauty of Cup-tie football that nothing can be predicted with absolute certainty, and so maybe it wasn't too unexpected that the 'Dragons' gave

their high-flying hosts such a difficult evening. The manner of the visitors display will also raise the question of just how a side can win so convincingly at Hillsborough, take Birmingham to extra time at St. Andrews, but concede five goals at both Accrington and Stockport in the space of three days?

Admittedly Steve Bruce chose the game to shuffle his talented squad around, but he

---

still included the likes of Sebastian Larsson, Gary McSheffrey, Mikael Forssell and Cameron Jerome. Denis Smith also made changes, in part due to injury, but also due to recent results. Josh Johnson came in for his first start, and John McAliskey, a loan signing from Huddersfield Town, was registered just in time, while Danny Williams dropped back into central defence.

There was little to separate the teams in the early exchanges - both sides settling down well to the task in hand, and having chances to open the scoring. From one such chance McAliskey's powerful header forced keeper Colin Doyle to concede a corner and from Darren Ferguson's flag kick Danny Williams flicked on for Chris Llewellyn to score from about eight yards.

The 'Blues' responded as you'd expected from such a talented side, and equalised when Jerome, who'd been guilty of wasting several opportunities, headed in a McSheffrey cross.

The home side predictably dominated the start of the second half, but the 'Dragons' stood firm and Johnson had a great chance to reclaim the lead on 63 minutes, but shot straight at Doyle.

Michael Ingham then brought DJ Campbell down to concede a penalty, but the substi-

tute's spot kick flew wide and, with Wrexham in resilient mood, the game moved into extra time.

Unfortunately the exertions in the 90 minutes possibly took their toll on Wrexham in extra time, and Birmingham grabbed the lead on 102 minutes when McSheffrey, unchallenged due to the referee seemingly blocking Lee Roche's progress, volleyed in spectacularly from 25 yards.

Nicklas Bendtner gave the scoreline an unfair look with a fourth on 117 minutes, but the 'Dragons' at least restored some pride and went home with heads held high.

Birmingham:
13 Colin Doyle, 02 Stephen Kelly, 04 Martin Taylor, 16 Olivier Tebily, 20 Marcos Painter, 07 Sebastian Larsson, 26 Fabrice Muamba (90), 15 Neil Kilkenny, 28 Gary McSheffrey, 09 Mikael Forssell (64), 10 Cameron Jerome (64).

Subs: 01 Maik Taylor (GK), 08 David Dunn (90), 14 Dudley Campbell (64), 17 Neil Danns, 27 Nicklas Bendtner (64).

Wrexham:
01 Michael Ingham, 02 Lee Roche, 05 Steve Evans, 08 Danny Williams, 15 Mike Williams ■, 07 Mark Jones (90), 12 Matt Crowell, 10 Darren Ferguson, 17 Josh Johnson (83), 11 Chris Llewellyn, 22 John McAliskey (110) ■.

Subs:13 Michael Jones (GK), 14 Simon Spender, 16 Levi Mackin (90), 18 Jon Newby (83), 24 Gareth Evans (110).

John McAliskey volleys at goal.

Shots on Goal:	20	11
Shots on Target:	10	6
Shots off Target:	10	5
Possession:	50%	50%
Fouls Conceded:	15	16
Corners:	9	5
Yellow Cards:	0	2
Red Cards:	0	0

Darren Ferguson dances past a Hereford defender

Coca Cola League 2: September 23rd, 2006

Wrexham 1   Hereford United 0

Steve Evans 28

Referee: Phil Joslin (Nottinghamshire)
Attendance (Away): 4,705 (663)

I t was home sweet home for Wrexham as they returned to winning ways following three successive away defeats, having conceded fourteen goals in the process! A first half header from Steve Evans proved to be decisive as the home side recorded a confidence boosting clean sheet.

Overall, this game was an even contest with the 'Dragons' having two shots cleared off the line, and Hereford hitting the woodwork. Both sides faded in the second half as their midweek cup adventures against Championship opponents took its toll.

Hereford looked dangerous on the break, and a well-worked move down the right got the better of Ryan Valentine and Evans, but Ingham just managed to punch Stuart Fleetwood's cross before Alan Connell could reach the ball.

From a corner Darren Ferguson's delivery to the far post was powered goalwards by

Evans. Simon Travis was unable to hack clear before the ball had crossed the line, with the referee awarding the goal following the signal from his assistant much to the delight of the home fans.

A few minutes later Chris Llewellyn noticed Wayne Brown off his line, but his shot from 45 yards just cleared the crossbar. The visitors responded at the other end when Richard Rose went close after cutting in from the left.

The 'Bulls' went even closer to equalising when Wrexham failed to deal with a set play. The ball was crossed back to the far post where Ingham managed to tip Tim Sills' header onto the bar, with Valentine clearing the rebound to safety.

Chances were few and far between in a lackluster second half, with both teams effectively canceling each other out. However, it was Matty Done who had the first chance following the restart. Good wing play allowed him to burst clear in the box, but he curled the ball agonizingly wide of the post.

Fleetwood had a couple of chances from free kicks, but hit the first straight into Ingham's arms and curled the second around the wall, narrowly missing the bar

with Ingham beaten.

Wrexham had a lucky escape with five minutes remaining. A clever corner was taken low to towards the edge of area and redirected into the six-yard box, but Fleetwood diverted the ball wide.

Josh Johnson gave away a free kick in final minute of injury time with a shoulder charge, but Matty Done cleared the danger by hacking the ball up field. The final whistle blew saw Wrexham maintain their unbeaten home run with a valuable win against their border rivals.

Wrexham:
01 Michael Ingham, 02 Lee Roche ■, 05 Steve Evans, 08 Danny Williams ■, 03 Ryan Valentine ■, 07 Mark Jones (74), 12 Matt Crowell, 10 Darren Ferguson, 20 Matt Done, 22 John McAliskey, 11 Chris Llewellyn.

Subs: 13 Michael Jones (GK), 14 Simon Spender, 15 Mike Williams, 17 Josh Johnson (74), 18 Jon Newby.

Hereford:
01 Wayne Brown, 28 Dean Beckwith ■, 05 Tamika Mkandawire, 17 Martin Giles, 20 Alex Jeannin, 09 Tim Sills, 06 Robert Purdie, 02 Simon Travis, 04 Richard Rose (81) ■, 10 Stuart Fleetwood, 12 Alan Connell (66).

Subs: 14 Glyn Thompson (GK), 07 Jon Wallis, 23 Philip Gulliver, 08 Andy Ferrell (66), 21 Luke Webb (81).

Matty Done unleashes a shot at goal.

	Wrexham	Hereford
Shots on Goal:	13	10
Shots on Target:	5	2
Shots off Target	8	8
Possession:	45%	55%
Fouls Conceded:	16	8
Corners:	6	5
Yellow Cards:	3	2
Red Cards:	0	0

Mark Jones leaves Rochdale's players standing as he heads for goal

Coca Cola League 2: September 27th, 2006

Wrexham 1   Rochdale 2

Chris Llewellyn 12   Chris Dagnall 48, 77

Referee: Steve Bratt (West Midlands)
Attendance (Away): 3,577 (261)

An unchanged Wrexham lost their undefeated home record, despite taking an early lead through Chris Llewellyn, as Rochdale fought back to claim the points with two goals in the second half from top scorer Chris Dagnall.

Steve Parkin's side had chalked up their first away win of the season in their previous fixture away at Boston, and started brightly enough.

The home side soon began to exert their influence with Llewellyn dragging a shot wide, and Steve Evans firing over from Darren Ferguson's corner. They did not need to wait long for the opening goal. The visitors' defence hesitated and allowed Llewellyn to collect the ball, and he turned quickly to fire a low left foot shot under Matthew Gilks in the Rochdale goal.

'Dale' enjoyed the better of the possession during the first half, but failed to carve out any guilt edge opportunities. A penalty appeal was turned down when Alan Goodall fired in a cross at the bodies of Steve Evans and Ryan Valentine, but the referee waived play on by indicating that the ball had struck the chests of the Wrexham defenders.

The home side forced an early corner in the second half following good work by Llewellyn, from which Ferguson curled the ball into the centre, but Danny William's header lacked the power to beat Gilks.

Rochdale broke quickly, and scored the goal their first half display had deserved. A slip by Evans allowed Gary Jones to pick out Dagnall, and he made no mistake with a shot from inside of the area.

With the Wrexham strikers finding it increasingly difficult to hold the ball up, Rochdale began to dominate the midfield, with Ferguson and Crowell struggling to win possession.

It got worse for the 'Dragons when the dangerous Dagnall scored his, and Rochdale's second of the night, as he followed up on a long range shot from Goodall that was spilled by Ingham.

John Johnson, Jon Newby and Mike Williams were all introduced late on, but Wrexham failed to create any real chances, and almost conceded a third, but Ingham did well to hold a shot from the right side of the area.

With four minutes of added time, Steve Evans climbed well to head a Ferguson free kick to the far post, but the ball was too far in front of Llewellyn for him to be able to steer it on target. The visitors celebrated their second consecutive away win at the expense of Wrexham's unbeaten home record.

Wrexham:
01 Michael Ingham, 02 Lee Roche, 05 Steve Evans, 08 Danny Williams, 03 Ryan Valentine, 07 Mark Jones ■, 12 Matt Crowell (84), 10 Darren Ferguson, 20 Matt Done (63), 22 John McAliskey (85), 11 Chris Llewellyn.

Subs: 13 Michael Jones (GK), 14 Simon Spender, 15 Mike Williams (84), 17 Josh Johnson (63), 18 Jon Newby (85).

Rochdale:
01 Matthew Gilks ■, 14 Gary Brown, 18 Nathan Stanton, 21 James Sharp, 12 Alan Goodall, 05 John Doolan (90) ■, 19 Lee Crooks, 08 Gary Jones, 16 Keith Barker (71), 26 Morike Sako, 09 Chris Dagnall.

Subs: 02 Simon Ramsden, 04 Ernie Cooksey (90), 07 Darrell Clarke, 06 Jon Boardman, 20 Clive Moyo-Modise (71).

Mark Jones brushes off a tackle

	Wrexham	Rochdale
Shots on Goal:	10	5
Shots on Target:	3	4
Shots off Target	7	1
Possession:	48%	52%
Fouls Conceded:	6	10
Corners:	5	6
Yellow Cards:	1	2
Red Cards:	0	0

Mark Jones runs the ball out of Wrexham's half and away from danger

Coca Cola League 2: September 30th, 2006

Hartlepool United 3   Wrexham 0

Jon Daly 20, 22, 68

Referee: Garry Sutton (Lincolnshire)
Attendance (Away): 4,452 (175)

Yet another depressing away defeat, but in all honesty there was generally very little to separate the two sides at Victoria Park. However, Hartlepool were clinical in front of goal and made the most of the opportunities that came their way, whereas the 'Dragons' never looked like scoring.

Again - as seems to be happening far too often - conceding one goal quickly led to the conceding of a second, which clearly demonstrates Wrexham's frailty.

Injuries again meant that Denis Smith had to shuffle his pack with Lee Roche occupying a central midfield role, and Simon Spender coming in at right back. The former clearly looked like someone playing in an unaccustomed position, while the latter paid for a torrid first half display by being substituted at the interval by Mike Williams.

It certainly seemed harsh on Spender who, it must be said, was offered very little protection by those ahead of him, and often found himself on the wrong end of two-on-one situations.

The architect of Wrexham's downfall was striker Jon Daly, who continued his rich vein of form going into the game, by netting all three of the home side's goals.

His first on 22 minutes came when he was left unmarked to head home a John Brackstone corner, and he quickly added a second when Joel Porter, looking suspiciously offside it has to be said, broke clear down the left and centred for Daly to have the simple task of side-footing home from close range.

Somehow Wrexham steadied the ship and the closest they came to scoring all afternoon was when Steve Evans rose to meet a Matty Crowell corner, but his header was cleared from near the goal line.

The opening moments of the second half finally saw 'Pools' keeper Dimitrios Konstantopoulos dirty his gloves, when Brackstone sliced an Evans header towards his own goal. Yes, Wrexham were better after the break, but their approach play failed to deliver any threat.

Other than a Mark Jones free kick that

Konstantopoulos got down low to save, it's difficult to recall anything else the keeper had to do that wasn't routine.

Daly completed his treble with another free header on 69 minutes, the ball ricocheting in off a post, to complete the scoring and cap yet another miserable afternoon on the north east coast.

"We were equal to them, but they scored the goals," reflected Denis Smith after the game. Heaven knows what would've happened if we'd been worse than them!

Hartlepool:
01 Dimitrios Konstantopoulos, 23 Darren Williams, 05 Michael Nelson, 06 Ben Clark, 19 John Brackstone, 24 Alistair Gibb, 17 Willie Boland, 18 Gary Liddle (30), 03 Matty Robson, 09 Joel Porter (84), 25 Jon Daly (73).

Subs: 11 Eifion Williams (73), 12 Gavin Strachan, 16 Lee Bullock (30), 20 James Brown (84), 21 Jim Provett (GK).

Wrexham:
01 Michael Ingham ■, 14 Simon Spender (45), 05 Steve Evans ■, 08 Danny Williams, 03 Ryan Valentine, 02 Lee Roche, 07 Mark Jones, 12 Matt Crowell, 20 Matt Done (73), 11 Chris Llewellyn, 22 John McAliskey.

Subs: 13 Michael Jones (GK), 15 Mike Williams (45), 17 Josh Johnson, 18 Jon Newby (73), 21 Marc Williams.

Michael Ingham and Ryan Valentine are not happy!

	Hartlepool	Wrexham
Shots on Goal:	12	3
Shots on Target:	8	1
Shots off Target	4	2
Possession:	63%	37%
Fouls Conceded:	11	20
Corners:	6	3
Yellow Cards:	0	1
Red Cards:	0	0

Neil Roberts celebrates Wrexham's first and only goal against the MK Dons

Coca Cola League 2: October 14th, 2006

Wrexham 1   Milton Keynes Dons 2

Neil Roberts 20   Izale McLeod 46
        Sean O'Hanlon 77

Referee: Uriah Rennie (Sheffield)
Attendance (Away): 3,828 (212)

After a promising start, Wrexham failed to capitalise on a deserved first half lead and a disappointing second half display from the home side allowed the visitors to take home three points to assist their promotion challenge.

The introduction of striker Izale McLeod at half time turned the game in the favour of the MK Dons as he scored within a minute and then set up the winning goal

for Sean O'Hanlon.

MK Dons were the quickest out of the blocks and had an early penalty appeal turned down by Uriah Rennie following a challenge by Gareth Evans on Clive Platt in the box.

After several long-range efforts, Wrexham got the goal their early dominance deserved, despite needing three attempts to get the ball across the line. Mike

---

William's shot on goal was blocked, and Crowell's strike on the rebound was deflected into the path of Neil Roberts who managed to force the ball past Aldolfo Baines.

This sparked the 'Dons' into life, and they went close to equalising when Lee Roche was penalised for a heavy challenge on Scott Taylor. From the resulting free-kick McGovern curled a shot narrowly wide.

'Dons' top goal scorer McLeod was brought on after the break, and Martin Allen's substitution paid immediate dividends with McLeod celebrating an equaliser with virtually his first touch of the game. He received the ball with his back to goal on the edge of the 18-yard box, and the 'Dragons' defence stood off him. He was allowed to turn and drill a shot through the legs of Steve Evans with Ingham rooted to his spot.

The home side started to stem the attacks as they got to grips with McLeod, but the loss of Neil Roberts was a crucial blow as he limped off to be replaced by Jon Newby.

With Wrexham looking the most likely side to grab the winner, it was the MK

Dons who took the lead when McLeod was played in down the right channel, and O'Hanlon who was virtually on the goal line tapped in his low cross.

Chris Llewellyn had a glorious opportunity to equalise with five minutes left as he tried to bend the ball inside of the top corner when a simple pass to Newby would have been a better option.

With the game ending in a sixth defeat in seven games, Wrexham continued their poor run of results and were left just three points above the relegation zone.

Wrexham:
01 Michael Ingham, 02 Lee Roche (71), 05 Steve Evans (80), 24 Gareth Evans ■, 15 Mike Williams, 07 Mark Jones ■, 12 Matt Crowell, 10 Darren Ferguson, 11 Chris Llewellyn, 20 Matt Done ■, 23 Neil Roberts (64).

Subs: 13 Michael Jones (GK), 14 Simon Spender (71), 16 Levi Mackin (80), 18 Jon Newby (64), 22 John McAliskey.

MK Dons:
31 Adolfo Baines, 02 Jamie Smith, 04 Drissa Diallo, 06 Sean O'Hanlon ■, 03 Dean Lewington, 07 Jon-Paul McGovern, 08 Paul Mitchell, 20 Aaron Wilbraham, 23 Lloyd Dyer (81), 09 Clive Platt, 19 Scott Taylor (45).

Subs: 01 Ademole Bankole (GK), 10 Izale McLeod (45), 12 Leon Crooks, 15 Gareth Edds, 17 Ben Chorley (81).

Mike Williams' shoots at goal.

Shots on Goal:	9	7
Shots on Target:	4	3
Shots off Target:	5	4
Possession:	57%	43%
Fouls Conceded:	16	9
Corners:	6	9
Yellow Cards:	4	1
Red Cards:	0	0

The Wrexham players prepare for the penalty shoot out

Johnstone Paint Trophy Round 1, October 17th, 2006.

Wrexham 1

Matt Crowell 80
(Rochdale win 5 - 3 on penalties)

Rochdale 1

Chris Dagnall 40

Referee: Mark Haywood (Wakefield)
Attendance (Away): 1,209 (79)

Wrexham's stay in this season's JP Trophy ended following a penalty shoot out. This closely fought game ended one apiece after 90 minutes with deflected goals late in each half. Unfortunately the visitors scored all five of their penalties against the Dragons' three to go through to round two.

The home side had the better of the opening ten minutes with Josh Johnson looking promising. The first chance came when the Trinidadian winger picked out Danny Williams, but he dragged his shot wide from the edge of the area on his weaker left foot.

Rochdale got more of a grip on the game, and limited the supply out to the Dragons' wide players Johnson and Matty Done. Michael Ingham did well to dive low to his left to collect a low shot from Gary Jones, but was backpedaling to reach his cross from the left that ended up on the roof of the net.

The opening goal came five minutes before half time when Mark Jones lost possession inside his own half. Rochdale worked the ball to the edge of the area with Chris Dagnall's low shot taking a deflection off Craig Morgan to wrong foot Ingham as it nestled into the corner of the net.

The home side started the second period positively with Steve Evans heading over from a Crowell corner, while a penalty appeal for a handball following Johnson's cross was turned down.

The most controversial moment of the game came when a routine cross from Done was dropped by Gilks, who was under no pressure. The ball looked to have crossed the goal line, but no goal was awarded to the disbelief of the home crowd.

Wrexham scored the equaliser their second half display deserved with ten minutes left. Mark Jones picked out Danny Williams on the edge of the area and his dummy allowed Crowell to shoot, but his effort took a deflection, and wrong-footed

Matthew Gilks. Within a minute Done went close to giving the home side the lead with a shot that narrowly missed the top corner.

Rochdale almost hit back immediately when substitute Morike Sako shot on the turn straight into the arms of Ingham.

With no extra-time, the game had to be decided on the night by the dreaded penalty shoot out. The visitors emphatically converted all of their five penalties with precision, but Llewellyn's miss proving decisive, denying Wrexham the prospect of progress towards another appearance at the Millennium Stadium.

Wrexham:
01 Michael Ingham, 03 Ryan Valentine, 05 Steve Evans, 06 Craig Morgan, 15 Mike Williams, 07 Mark Jones, 12 Matt Crowell, 08 Danny Williams, 20 Matt Done, 17 Josh Johnson (90), 11 Chris Llewellyn.

Subs: 13 Michael Jones (GK), 14 Simon Spender, 16 Levi Mackin, 18 Jon Newby (90), 24 Gareth Evans.

Rochdale:
01 Matthew Gilks, 02 Simon Ramsden, 06 Jon Boardman, 21 James Sharp ■, 12 Alan Goodall, 05 John Doolan, 08 Gary Jones, 19 Lee Crooks (83), 20 Clive Moyo-Modise (85), 09 Chris Dagnall, 16 Keith Barker.

Subs: 04 Ernie Cooksey (83), 11 Adam Rundle, 15 Joe Thompson, 25 Theo Coleman, (26) Morike Sako (85).

Matt Crowell celebrates his equaliser.

Shots on Goal:	12	9
Shots on Target:	6	4
Shots off Target:	6	5
Possession:	67%	33%
Fouls Conceded:	7	10
Corners:	3	4
Yellow Cards:	0	1
Red Cards:	0	0

The Wrexham players line up in a wall for a Mansfield free kick

Coca Cola League 2: October 28th, 2006

Mansfield Town 3   Wrexham 0

Richie Barker 21, 36
Danny Reet 69

Referee: Andy Penn (West Midlands)
Attendance (Away): 2,941 (254)

Yet another miserable away day as Wrexham were well beaten at Field Mill. It's fair to say that Mansfield were hardly impressive, but the ease by which they dismantled Denis Smith's side will once again set alarm bells ringing amongst the travelling support.

Losing so easily - and it looked from the start that there was never going to be any other result - is bad enough against one of the top sides, but when it happens against a side just two points above the 'Dragons' in the table then it's simply unacceptable. Unfortunately, heavy away defeats have been seen far too often during Denis Smith's five-year tenure in the hot seat.

The problems are quite clear. Poor defending at one end, and no cutting edge whatsoever at the other, are hardly the recipe for success, and both were visibly evident once again during this forgettable afternoon.

It had all started encouragingly though, with Wrexham taking the upper hand in the opening 20 minutes or so. Then Mansfield scored - and everyone, including the players it seemed, expected the worst from then on.

The 'Stags' had done nothing in the early stages to hint that'd they'd win so easily, but on 21 minutes one simple pass put Ritchie Barker through on goal, and the striker neatly rounded Ingham to score.

Chris Llewellyn, who again worked tirelessly for the cause, almost restored parity soon afterwards, but Jon Olav Hjelde was in the right place to concede a corner. But this was a rare foray forward, and Mansfield quickly got back on the front foot and doubled their lead in the 36th minute when Barker again rounded Ingham before slotting the ball home.

That was the signal for Denis to immediately replace Lee Roche with Mike Williams, before Jon Newby replaced Matty Done at the interval as the manager changed the formation in an attempt to change the course of the game. The attempt failed - and if anything the Dragons were even worse after the break!

Again the home side were the only ones that posed any threat on goal. Only the bar and then the post prevented Alex John-Baptiste from adding to Wrexham's woes on 55 minutes.

A third goal looked inevitable, and it duly arrived in the 69th minute when Wrexham's offside trap failed miserably, and left no fewer than three Mansfield players unmarked inside the penalty area! One of them, Hjelde, brought the ball down, and Danny Reet hammered the ball past Ingham from six yards out.

Mansfield:
19 Carl Muggleton, 02 Johnny Mullins, 05 Jon Olav Hjelde, 06 Alex Baptiste, 20 Alan Sheehan, 07 Matthew Hamshaw (85), 04 Jonathan D'Laryea, 08 Stephen Dawson (68), 03 Gareth Jelleyman, 09 Richard Barker, 31 Danny Reet (78).

Subs: 01 Jason White (GK), 12 Jake Buxton, 14 Chris Beardsley (78), 15 Giles Coke (68), 16 Nathan Arnold (85).

Wrexham:
01 Michael Ingham, 02 Lee Roche (38), 05 Steve Evans, 06 Craig Morgan, 03 Ryan Valentine, 17 Josh Johnson (63), 08 Danny Williams, 10 Darren Ferguson, 20 Matt Done (46), 07 Mark Jones, 11 Chris Llewellyn.

Subs: 12 Matt Crowell (63), 13 Michael Jones (GK), 15 Mike Williams (38), 18 Jon Newby (46), 21 Marc Williams.

Mark Jones fights off a Mansfiled player.

Shots on Goal:	11	4
Shots on Target:	5	0
Shots off Target	6	4
Possession:	50%	50%
Fouls Conceded:	7	9
Corners:	11	3
Yellow Cards:	0	0
Red Cards:	0	0

New loan signing Tom Craddock scored on his debut for Wrexham

Coca Cola League 2: October 28th, 2006

Wrexham 2   Bristol Rovers 0

Chris Llewellyn 22
Tom Craddock 90

Referee: Russell Booth (Nottinghamshire)
Attendance (Away): 3,803 (306)

After four straight league defeats Denis Smith was glad to welcome back Shaun Pejic from injury and Tom Craddock on loan from Middlesbrough. With Mike Williams also replacing the injured Lee Roche, there were three changes from the side beaten at Mansfield.

The 'Pirates' dominated the opening twenty minutes with the home side often gifting the ball away inside their own half. Ryan Valentine was the first culprit losing possession to allow Rovers a strike on goal. Danny Williams then gave the ball away just inside his own half, which led to a good run by Stuart Campbell, whose cross was poorly finished by Lewis Haldane, who passed the ball into the arms of Ingham.

The Dragons opened the scoring against the run of play midway through the first half. This time it was the visitors giving away possession to allow Mark Jones to send Chris Llewellyn away down the right channel. The striker cut in from the touch-line, skipping past one defender before unleashing an unstoppable shot from the edge of the area to beat Phillips at his near post.

The goal gave the home side a much needed confidence boost, and Danny Williams went close to increasing the margin as he smacked a fantastic first time volley from 30-yards against the inside of the far post, and across the face of goal to safety.

After the break Sammy Igoe's cross was delivered to the near post where Richard Walker lost his marker to glance his header wide.

Just after the hour Llewellyn received a straight red card. Despite winning the ball, referee Russell Booth saw the two-footed lunge on Elliott as a red card offence, much to the annoyance of the home crowd.

Despite the reduction in numbers, Wrexham coped well with Craddock fighting for every ball on his own up front as the 'Pirates' failed to make their advantage count.

In injury time, a long Wrexham clearance

found Craddock isolated up front. He managed to advance to the edge of the penalty area, but with no support on offer from red shirts he turned and held the ball up. He then turned his man again to fire a superb left footed shot low across the face of Phillips and inside of the far post for a well-taken debut goal.

Despite his red card, the match sponsors named Llewellyn as man of the match as players and fans celebrated a home victory that finally ended a terrible series of results.

Wrexham:
01 Michael Ingham, 03 Ryan Valentine, 05 Steve Evans, 04 Shaun Pejic, 15 Mike Williams, 07 Mark Jones, 08 Danny Williams ■, 10 Darren Ferguson, 20 Matt Done, 11 Chris Llewellyn ■, 22 Tom Craddock.

Subs: 13 Michael Jones (GK), 06 Craig Morgan, 14 Simon Spender, 16 Levi Mackin, 21 Marc Williams.

Bristol Rovers:
01 Steve Phillips, 02 Ryan Green, 15 Byron Anthony, 06 Steve Elliott, 32 Aaron Lescott, 04 Sammy Igoe (76), 07 Stuart Campbell, 08 James Hunt, 26 Lewis Haldane (69) ■, 10 Richard Walker, 27 Sean Rigg (59).

Subs: 05 Craig Hinton, 11 Chris Carruthers, 17 Andy Sandell (69), 20 Craig Disley (76), 18 Jamal Easter (59).

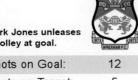

Mark Jones unleases a volley at goal.

	Wrexham	Bristol Rovers
Shots on Goal:	12	6
Shots on Target:	5	2
Shots off Target	7	4
Possession:	54%	46%
Fouls Conceded:	9	13
Corners:	3	7
Yellow Cards:	1	1
Red Cards:	1	0

Maheta Molango's shot is blocked at the feet of Macclesfield keeper Jonathon Brain

Coca Cola League 2: November 4th, 2006

Wrexham 0   Macclesfield Town 0

Referee: Eddie Ilderton (Tyne & Wear)
Attendance (Away): 3,568 (286)

Newly appointed manager Paul Ince's Macclesfield arrived at the Racecourse without a win this season and, coupled with Wrexham's recent poor run of form, this goalless draw was a predictable outcome and consistent with the current league positions of both teams.

Despite the all-new strike force of Kevin Smith and Maheta Molango, Wrexham were unable to break the deadlock, and had to rely on some near misses from the 'Silkmen' to take a point from this dull game.

Steve Evans had a great chance to open the scoring, but put his free header over the bar. The best that the visitors had to offer was when Colin Heath latched onto a misplaced pass from Evans, but he shot straight at Michael Ingham in the Wrexham goal.

The best chance of the game came when Darren Ferguson set Molango clean through with a weighted through ball, but his shot was blocked by the feet of

Jonathan Brain.

Macclesfield forced their first corner of the game towards the end of the first half. Matthew Tipton swung it over; the ball was going straight in at the near post, but Ferguson was on hand to head clear.

The 'Silkmen' made the early running after the break, and a dangerous cross, flashed across the face of Wrexham's goal, and Ingham was grateful that Heath shot straight at him.

It was the 'Dragons' who had the best chance of the half following more quick thinking from Ferguson. His quickly taken free kick set Molango through down the right channel, but the on loan striker wasted his third opportunity of the afternoon, as he blasted woefully high into the back of the Kop.

With twelve minutes remaining, Wrexham lost possession on the left touchline, and the ball was quickly switched for Martin Bullock to pick out Matty McNeil in acres of space. He advanced to the edge of the area and tucked the ball under Ingham, but his effort rebounded off the far post and Mike Williams was on hand to force the rebound high over the bar.

Williams again saved the 'Dragons' when the 'Silkmen' forced another corner towards the end of the game. The Wrexham defender heading off the line after John Murphy connected.

Jon Newby had a right-footed shot saved by Brain, and the final chance fell to Mark Jones, but he dragged his right-footed shot wide of the near post.

Three minutes of injury time were played without real incident, and with the game goalless, a chorus of boos greeted the final whistle.

Wrexham:
01 Michael Ingham, 03 Ryan Valentine, 04 Shaun Pejic, 05 Steve Evans ■, 15 Mike Williams, 07 Mark Jones, 08 Danny Williams, 10 Darren Ferguson ■, 20 Matt Done, 26 Maheta Molango, 25 Kevin Smith (66).

Subs: 02 Lee Roche, 06 Craig Morgan, 12 Matt Crowell, 13 Michael Jones (GK), 18 Jon Newby (66).

Macclesfield:
01 Jonny Brain, 03 David Morley ■, 05 Danny Swailes (90), 24 Robert Scott, 02 Carl Regan, 06 Martin Bullock, 07 Alan Navarro, 14 Kevin McIntyre, 21 James McNulty, 08 Colin Heath (73), 12 Matthew Tipton (46).

Subs: 09 Matty McNeil (73), 10 Simon Miles, 13 Tommy Lee (GK), 18 Andrew Teague (90), 26 John Murphy (46).

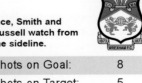

Ince, Smith and Russell watch from the sideline.

Shots on Goal:	8	9
Shots on Target:	5	5
Shots off Target:	3	4
Possession:	53%	47%
Fouls Conceded:	9	10
Corners:	4	3
Yellow Cards:	2	1
Red Cards:	0	0

Loan striker Kevin Smith powers towards the Stevange goal

FA Cup Round 1: November 11th, 2006

Wrexham 1   Stevenage Borough 0

Danny Williams 40

Referee: Matt Haywood (Leeds)
Attendance (Away): 2,873 (332)

Wrexham progressed safely into the second round of the FA Cup, but missed enough chances to make the victory more comfortable against a Conference side, who almost snatched a last gasp equaliser.

Lee Roche returned to replace the injured Ryan Valentine, and Darren Ferguson returned from illness to replace Matt Crowell. A minute's silence for Remembrance Day was observed before

Wrexham kicked off, attacking the 'Tech End' of the ground.

Stevenage started well enough, forcing two early corners, but Wrexham defended these well and started to dominate proceedings after ten minutes.

The Dragons should have lead following a foul on striker Kevin Smith, as Ferguson delivered a decent ball for Danny Williams, who rose to plant his free header over the bar.

With Ferguson dominating the midfield area it was no surprise when the only goal of the game finally came. Good play from Mark Jones forced a corner and 'Fergie' floated the ball across for Danny Williams to loop a header beyond Julian to give Wrexham a deserved lead.

Stevenage's only real threat of the first half came in added time when Ingham did well to save at the feet of George Boyd as Pejic reacted quickly to clear the danger.

Wrexham continued the second half as they finished the first with a string of decent chances with the enigmatic Molango failing to convert several excellent opportunities following good approach play.

The Stevenage players began to get frustrated and a flurry of cynical challenges resulted in three yellow cards for the visitors. Wrexham's only real scare came in the final minutes of the game as Morrison glanced his header narrowly wide of the far post from a set play.

Borough forced another corner in stoppage time and keeper Julian left his goal to march up field to add an extra attacking threat. This proved to be an anti-climax as

Ingham came and collected the ball comfortably. The crowd urged Ingham to shoot at the open goal, but his effort from his own six-yard box went well wide of the target.

There was still time for Molango to endanger the lives of the fans on the Kop as he fired high and wide to much amusement from the home crowd, although the on-loan Brighton striker did not seem to see the funny side of it.

In the final moments Ingham collected another shot, but Wrexham booked a safe passage into the second round with Denis Smith delighted at a third successive clean sheet at the Racecourse.

Wrexham:
01 Michael Ingham, 02 Lee Roche, 04 Shaun Pejic, 05 Steve Evans, 15 Mike Williams, 07 Mark Jones ■, 08 Danny Williams, 10 Darren Ferguson (90), 20 Matt Done, 26 Maheta Molango, 25 Kevin Smith (83).

Subs: 13 Michael Jones (GK), 14 Simon Spender, 16 Levi Mackin (90), 17 Josh Johnson, 21 Marc Williams (83).

Stevenage:
01 Alan Julian, 02 Barry Fuller ■, 25 Ronnie Henry, 06 Santos Gaia ■, 03 John Nutter, 09 Jon Nurse (74), 26 Mark Beard ■, 10 Adam Miller, 23 Dale Binns (66), 11 George Boyd, 20 Steve Morison.

Subs: 04 Luke Oliver (74), 16 Danny Potter, 22 Craig Dobson (66), 27 Hasim Deen, 30 Tyron Scaley.

Kevin Smith heads for goal.

Shots on Goal:	16	3
Shots on Target:	8	2
Shots off Target	8	1
Possession:	59%	41%
Fouls Conceded:	14	10
Corners:	5	10
Yellow Cards:	1	3
Red Cards:	0	0

Shaun Pejic watches Steve Evans' header go wide of County's goal

Coca Cola League 2: November 18th, 2006

Notts County 2   Wrexham 1

Andy Parkinson 37   Chris Llewellyn 65
Jason Lee 60

Referee: Ray Lee (Essex)
Attendance (Away): 4,416 (292)

With Chris Llewellyn returned to the side after suspension and Josh Johnson getting his second League start, the 'Dragons' looked a lot more threatening than on recent away trips. But a failure to turn possession, creativity and chances into goals proved costly as County grabbed the points thanks to goals either side of half time.

It would have been a different story had the 'Dragons' taken their chances, with the stats showing that they had more shots on target (9) than County had in total (8).

Johnson should have opened the scoring in the first minute, but after skinning the full back his shot lacked the power to trouble Kevin Pilkington. Mark Jones then volleyed just wide, and at the other end Michael Ingham saved well from Junior Mendes. Johnson then wasted a glorious

---

chance to open the scoring... not once, but twice!

On both occasions he was put through on goal, but couldn't find the finish the rest of his enterprising performance deserved. Mark Jones then had Pilkington at full stretch conceding a corner, as the 'Dragons' looked the side most likely to break the deadlock.

Almost inevitably they paid the price for this profligacy in front of goal on 37 minutes. Jason Lee brought the ball down and laid it off to Mendes, who expertly picked out Andy Parkinson's run, and the striker emphatically buried the ball past Ingham.

But Wrexham could, maybe should, have been level by the break, but Johnson's touch let him down after Alan White's poor back header had presented him with an opportunity to beat Pilkington to the ball.

Wrexham again started sprightly in the second half, but for the second time in the game conceded a goal against the run of play on the hour mark. Steve Evans' clearance was charged down by David Pipe who squared for Lee to easily beat Ingham from ten yards out.

The Dragons kept fighting, and pulled a goal back within five minutes. Johnson bamboozled two defenders down the left, and crossed to the far post where Llewellyn was perfectly positioned to head the ball home from close range.

The pressure was now firmly on the home side. An Evans header was cleared off the line, a Kevin Smith header was tipped around the post by the alert Pilkington, and another Evans header flew wide deep into added-on time as the Dragons pushed for the point their efforts at the very least deserved. But it wasn't to be!

Notts County:
01 Kevin Pilkington, 22 Dan Gleeson (68), 04 Mike Edwards, 05 Alan White, 03 Austin McCann, 02 David Pipe, 06 Matthew Somner ■, 24 Ian Ross (75), 11 Andy Parkinson, 20 Junior Mendes (86), 09 Jason Lee ■.

Subs: 08 Daniel Martin, 10 Lawrie Dudfield (86), 23 Saul Deeney (GK), 26 Daryl McMahon (68), 27 Jay Smith (75).

Wrexham:
01 Michael Ingham, 02 Lee Roche ■, 04 Shaun Pejic ■, 05 Steve Evans, 15 Mike Williams, 07 Mark Jones, 08 Danny Williams, 10 Darren Ferguson, 17 Josh Johnson, 11 Chris Llewellyn, 26 Maheta Molango (59).

Subs: 13 Michael Jones (GK), 14 Simon Spender, 16 Levi Mackin, 24 Gareth Evans, 25 Kevin Smith (59).

Josh Johnson runs at County's defence.

	Notts County	Wrexham
Shots on Goal:	11	9
Shots on Target:	9	9
Shots off Target	2	9
Possession:	38%	62%
Fouls Conceded:	20	15
Corners:	1	8
Yellow Cards:	2	2
Red Cards:	0	0

Trinidadian Josh Johnson skips through two Lincoln defenders

Coca Cola League 2: November 25th, 2006

Wrexham 2   Lincoln City 1

Mark Jones 24   Mark Stallard 64
Chris Llewellyn 44

Referee: Trevor Kettle (Berkshire)
Attendance (Away): 3,619 (221)

The Reds produced one of their best performances of the season to send second placed Lincoln City home with their tails between their legs.

Denis Smith made one change from the defeat at Notts County, with Kevin Smith starting and Maheta Molango dropping to the bench, but the excellent news for 'Dragons' fans was that Lee McEvilly was considered fit enough for a place on the bench after his long injury lay off.

Wrexham had early chances as both Chris Llewellyn and Josh Johnson threatened, but they soon led when Mark Jones cut in from his right flank, and shot from the edge of the area. The ball took a wicked deflection and looped past Alan Marriott and into the net.

The 'Red Imps' played some neat football, but lacked quality in their final delivery and failed to trouble the Wrexham goal. They almost found a way through when Mark Stallard was given space in the box, but was blocked by Lee Roche. At the other end Smith fired in a low free kick to force a good save from Marriott.

Just before the break, Darren Ferguson delivered a corner to the back post for Steve Evans to head back across goal for Chris Llewellyn to finish from close range.

Early in the second-half Marriott spilled Kevin Smith's twenty-five yard shot behind for a corner. Wrexham continued to dominate and following a foul on Mark Jones, Smith curled the free kick around the wall, but Marriott was able to make a simple save.

Lincoln replaced defender Adie Moses with striker Nat Brown and within a minute Stallard found himself clean through on goal. An attempted clearance was deflected off a Lincoln player, and the experienced striker finished past Ingham.

Wrexham then found themselves under pressure, but Ingham dealt with some routine saves. Eventually the home side recovered as Llewellyn fired in a twenty-five yard shot that just cleared the bar and Williams had a shot held by Marriott.

The introduction of Lee McEvilly for Smith brought a huge applause from the home crowd, and he immediately made his presence felt by being involved in several good moves. Late in the game he picked out Mark Jones in open space who dragged his low shot wide of the post.

Lincoln introduced two more late substitutes, and their final chance came from a corner that was well claimed by Ingham. As he cleared up field the final whistle confirmed a deserved home victory that could have been more emphatic with better finishing.

Wrexham:
01 Michael Ingham, 02 Lee Roche, 04 Shaun Pejic, 05 Steve Evans, 15 Mike Williams, 07 Mark Jones, 08 Danny Williams, 10 Darren Ferguson, 17 Josh Johnson, 25 Kevin Smith (80), 11 Chris Llewellyn.

Subs: 13 Michael Jones (GK), 03 Ryan Valentine, 09 Lee McEvilly (80), 26 Maheta Molango, 16 Levi Mackin.

Lincoln:
01 Alan Marriott, 02 Lee Beevers, 04 Adie Moses (63), 12 Nicky Eaden, 03 Paul Mayo, 14 Ryan Amoo, 07 Lee Frecklington (87), 31 Shane Nicholson (82), 33 Matthew Birley, 09 Mark Stallard, 22 Jamie Forrester.

Subs: 05 Paul Morgan (87), 13 Simon Rayner (GK), 15 Martin Gritton (82), 23 Nat Brown (63), 27 Leon Mettam.

Wrexham's players celebrate Chris Llewellyn's goal.

Shots on Goal:	17	5
Shots on Target:	2	1
Shots off Target	15	4
Possession:	50%	50%
Fouls Conceded:	12	12
Corners:	8	5
Yellow Cards:	0	0
Red Cards:	0	0

Kevin Smith leads Wrexham's shout for a hand ball

FA Cup Round 2: December 2nd, 2006

Scunthorpe United 0   Wrexham 2

Mark Jones 49
Kevin Smith 66

Referee: Kevin Friend (Leicestershire)
Attendance (Away): 5,054 (359)

How fitting that almost two years to the day since the club went into administration in the morning and lost a second round tie at Glanford Park in the evening, Wrexham returned to the same venue at the same stage of the competition and won in style.

This was certainly a real coupon-buster if ever there was one as the 'Dragons' produced a performance that deservedly booked a place in the third round for the

first time since 1999 with an unexpected 2-0 victory against a Scunthorpe side lying 2nd in League One.

It was no fluke either, and second half Kevin Smith and Mark Jones goals were the rewards for an outstanding team display, though special praise is due in particular to central defenders Shaun Pejic and Steve Evans. The pair was awesome against Scunny's prolific strike force of Billy Sharp and Andy Keogh and laid the foundations for what happened further up the field.

Scunthorpe started like a side oozing confidence from such a lofty position and impressive home record (just one defeat going into the tie). But they found Wrexham's rearguard in defiant mood, and other than a Richard Hinds header that was disallowed for an obvious foul on Steve Evans, and a hasty shot from Sharp when well placed, they rarely looked like making a breakthrough.

Little was seen of Wrexham as an attack-ing force in the opening period, but it was a different story after the break. 'Iron' keeper Joe Murphy saved a Danny Williams header and hastily threw the ball out to launch a quick counter attack, but his throw was picked off by Mark Jones who sent an unstoppable 25-yard left foot shot fizzing into the net.

Murphy then saved low down to deny Chris Llewellyn from adding a second and, with Wrexham on top, the Welsh international had another effort saved by the busy home 'keeper. The second goal eventually arrived on 64 minutes. Evans headed down Darren Ferguson's corner and Kevin Smith turned and shot goal-wards in one movement. The ball

appeared to strike the hand of Scunny captain Andy Crosby, but the assistant referee adjudged that the ball had already crossed the line.

Mark Jones sensed the opportunity to kill the game off with a third goal, but after beating two defenders his shot was saved by Murphy. The home side rallied towards the end, but couldn't find a way past the unyielding Wrexham defence. And there was also a fleeting glimpse of Juan Ugarte as a late substitute. C'mon the Town!

Scunthorpe:
01 Joe Murphy, 06 Cliff Byrne, 04 Andy Crosby, 12 Stephen Foster, 05 Richard Hinds (72), 15 Cleveland Taylor, 07 Matthew Sparrow, 11 Ian Baraclough, 27 Ian Morris (67), 09 Billy Sharp, 19 Andrew Keogh,

Subs: 02 Dave Mulligan, 08 Jim Goodwin, 10 Steve Torpey (67), 17 Marcus Williams (72), 22 Josh Lillis (GK).

Wrexham:
01 Michael Ingham, 02 Lee Roche, 04 Shaun Pejic, 05 Steve Evans, 15 Mike Williams, 07 Mark Jones ▪, 08 Danny Williams, 10 Darren Ferguson, 17 Josh Johnson (90), 11 Chris Llewellyn, 25 Kevin Smith (77).

Subs: 03 Ryan Valentine, 09 Lee McEvilly (77) ▪, 12 Matt Crowell, 13 Michael Jones (GK), 32 Juan Ugarte (90).

Steve Evans heads down Darren Ferguson's corner.

Shots on Goal:	7	18
Shots on Target:	2	8
Shots off Target:	5	3
Possession:	53%	47%
Fouls Conceded:	13	14
Corners:	6	1
Yellow Cards:	0	2
Red Cards:	0	0

Lee McEvilly unleases a shot at Torquay's goal

Coca Cola League 2: December 5th, 2006

Torquay United 1   Wrexham 1

Jordan Robertson 51   Kevin Smith 07

Referee: Steve Tanner (Somerset)
Attendance (Away): 1,588 (75)

Expectations on the long trek down the M5 had been raised by the FA Cup win over Scunthorpe, and a sixth minute lead for the 'Dragons' should have been good enough to claim their first away League win since August.

However, even at this early stage Torquay look a side with a long struggle ahead to avoid relegation to the Conference so, given the perfect start courtesy of Kevin Smith's goal, three points should have

been a formality. But football isn't like that, and Torquay were full value for their point.

Conditions were dreadful, with strong winds and torrential rain a feature of the evening. So anything approaching good football was inevitably going to be at a premium. But with the strong wind behind them in the first half Wrexham looked keen to continue on from where they'd left off at Glanford Park, and Chris Llewellyn quickly called 'Gulls' 'keeper Nathan

Abbey into action.

The visitors led with their very next attack when Darren Ferguson's early ball was helped on by Llewellyn to Smith, the striker's shot was blocked, but he reacted quickly and headed the rebound into the empty net for his second goal in successive games.

Torquay struggled to make any impact against a solid Wrexham unit, though Steve Evans was fortunate to get away with pulling Lee Thorpe back inside the penalty area after an offside flag saw play called back by the referee.

Conditions deteriorated for the start of the second half with the wind and rain now driving into Wrexham's faces. And there was also an enforced personnel change with the injured Mark Jones being replaced by Lee McEvilly, forcing Llewellyn to drop back into a midfield role. And the substitute was quickly in the action with a 25-yard shot that flew wide.

But the home side were level on 51 minutes when Shaun Pejic fouled Jordan Robertson, and the loanee striker picked himself up and curled a superb free kick perfectly into the top corner of the net.

Ingham had no chance.

Wrexham struggled to retain any quality possession and the best chance fell to win the game fell to 'Gulls' substitute Kyle Critchell on 74 minutes, but he blasted high over the bar with just Ingham to beat.

In a late rally McEvilly had a volley blocked, and substitute Juan Ugarte fired a free kick into the side netting, but a draw was, in the end, a fair reflection of the game.

Torquay:
01 Nathan Abbey, 02 Lee Andrews, 18 Steve Woods, 06 Matt Villis, 03 Steve Reed, 10 Lee Mansell, 04 Matt Hockley (72) ■, 11 Kevin Hill (28), 21 Adam Murray, 09 Lee Thorpe (46), 15 Jordan Robertson.

Subs: 07 Jamie Ward, 16 Carl Motteram (28), 19 Chris McPhee (46), 20 Martin Horsell (GK), 23 Kyle Critchell (72).

Wrexham:
01 Michael Ingham, 02 Lee Roche, 04 Shaun Pejic, 05 Steve Evans, 15 Mike Williams, 07 Mark Jones (46), 08 Danny Williams, 10 Darren Ferguson, 17 Josh Johnson (83), 11 Chris Llewellyn, 25 Kevin Smith (83).

Subs: 03 Ryan Valentine (83), 09 Lee McEvilly (46), 12 Matt Crowell, 13 Michael Jones (GK), 30 Juan Ugarte (83).

Kevin Smith opens the scoring.

Shots on Goal:	7	8
Shots on Target:	2	5
Shots off Target:	5	3
Possession:	58%	42%
Fouls Conceded:	9	12
Corners:	2	6
Yellow Cards:	1	0
Red Cards:	0	0

Former Wrexham keeper Andy Marriot thanks old friends after the game

Coca Cola League 2: December 9th, 2006

Boston United 4   Wrexham 0

Anthony Elding 22, 83
Drew Broughton 48, 69

Referee: Dean Whitestone (Northamptonshire)
Attendance (Away): 1,708 (194)

You can argue as long as you want whether the 22nd minute dismissal of Steve Evans, for a retaliatory kick out at Drewe Broughton after a nasty foul by the striker, was the turning point in this game. But the reality is that Wrexham had started so poorly that Boston had already looked the more likely winners even before Evans' red card.

Preparations were hardly helped by the late withdrawal of Mark Jones, who injured a knee in the warm-up. But even taking the early sending-off into account, there can be no excuse for such a lethargic and disappointing display, especially coming only a week after the performance at Scunthorpe.

Maybe if the 'Dragons' had maintained a modicum of composure after Anthony Elding had opened the scoring from close range after 21 minutes, it could still have been a different outcome. But almost immediately Evans saw red and maybe with it went any hopes of staging a come-back.

Danny Williams dropped back into the defence to cater for the loss of Evans and, to be fair, other than a Broughton effort that clipped the bar on 41 minutes the 'Dragons' saw things through to the interval without any further scares. However, with Chris Llewellyn also forced to drop deeper in the re-shuffle, the problem facing Denis Smith's side was how to create problems for Andy Marriott in the home goal.

Any fleeting hopes of mounting a second half recovery drive were dispelled three minutes after the restart when Broughton, who admittedly looked yards offside, turned home a Francis Green centre.

Kevin Smith then forced Marriott's first save of the afternoon before Denis Smith introduced both Neil Roberts and Juan Ugarte in a desperate attempt to find a way back into the game.

Unfortunately, it had little impact on pro-ceedings and within twelve minutes of the double substitution Broughton took

Elding's pass in his stride and drove the ball low past Ingham. Elding then com-pleted the scoring, and the 'Dragons' mis-ery, with a fourth goal on 83 minutes, the striker neatly glancing a header from David Rowson's cross beyond Ingham and into the corner of the net.

Only a week ago, after the resilient dis-play at Glanford Park, Denis Smith was eulogising about how there's "every chance of getting more results away from home" and "we are a hard team to break down". Isn't a week a long time in foot-ball!

Boston:
01 Andy Marriott, 02 Lee Canoville (58), 24 Ian Miller, 04 Paul Ellender, 03 Tim Ryan, 08 Anthony Elding, 05 Mark Greaves, 25 Jason Kennedy, 27 David Rowson, 10 Francis Green (88), 09 Drewe Broughton (84) ■.

Subs: 07 Brad Maylett (84), 15 David Farrell (88), 16 Jamie Clarke (58), 19 Richie Ryan, 22 Dany N'Guesson.

Wrexham:
01 Michael Ingham, 02 Lee Roche, 04 Shaun Pejic, 05 Steve Evans ■, 15 Mike Williams, 17 Josh Johnson (57) ■, 10 Darren Ferguson, 08 Danny Williams, 16 Levi Mackin (73), 25 Kevin Smith (57), 11 Chris Llewellyn ■.

Subs: 03 Ryan Valentine (73), 13 Michael Jones (GK), 20 Matty Done, 23 Neil Roberts (57), 30 Juan Ugarte (57).

Steve Evans is sent off as Wrexham crash to defeat.

Shots on Goal:	10	1
Shots on Target:	3	1
Shots off Target	7	0
Possession:	43%	57%
Fouls Conceded:	15	15
Corners:	1	4
Yellow Cards:	1	2
Red Cards:	0	1

Matty Done breezes past a Walsall defender

Coca Cola League 2: December 16th, 2006

Wrexham 1
Chris Llewellyn 68

Walsall 1
Hector Sam 27

Referee: Colin Webster (Tyne & Wear)
Attendance (Away): 4,270 (677)

I n a game of two contrasting halves, the 'Dragons' fought back against the league leaders to earn a deserved point after going a goal behind.

Overall, there was little to choose between the two teams with Wrexham not looking out of their depth against a Walsall team five points clear at the top of League Two.

Injuries and suspension left Denis Smith needing to make three changes from the

side beaten comprehensively at Boston. With Steve Evans suspended after his sending off Mike Williams moved to centre back and Ryan Valentine replaced him at left back. Matty Done and Marc Williams came into the side replacing Levi Mackin and Kevin Smith.

Walsall started the game the brighter and set the tone for the first half. Ingham was a spectator as he watched Kris Taylor curl a free kick narrowly wide of the near post. Wrexham's best effort in the first half was from Matty Done who shot wide following a lay off by Chris Llewellyn.

The opening goal came from a corner that the Wrexham defence failed to deal with effectively. Gerrard won the initial header and Hector Sam, in the six-yard box, flicked this in. He kept a promise that he had made to supporters of his former club as he refused to celebrate his goal. He then came close to extending the 'Saddlers' lead, but he failed to connect with a corner at the back post.

The second half started in the same vein as the first until the introduction of Lee McEvilly. The burly striker began to terrorise the Walsall defence and it was no surprise when cracks started to appear.

The equaliser came when Marc Williams skipped past his marker on the left touchline, and quickly raced to the edge of the area. He showed great composure in laying the ball back for Llewellyn to whip in a great finish from inside of the 'D', giving Clayton Ince no chance of saving at his near post.

Wrexham then dominated proceedings for the final twenty minutes, and almost took the lead when Pejic connected powerfully with a Ferguson corner.

The 'Saddlers' could have been celebrating an undeserved winner in the last minute when they broke quickly down the Wrexham right. A cross was swung into the far post, but Wright completely missed his header despite being unmarked.

The last chance of the match fell to Wrexham deep into injury time when McEvilly volleyed inches wide from Llewellyn's cross, but overall the score line was a fair reflection of a decent game of football.

Wrexham:
01 Michael Ingham, 02 Lee Roche, 15 Mike Williams, 04 Shaun Pejic ■, 03 Ryan Valentine ■, 20 Matty Done, 10 Darren Ferguson, 08 Danny Williams, 17 Josh Johnson (62), 21 Marc Williams, 11 Chris Llewellyn.

Subs: 09 Lee McEvilly (62), 12 Matt Crowell, 13 Michael Jones (GK), 14 Simon Spender, 24 Gareth Evans.

Walsall:
01 Clayton Ince, 05 Chris Westwood, 06 Ian Roper ■, 04 Anthony Gerrard, 15 Kris Taylor, 11 Tony Bedeau (59), 02 Craig Pead (90) ■, 03 Daniel Fox ■, 14 Mark Wright, 09 Martin Butler ■, 10 Hector Sam (66).

Subs: 18 Tommy Wright (66), 20 Ishmel Demontagnac (90), 24 Scott Dann, 26 Mark Bradley, (59), 41 Bertrand Bossu (GK).

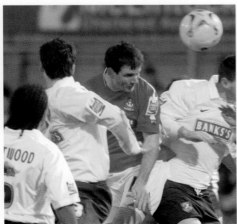

Chris Llewellyn heads towards goal

	Wrexham	Walsall
Shots on Goal:	10	7
Shots on Target:	5	3
Shots off Target	5	4
Possession:	53%	47%
Fouls Conceded:	12	15
Corners:	6	4
Yellow Cards:	2	4
Red Cards:	0	0

Chris Llewellyn's pass to Marc Williams is turned into Darlington's net by Darren Holloway

Coca Cola League 2: December 23rd, 2006

Wrexham 1   Darlington 0

Darren Holloway 19 (og)

Referee: Ray Olivier (West Midlands)
Attendance (Away): 3,401 (104)

Wrexham ended 2006 at the Racecourse with a hard fought, but deserved victory decided by an own goal to start the Christmas festivities off with a bang for Denis Smith's side.

Darlington had the better of the opening exchanges, and a positive run and shot by former 'Dragons' winger Neil Wainwright created the game's first opportunity as Michael Ingham made a comfortable diving save.

Wainwright found himself with an open goal a few minutes later, as Ingham left his area to head clear, but the ex-Dragon elected to pass to Simon Johnson who headed over the Wrexham bar.

Darlington continued to dominate the early proceedings with the home side struggling to cross the halfway line, but young centre-back's Gareth Evans and Mike Williams coped well with the 'Quakers' attacks.

It was Wrexham who celebrated the open-

---

ing goal of the game, when the visitors failed to deal with a long ball out of defence that was flicked on by Marc Williams into the path of Chris Llewellyn. His square pass was aimed at Williams, but Darren Holloway turned it into his own net.

Darlington should perhaps have equalised on the stroke of half time after Johnson turned Gareth Evans, but Ingham reacted well by sticking out his leg to divert the shot behind for a corner.

Wrexham started slowly after the break, but the lead never looked to be in any real danger with the 'Quakers' struggling to record any serious attempts on Ingham's goal.

Matty Done force a string of corners, and from of these Danny Williams powered a header that David Stockdale struggled to gather on his line.

The Wrexham goal lived dangerously for a fifteen-minute spell with Ingham pulling off a good save to deny Martin Smith with the Wrexham 'keeper blocking his shot only to see Clark Keltie fire the rebound hopelessly over the bar.

Alun Armstrong's appearance off the bench

saw him immediately combine well to set up Julian Joachim, who initially got the better of Evans, but the Wrexham defender put the striker under enough pressure to force him to shoot wide with Ingham narrowing down the shooting angle.

As the game went into the final ten minutes, there were some nervous moments with Wrexham defending their slender one goal lead, but Darlington's only real threat came from a couple of late corners, and the 'Dragons' defence comfortably held on as the final whistle was welcomed by the home crowd.

Wrexham:
01 Michael Ingham, 02 Lee Roche, 24 Gareth Evans ■, 15 Mike Williams, 03 Ryan Valentine, 17 Josh Johnson (67), 08 Danny Williams, 10 Darren Ferguson, 20 Matty Done, 11 Chris Llewellyn, 21 Marc Williams.

Subs: 09 Lee McEvilly (67), 12 Matt Crowell, 13 Michael Jones (GK), 14 Simon Spender, 28 Alex Darlington.

Darlington:
01 David Stockdale, 18 Brian Close, 05 Patrick Collins, 04 Darren Holloway (29), 03 Craig James ■, 07 Neil Wainwright (55), 08 Micky Cummins, 10 Clark Keltie, 19 Martin Smith, 11 Simon Johnson (81), 12 Julian Joachim.

Subs: 02 David Duke (29) ■, 14 Carlos Logan (81) ■, 31 Jack Norton (GK), 25 Alun Armstrong (55), 30 Anthony Griffin.

Mike Williams lays off a pass		
Shots on Goal:	16	8
Shots on Target:	8	5
Shots off Target	8	3
Possession:	54%	46%
Fouls Conceded:	15	14
Corners:	4	10
Yellow Cards:	0	1
Red Cards:	0	0

The Wrexham players celebrate Lee McEvilly's opening goal against Rochdale

Coca Cola League 2: December 26th, 2006

Rochdale 2   Wrexham 2

John Doolan 63   Lee McEvilly 48
Glen Murray 78   Chris Llewellyn 55

Referee: Jonathon Moss (Yorkshire)
Attendance (Away): 2,837 (approx. 700)

Wrexham will probably never have a better chance of getting that elusive first away League victory since August after throwing away a two-goal lead at Spotland.

Rochdale impressed on both their visits to the Racecourse this season, and finished the game strongly. Indeed, it was the 'Dragons' that were the more grateful side to hear the final blast of the referee's whistle. But ten minutes into the second period

there looked like there'd only be one winner - after goals from substitute Lee McEvilly and Chris Llewellyn had given the travelling support some Boxing Day cheer.

The first half was a lacklustre affair with goalmouth incident at a premium. The best of the few opening chances fell generally to the home side, with Glen Murray failing to hit the target with a header from a Chris Dagnall centre, and then seeing a shot lack the power to seriously test Michael

---

Ingham. Wrexham's best chance came on 27 minutes when Ryan Valentine's shot from the edge of the box flew narrowly wide.

Denis Smith responded to the lack of a cutting edge in the first half by replacing Williams with McEvilly at the break, and the former 'Dale' man had an immediate impact. Ingham launched the ball forward, Llewellyn headed on, and McEvilly raced clear to fire past Matthew Gilks from just inside the area.

Chances were then spurned at both ends - McEvilly heading straight at Gilks at one end, Clive Moyo-Modise firing wide at the other - before Wrexham doubled their lead in the 55th minute. Darren Ferguson crossed, Danny Williams headed down, and McEvilly shot at goal. Gilks saved, but could only parry it, and Llewellyn was on hand to convert the rebound from close range.

That should have been enough, but Rochdale refused to accept defeat and responded by pulling a goal back after 63 minutes. Ingham failed to deal with Gary Jones' cross, and was beaten to the ball by Murray who accepted the opportunity to head into the empty net.

Wrexham were now well and truly on the back foot, and it took a Lee Roche goal line clearance to deny the dangerous Dagnall an equaliser. The pressure finally took its toll on 78 minutes when Joe Doolan's powerful header struck the bar, and dropped down just over the goal line despite sterling efforts by the 'Dragons' defence to clear.

Rochdale came closest to winning the game in the time left, but Wrexham were still left to reflect on two points that got away.

Rochdale:
01 Matthew Gilks, 02 Simon Ramsden, 12 Alan Goodall, 18 Nathan Stanton, 23 Rory McArdle, 08 Gary Jones, 05 John Doolan, 24 Callum Warburton (57), 09 Chris Dagnall, 20 Clive Moyo Modise (57), 17 Glen Murray.

Sub: 13 Lloyd Rigby (GK), 14 Gary Brown, 15 Joe Thompson (57), 19 Lee Crooks (27), William Macquet (57).

Wrexham:
01 Michael Ingham, 02 Lee Roche ■, 04 Shaun Pejic, 15 Mike Williams, 03 Ryan Valentine, 17 Josh Johnson (86), 10 Darren Ferguson, 08 Danny Williams, 20 Matty Done, 11 Chris Llewellyn, 21 Marc Williams (46).

Subs: 09 Lee McEvilly (46), 12 Matt Crowell (86), 13 Michael Jones (GK), 14 Simon Spender, 24 Gareth Evans.

Chris Llewellyn celebrates the second goal.

	Rochdale	Wrexham
Shots on Goal:	7	13
Shots on Target:	8	5
Shots off Target:	6	6
Possession:	55%	45%
Fouls Conceded:	16	18
Corners:	4	10
Yellow Cards:	0	1
Red Cards:	0	0

The Hereford keeper, Wayne Brown, blocks a header from Chris Llewellyn

Coca Cola League 2: December 30th, 2006

Hereford United 2   Wrexham 0

Alan Connell 37, 88

Referee: Anthony Taylor (Manchester)
Attendance (Away): 3,444 (519)

It was home sweet home for Wrexham as they returned to winning ways following three successive away defeats, having conceded fourteen goals in the process! A first half header from Steve Evans proved to be decisive as the home side recorded a confidence boosting clean sheet.

Overall, this game was an even contest with the 'Dragons' having two shots cleared off the line, and Hereford hitting the woodwork. Both sides faded in the second half as their midweek cup adventures against Championship opponents took its toll.

Hereford looked dangerous on the break, and a well-worked move down the right got the better of Ryan Valentine and Evans, but Ingham just managed to punch Stuart Fleetwood's cross before Alan Connell could reach the ball.

From a corner Darren Ferguson's delivery to the far post was powered goalwards by

Evans. Simon Travis was unable to hack clear before the ball had crossed the line, with the referee awarding the goal following the signal from his assistant much to the delight of the home fans.

A few minutes later Chris Llewellyn noticed Wayne Brown off his line, but his shot from 45 yards just cleared the crossbar. The visitors responded at the other end when Richard Rose went close after cutting in from the left.

The 'Bulls' went even closer to equalising when Wrexham failed to deal with a set play. The ball was crossed back to the far post where Ingham managed to tip Tim Sills' header onto the bar, with Valentine clearing the rebound to safety.

Chances were few and far between in a lackluster second half, with both teams effectively canceling each other out. However, it was Matty Done who had the first chance following the restart. Good wing play allowed him to burst clear in the box, but he curled the ball agonizingly wide of the post.

Fleetwood had a couple of chances from free kicks, but hit the first straight into Ingham's arms and curled the second

around the wall, narrowly missing the bar with Ingham beaten.

Wrexham had a lucky escape with five minutes remaining. A clever corner was taken low to towards the edge of area and redirected into the six-yard box, but Fleetwood diverted the ball wide.

Josh Johnson gave away a free kick in final minute of injury time with a shoulder charge, but Matty Done cleared the danger by hacking the ball up field. The final whistle blew saw Wrexham maintain their unbeaten home run with a valuable win against their border rivals.

Hereford:
01 Wayne Brown, 05 Tamika Mkandawire, 23 Phil Gulliver, 04 Richard Rose, 18 Trent McClenahan, 21 Luke Webb, 08 Andrew Ferrell, 02 Simon Travis, 12 Alan Connell, 09 Tim Sills (79) ■, 10 Stuart Fleetwood (59),

Subs: 14 Glyn Thompson (GK), 16 Andrew Williams (59), 17 Martin Giles, 20 Alex Jeannin, 11 Gareth Sheldon (79),

Wrexham:
01 Michael Ingham, 14 Simon Spender, 04 Shaun Pejic, 24 Gareth Evans, 15 Mike Williams, 17 Josh Johnson (46), 02 Lee Roche ■, 12 Matt Crowell (74), 20 Matt Done, 11 Chris Llewellyn ■, 21 Marc Williams (46).

Subs: 06 Brian Carey, 09 Lee McEvilly (46), 10 Darren Ferguson (74), 13 Michael Jones (GK), 25 Kevin Smith (46).

Mike Williams is tackled by a Hereford player.

	Hereford	Wrexham
Shots on Goal:	4	10
Shots on Target:	1	6
Shots off Target	3	4
Possession:	57%	43%
Fouls Conceded:	6	7
Corners:	3	10
Yellow Cards:	1	2
Red Cards:	0	0

Chris Llewellyn runs at the Accrington defence in search of an opening

Coca Cola League 2: January 1st, 2007

Wrexham 1   Accrington Stanley 3

Josh Johnson 45   Paul Mullin 17
David Brown 83, 88

Referee: Mike Dean (Wirral)
Attendance (Away): 3,805 (161)

Wrexham suffered a New Year hang over as recent optimistic thoughts of a push towards a play off spot were brought back to earth by a workmanlike performance from Accrington Stanley, who showed the 'Dragons' how to play and win at this level for the second time this season.

The home side struggled early on with 'Stanley' making good use of both flanks throughout. James Harris dominated proceedings in the middle, and the experience of Andy Todd was always an option on the right, while Shaun Whalley continually caused problems down the left flank.

It was Whalley who got the better of Lee Roche to deliver a cross into the near post that forced Steve Evans to head against his own bar, but Paul Mullin reacted quickest to the rebound to score from close range.

Accrington almost doubled their advantage when a dangerous free kick from Whalley was glanced goal wards, but Roche did well to scramble the ball behind for a corner at the back post.

However, on the stroke of half-time the home side leveled when Michael Ingham delivered a huge kick and Josh Johnson battled with Richardson on the edge of the area. The Accrington defender lost his footing, which gave Johnson space to steer the ball past Elliot for his first goal in a Wrexham shirt.

That goal spurred the 'Dragons' to begin the second period more positively, and they threatened from set plays. From one Steve Evans played in Lee McEvilly, but his attempted chip from inside of the area failed to clear Elliott who took a simple catch. McEvilly had a goal disallowed following a challenge that left an Accrington defender and Elliott flat out on the edge of the area.

'Stanley' could have been down to ten men when Williams appeared to haul down Kevin Smith, but referee Mike Dean waved play on. With seven minutes remaining, Brown had the better of Ingham with a cool finish.

Wrexham almost struck back when Smith picked out McEvilly who fired a fierce volley that Elliott could only palm away. The result was put beyond doubt when Roche brought down Whalley. Ingham did well to save the resultant penalty from Todd, but his efforts were in vein as Brown was quickest to follow up with a simple tap in.

There were chances for either side in the time remaining, but Wrexham left the field to a chorus of boos and the harsh realisation that a relegation battle looked more likely than a dash for promotion.

Wrexham:
01 Michael Ingham, 02 Lee Roche, 05 Steve Evans ■, 04 Shaun Pejic, 03 Ryan Valentine ■, 17 Josh Johnson, 12 Matt Crowell ■, 10 Darren Ferguson (78), 20 Matty Done (78), 11 Chris Llewellyn, 21 Marc Williams (46).

Subs: 09 Lee McEvilly (46), 13 Michael Jones (GK), 15 Mike Williams (78), 24 Gareth Evans, 25 Kevin Smith (78).

Accrington:
01 Rob Elliott, 24 Ricky Baines, 05 Robbie Williams, 05 Michael Welch, 03 Leam Richardson, 17 Andy Todd, 06 Andy Proctor, 20 Jay Harris ■, 26 Shaun Whalley, 10 Paul Mullin, 18 David Brown.

Subs: 32 Andy Smith, 33 Jimmy Bell, 34 Peter Murphy, 35 Martin Fearon (GK), 28 Joe Jacobson.

Josh Johnson goes in for a tackle

Shots on Goal:	8	10
Shots on Target:	4	4
Shots off Target	4	6
Possession:	58%	42%
Fouls Conceded:	16	9
Corners:	5	8
Yellow Cards:	3	1
Red Cards:	0	0

Lee McEvilly pulls a goal back for Wrexham against Derby County in the FA Cup

FA Cup Round 3: January 6th 2007

Derby County 3   Wrexham 1

Arturo Lupoli 32, 56, 85   Lee McEvilly 61

Referee: Richard Beeby (Northamptonshire)
Attendance (Away): 15,609 (2,922)

Roared on by nearly 3,000 fans the 'Dragons' delivered a performance that belied their lowly position and recent away form. But Championship high-fliers Derby County proved just too good.

Had Steve Evans' 69th minute effort not been contentiously ruled out for offside then a draw, or even a shock win, may have been on the cards. We'll never know!

That Derby were deserved winners cannot

be questioned, but they will know that Denis Smith's side gave them a serious run for their money. Nevertheless, the 'Dragons' were the first side to show and Chris Llewellyn shot just wide and Lee McEvilly had a shot parried to safety by 'Rams' 'keeper Stephen Bywater.

Derby's trademark slick passing had struggled to find any rhythm against a determined and hard-working Wrexham but, gradually, they began finding more space and made the breakthrough in the 32nd

---

minute. David Jones, from Gresford, released Morten Bisgaard and the Dane in turn found Arturo Lupoli and the on-loan Arsenal striker emphatically beat Michael Ingham.

The 'Dragons' held firm until the interval, following which Evans jumped to meet a Darren Ferguson free kick, but Bywater easily saved his near post header. Immediately though Derby went up the field and forced a corner that Bisgaard delivered and Lupoli, unmarked, had the simple task of heading past Ingham on 56 minutes.

Surely there was no way back after this second setback but, remarkably, in the 61st minute McEvilly latched onto Bob Malcolm's poor back header and rounded Bywater before rolling the ball into the empty net.

Manic celebrations followed in the massed ranks of the Red Army behind the goal, and things almost got even better two minutes later but Evans' header from Fergie's free kick flew just wide of the far post. For the first time in the game the home side were starting to look nervy and from another Fergie free kick Llewellyn powered a header back across goal and Evans, running from deep, hammered the ball into the

net from close range. More mad celebrations followed, only for them to be quickly cut short by the assistant's flag.

Wrexham continued to press with McEvilly's shot blocked, and an Evans header saved by Bywater as the home side's concerns remained. However, the need for an equaliser obviously left the 'Dragons' prone to rapid counter-attacks, and from one such break Ryan Smith crossed from the left, Steve Howard headed against the bar, and Lupoli completed his hat trick with a simple header.

Defeated - but certainly not disgraced.

Derby:
43 Stephen Bywater, 02 Marc Edworthy, 23 Darren Moore, 06 Michael Johnson ■, 03 Mohammed Camara, 07 David Jones, 22 Matt Oakley (90), 08 Morten Bisgaard (76), 21 Bob Malcolm (71), 09 Steve Howard, 16 Arturo Lupoli.

Subs: 11 Paul Peschisolido (90), 14 Richard Jackson, 15 Ryan Smith (71), 18 Seth Johnson, 28 Giles Barnes (76).

Wrexham:
01 Michael Ingham, 03 Ryan Valentine ■, 04 Shaun Pejic, 05 Steve Evans, 15 Mike Williams, 12 Matt Crowell (58), 08 Danny Williams, 10 Darren Ferguson, 20 Matty Done, 11 Chris Llewellyn, 09 Lee McEvilly.

Subs: 13 Michael Jones (GK), 14 Simon Spender, 17 Josh Jonson (58), 21 Marc Williams, 24 Gareth Evans.

Chris Llewellyn brushes off a Derby defender.

Shots on Goal:	13	12
Shots on Target:	11	5
Shots off Target	2	7
Possession:	51%	49%
Fouls Conceded:	19	11
Corners:	4	2
Yellow Cards:	1	1
Red Cards:	0	0

Joey and Fergie shout instructions to the Wrexham players

Coca Cola League 2: January 13th 2007

Swindon Town 2   Wrexham 1

Sofiene Zaaboub 9   Marc Williams 8
Christian Roberts 71p

Referee: Phil Taylor (Hertfordshire)
Attendance (Away): 6,130 (Approximately 200)

What a week it's been? First the FA Cup exit at Derby, then the sacking of Denis Smith and Kevin Russell on Thursday, and the subsequent appointment of Brian Carey as manager, and finally this cruel defeat at the County Ground. Yes, it's true. A week can be a long time in football!

Carey's first team sheet as boss certainly had chins wagging, with Darren Ferguson dropped to the substitute's bench, with new loan signing Paul Mitchell from MK Dons starting in midfield, and young striker Marc Williams given a starting berth alongside Lee McEvilly as the 'Dragons' went in search of goals.

The bold team selection reaped early rewards as the 'Dragons' roared into an eighth minute lead. McEvilly, enjoying his first League start of the campaign, swept the ball out to Simon Spender on the right, and playing in a more advanced role than normal, delivered an inch-perfect cross for Marc Williams to direct a firm header past Phil Smith for his first goal of his fledgling career.

But, typically, there was no time to enjoy the lead as Swindon equalised almost immediately. An uncharacteristic mix-up between Chris Llewellyn and Ryan Valentine near the corner flag gave Curtis Weston the chance to get to the by-line and pull the ball back invitingly to the edge of the box for Sofiene Zaaboub to hammer the ball past Ingham and into the top corner.

Williams and Llewellyn both went close to restoring Wrexham's lead, and at the other end it took a spectacular save from Ingham to keep out Jack Smith's quickly taken free kick.

With the strong wind in their favour, Swindon upped the tempo after the break, with Ingham having to be in top form to stop Zaaboub giving them an early second half lead. He denied the Frenchman again as the home side continued to pile on the pressure. But the 'Dragons' stood strong, and it took a dubious penalty decision in the 70th minute to turn the game irretrievably in Swindon's favour. There's no doubt that Michael Pook's cross struck Valentine's hand, but there was little the full back could do to get out of the way of the ball. When you're struggling down the bottom it's the kind of decision that goes against you, as Christian Roberts converted the spot kick with ease.

There was no way back and despite the best efforts of all concerned an equaliser never looked likely, leaving Wrexham just two points and two places above the relegation zone.

Swindon:
25 Phil Smith, 02 Jack Smith, 03 Jamie Vincent, 04 Sofiene Zaaboub (82), 05 Jerel Ifil, 06 Ady Williams, 23 Curtis Weston (85) ■, 19 Michael Pook, 09 Christian Roberts, (78), 10 Lee Peacock, 12 Ricky Shakes.

Subs: 08 Aaron Brown (82), 13 Jon Stewart (GK), 15 Andy Nicholas, 21 Lucas Jutkiewicz (78), 22 Blair Sturrock (85).

Wrexham:
01 Michael Ingham, 02 Lee Roche ■, 04 Shaun Pejic, 05 Steve Evans, 03 Ryan Valentine, 14 Simon Spender ■, 18 Paul Mitchell ■, 08 Danny Williams, 11 Chris Llewellyn, 09 Lee McEvilly (78), 21 Marc Williams (88).

Subs: 10 Darren Ferguson, 13 Michael Jones (GK), 16 Levi Mackin, 17 Josh Johnson (78), 24 Gareth Evans (88).

Marc Williams opens the scoring.

Shots on Goal:	7	2
Shots on Target:	3	1
Shots off Target	4	1
Possession:	60%	40%
Fouls Conceded:	11	9
Corners:	6	4
Yellow Cards:	1	3
Red Cards:	0	0

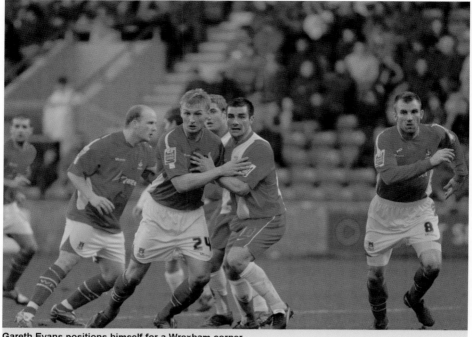

Gareth Evans positions himself for a Wrexham corner

Coca Cola League 2: January 20th 2007

Wrexham 1   Hartlepool United 1

Chris Llewellyn 64   Richard Barker 9

Referee: Graham Salisbury (Preston)
Attendance (Away): 3,828 (330)

A much-improved second-half display from Wrexham was more than enough to earn a point against an in-form Hartlepool side that had won 10 of their last 11 games.

Hartlepool started the game strongly, and with the home side struggling to cope, the visitors opened the scoring after just eight minutes when Richard Barker side-footed home from close range after he was picked out by James Brown.

Wrexham looked nervous at the back, and almost found themselves two down within fifteen minutes. Ingham was at full stretch as he turned a side-footed effort from Barker around the post after the Hartlepool striker had been left unmarked on the edge of the area.

The home side struggled to create chances, and registered their first meaningful shot late in the first half when Lee McEvilly fired in a low left footed effort from just outside of the area.

Konstantopoulos did well to turn the ball around the post, and then collected confidently from the resultant corner

The 'Dragons' had a lucky escape early on in the second half when Valentine cleared Barker's glanced header off the goal line. The introduction of Matty Done to replace Spender began to swing the game in Wrexham's favour, with Done a constant threat.

In a rare attack Sweeney failed to capitalise on an error by Shaun Pejic, when he fired wide of Ingham's left hand post.

The richly deserved equaliser came in the 64th minute. Done was played in by Valentine down the left, and this time the young winger delivered a perfect ball to pick out Chris Llewellyn at the far post, who slammed the ball home from close range against his former club.

With the goal lifting the home crowd Wrexham pressed for all three points, and the Hartlepool defence was clearly rattled. Done continued to torment, with Konstantopoulos requiring two attempts to gather a well struck long range shot from the lively winger.

Llewellyn was also a threat on the right

wing, and one of his crosses should have resulted in Wrexham's second goal, unfortunately Marc Williams took the ball off the head of McEvilly when his strike partner was better positioned.

Konstantopoulos then claimed Marc Williams powerful shot, and a good run from Valentine earned another corner that resulted in a scramble at the near post, with the ball finally cleared.

Wrexham appeared to take their foot off the gas, and some desperate defending was required to keep the game at 1-1, but the game ended with the points shared.

Wrexham:
01 Michael Ingham, 02 Lee Roche, 04 Shaun Pejic, 24 Gareth Evans, 03 Ryan Valentine ■, 14 Simon Spender (53), 08 Danny Williams, 18 Paul Mitchell ■, 11 Chris Llewellyn, 09 Lee McEvilly, 21 Marc Williams.

Subs: 13 Michael Jones (GK), 16 Levi Mackin, 17 Josh Johnson, 20 Matty Done (53), 27 Jamie Reed.

Hartlepool:
01 Dimitrios Konstantopoulos, 02 Micky Barron (65), 06 Ben Clark, 18 Gary Liddle, 08 Ritchie Humphreys ■, 35 Andy Monkhouse (75), 16 Lee Bullock, 15 Antony Sweeney, 20 James Brown, 11 Eifion Williams (56), 10 Richard Barker.

Subs: 03 Matty Robson (56), 21 Jim Provett (GK), 23 Darren Williams (65), 24 Ali Gibb (75), 28 David Foley.

Chris Llewellyn equalises for Wrexham.

Shots on Goal:	13	7
Shots on Target:	6	4
Shots off Target	7	3
Possession:	55%	45%
Fouls Conceded:	13	8
Corners:	6	5
Yellow Cards:	2	1
Red Cards:	0	0

The Wrexham players celebrate Simon Spender's opening goal

Coca Cola League 2: January 27th 2007

Darlington 1   Wrexham 1

Tommy Wright 45p   Simon Spender 31

Referee: Jon Moss (Yorkshire)
Attendance (Away): 3,301 (approx. 200)

Given the 'Dragons' dismal record on the road going into the game - six points (one win and three draws) from thirteen outings - nobody could really argue if you considered this a valuable point gained. But, on the other hand, you could also understand if someone took the attitude of it being two points lost, such was the number of opportunities that Brian Carey's side had to win the game.

The first half in particular saw the

'Dragons' rarely troubled, and not even the 14th minute injury to Steve Evans - that forced a reshuffle in the ranks, with Danny Williams dropping back into defence, and trainee Andy Fleming coming on for his first team debut - seemed to affect them unduly.

Indeed, Fleming appeared to grow in confidence the longer the game went on, and he certainly didn't look out of place. His tigerish determination and commitment earned him an early booking, but he didn't let it affect his style of play, and he delivered a performance that would suggest he has a bright future ahead of him.

Young striker Marc Williams tested Sam Russell with a 25-yarder early on, and with the 'Dragons' having made a promising start, the same player was unlucky to reach Simon Spender's pull back from a Ryan Valentine free kick.

Any disruption caused by the departure of Evans didn't surface, and it was no more than the 'Dragons' deserved when they took a 31st minute lead. Former Red, Neil Wainwright's clearance, was charged down by McEvilly, and Spender quickly latched onto the loose ball to slip it past Russell.

The Darlo keeper then denied Marc Williams with a smart backtracking save, before the home side finally managed to trouble Michael Ingham's goal in the closing minutes of the half. The 'Dragons' keeper saved from both Martin Smith and Mickey Cummins, but he was finally beaten in the fourth minute of added time when, despite vehement protests for offside, he was adjudged to have brought down Tommy Wright just inside the area, and Wright stepped up to score from the spot.

After an enterprising first half, the second was devoid of much goalmouth incident until the closing stages when the 'Dragons' pressed hard for a winner. Marc Williams just cleared the bar with one effort, and McEvilly failed to hit the target with another.

The introduction of Jamie Reed for the closing ten minutes gave the 'Dragons' fresh impetus, and the young striker had three opportunities to make a name for himself - two in injury time - but he couldn't force a winner.

Darlington:
23 Sam Russell, 18 Brian Close, 30 Dave Wheater, 04 Darren Holloway (46), 03 Craig James, 07 Neil Wainwright (77), 08 Mickey Cummins, 31 Ricky Ravenhill, 19 Martin Smith (87), 11 Julian Joachim, 27 Tommy Wright.

Subs: 01 David Stockdale (GK), 05 Patrick Collins (46), 25 Alun Armstrong (77), 26 Dave Rowson (87), 32 Shaun Reay.

Wrexham:
01 Michael Ingham, 02 Lee Roche, 04 Shaun Pejic, 05 Steve Evans (14), 03 Ryan Valentine, 14 Simon Spender (60), 08 Danny Williams, 18 Paul Mitchell, 11 Chris Llewellyn, 21 Marc Williams (81), 09 Lee McEvilly,

Subs: 13 Michael Jones (GK), 15 Mike Williams, 19 Andy Fleming (14), 20 Matt Done (60), 27 Jamie Reed (81),

Simon Spender opens the scoring for Wrexham

Shots on Goal:	3	10
Shots on Target:	2	4
Shots off Target	1	6
Possession:	50%	50%
Fouls Conceded:	16	13
Corners:	5	4
Yellow Cards:	0	2
Red Cards:	0	0

Loan star Robbie Garrett unleashes a shot at the County goal

Coca Cola League 2: January 30th 2007

Wrexham 0   Stockport County 1

Liam Dickenson 90

Referee: Andy Hall (West Midlands)
Attendance (Away): 4,060 (937)

With Wrexham seconds away from recording a third successive league draw, visitors Stockport County snatched all three points with virtually the last touch of the match. The score line was cruel on an industrious Wrexham side that had edged the game and deserved at least a point for their efforts.

The Dragons had started brightly and dominated the early exchanges. This set the tone for an entertaining game played at a high tempo, but good approach play from both sides was frequently let down by the final ball, as defences remained on top.

On loan Paul Mitchell and Robbie Garrett combined well in midfield, but Wrexham's wide players Llewellyn and Done were contained in the first half. McEvilly tested Hennessey in the Stockport goal with a shot that the keeper did well to hold, and County also went close when Ingham held well from a long range shot.

Wrexham had the best chance of the game as Done curled a corner into the near post for Mitchell to divert his header into the hands of Stockport's on loan Welsh keeper. Poole then broke clear of the 'Dragons' midfield to fire narrowly wide after the home defence had been slow in closing him down.

After the break Stockport began in positive fashion with a shot that flashed across the six-yard box and evaded the waiting strikers. Llewellyn took advantage of a mis-timed clearance, but fired disappointingly high. Another loan signing, Cherno Samba, made his Wrexham debut just before the half way point to replace Marc Williams.

Stockport's attacks were few in the second-half, but Ingham did well to parry a powerful shot from Poole and the Wrexham defence managed to clear the danger.

'The Dragons' seemed the team most likely to break the deadlock, and in the final ten minutes Done set up a chance for substitute Jamie Reed to fire over at the back post. Done delivered another excellent ball for Mitchell, who unfortunately lost his footing on the edge of the

six-yard box with the goal at his mercy. Ryan Valentine twice rescued Wrexham with well time blocks but they conceded one free kick too many in the final attack of the game. Substitute Liam Dickinson made the most of his short time on the pitch by heading in from close range after a deep cross was flicked on inside of the area.

Stunned silence marked the final whistle as the home fans looked on in disbelief, reflecting on how Wrexham had managed to throw a point away when they probably deserved all three.

Wrexham:
01 Michael Ingham, 02 Lee Roche, 04 Shaun Pejic, 08 Danny Williams ■, 03 Ryan Valentine, 11 Chris Llewellyn, 26 Robbie Garrett, 18 Paul Mitchell, 20 Matty Done, 09 Lee McEvilly (77), 21 Marc Williams (64).

Subs: 13 Michael Jones (GK), 15 Mike Williams, 19 Andy Fleming, 22 Cherno Samba (64), 27 Jamie Reed (77).

Stockport:
29 Wayne Hennessy, 02 Rob Clare, 06 Ashley Williams, 16 Gareth Owen, 03 Michael Rose (64), 26 David Poole, 20 Jason Taylor ■, 30 Stephen Gleeson, 24 Adam Griffin, 31 Adam Proudlock (64), 32 Anthony Elding (90).

Subs: 01 James Spencer (GK), 04 Tony Dinning, 09 Tesfaye Bramble (64), 10 Liam Dickinson (90), 21 Anthony Pilkington (64).

Matty Done fights off a tough challenge.

Shots on Goal:	16	7
Shots on Target:	7	4
Shots off Target	9	3
Possession:	51%	49%
Fouls Conceded:	19	11
Corners:	7	0
Yellow Cards:	1	1
Red Cards:	0	0

Stockport's keeper, Ricardo Batista, is sent off for kicking the ball into the crowd.

Coca Cola League 2: February 3rd 2007

Wrexham 0   Wycombe Wanderers 2

Mike Williamson 23
Jermaine Easter 52

Referee: Clive Oliver (Tyne & Wear)
Attendance (Away): 3,607 (141)

A disappointing display saw Brian Carey's side drop to next from bottom of the Football League. Two soft goals proved Wrexham's downfall, with the visitors goal only threatened for a late ten minute spell after the 'Chairboys' were reduced to ten men.

The first half was forgettable for Wrexham fans with the highlight being the mascot 'Wrex the Dragon's' banishment to the stands after his kit clashed with the home shirt and confused the linesman! It was really that bad as the 'Dragons' failed to direct a decent shot on target as Wycombe controlled the game and created the best openings.

The visitors took the lead midway through the first half. A free-kick was delivered deep into the box, and Mike Williamson got behind Steve Evans to loop a header over the stranded Ingham. Wycombe should have been celebrating a second following a powerful run by Grant down the right as he jinked past the static Wrexham defence, and picked out Jermaine Easter unmarked ten yards out, who took too long to shoot, and Ingham saved comfortably.

Wrexham won a couple of corners towards the end of the first half, but failed to test Ricardo Batista in the Wycombe goal, though Pejic soon after headed wide from Samba's free-kick.

Seven minutes after the restart, some poor defending saw Easter score his 21st goal of the season. Mooney flicked Grant's cross to an unmarked Easter who smashed the ball past the exposed Ingham.
Golbourne went close to making it 3-0 as his shot rebounded out off the far post after the Wycombe player was left unchallenged inside the Wrexham area.

Llewellyn had a rare opportunity for the home side, but his right footed shot from outside of the area was never really going to trouble Batista in the Wycombe goal. However, his two-footed challenge on Oakes soon after sparked a melee, and he was lucky to get away with a yellow card. McEvilly and Grant were also booked for

their part in the confrontation, but as the situation calmed down, Batista inexplicably blasted the ball into the crowd, and the keeper was show a straight red.

The home side played with more purpose against ten men for the final few minutes, with McEvilly twice going close and Danny Williams firing wide of the far post following a quickly taken Valentine free-kick.

There were six minutes of injury time, but like the ninety before it, Wrexham struggled to test the Wycombe defence, and left the pitch to a chorus of boos from the home fans.

Wrexham:
01 Michael Ingham, 02 Lee Roche ■, 04 Shaun Pejic ■, 05 Steve Evans, 03 Ryan Valentine, 26 Robbie Garrett, 18 Paul Mitchell (67), 08 Danny Williams, 22 Cherno Samba (53), 21 Marc Williams (45), 11 Chris Llewellyn ■.

Subs: 09 Lee McEvilly (45) ■, 13 Michael Jones (GK), 15 Mike Williams, 20 Matty Done (53), 27 Jamie Reed (67).

Wycombe:
31 Ricardo Batista ■, 04 Russell Martin, 06 Mike Williamson, 25 Sam Stockley ■, 18 Scott Golbourne, 10 Matt Bloomfield, 30 Anthony Grant (83) ■, 15 Tommy Doherty, 08 Stefan Oakes, 16 Tommy Mooney (76), 09 Jermaine Easter (65).

Subs: 26 Leon Crooks, 17 Scott McGleish (76), 19 Tony McParland, 22 Sergio Torres (83), 32 Jamie Young (GK) (65).

McEvilly powers a header towards goal

	Wrexham	Wycombe
Shots on Goal:	11	10
Shots on Target:	2	3
Shots off Target	9	7
Possession:	40%	60%
Fouls Conceded:	20	17
Corners:	2	3
Yellow Cards:	4	2
Red Cards:	0	1

Former Wrexham legends Darren Ferguson and Kevin Russell with new Wrexham manager Brian Carey

Coca Cola League 2: February 10th, 2007

Peterborough United 3   Wrexham 0

Aaron McLean 23
George Boyd 53
Steve Evans 82 (og)

Referee: PW Melin (Surrey)
Attendance (Away): 3,839 (291)

Wrexham came up against the new management team at London Road of former Racecourse Legends, Darren Ferguson and Kevin Russell.

Following Denis Smith's departure, many thought Ferguson was the obvious choice to take over, but with his playing career obviously nearing an end, he jumped at the chance of stepping into football man-agement with Peterborough United when offered.

However, he didn't have the best of starts, but he showed no mercy towards his former club as the 'Posh' won their first game in 12, much to the delight of 'Daz' and 'Rooster'.

Wrexham were disappointing to say the least; was it down to the fact that there seems to be a new unfamiliar face or two each week in Brian Carey's starting eleven. His search for players to ignite a spark in his team, this week saw the turn of 'keeper John Ruddy, and left-sided defender-cum-midfielder Scott Barron to introduce themselves to the travelling faithful. What they must have been thinking after this performance (or non-performance) is anyone's guess?

Neil Roberts and Mark Jones returned to the side after lengthy injury absences, and the opening exchanges didn't hint on what was going to happen later as the early impetus was actually with Wrexham. But Lee McEvilly wasted the one gilt-edged chance that came the 'Dragons' way during this period, ignoring Roberts who was better positioned to his left, and instead deciding to go it alone, only to run into former Red Craig Morgan.

Had we scored then, who knows what might have happened? And both managers were quick to testify after the game how important getting the first goal was. That goal came for the 'Posh' on 23 minutes, when Adam Newton was too hot for Mike Williams to handle on the 'Dragons' left, and his cross was deflected off Shaun Pejic into the path of Aaron McLean who

netted in convincing fashion.

McEvilly shot wide a few minutes later, but it was the home side that were now firmly on the front foot, and it was no surprise when George Boyd doubled their lead in the 53rd minute racing on to a long ball from Morgan, outpacing Steve Evans, and rifling the ball past Ruddy, and into the bottom right-hand corner of the net.

When Evans sliced a Newton cross into his own net eight minutes from time, the game was well and truly up, and the final whistle just couldn't come quickly enough. Another bad away day!

Peterborough:
01 Mark Tyler, 28 Craig Morgan, 04 Mark Arber, 03 Shane Blackett (90), 07 Adam Newtown, 06 Micah Hyde, 02 Josh Low, 08 Richard Butcher, 17 Jamie Day, 30 George Boyd (80), 14 Aaron McLean (80).

Subs: 12 Craig Mackail-Smith (80), 16 Danny Crow (80), 23 Ben Futcher (90), 29 Gavin Strachan, 31 Shwan Jalal (GK).

Wrexham:
33 John Ruddy, 14 Simon Spender, 04 Shaun Pejic (43), 05 Steve Evans, 15 Mike Williams, 07 Mark Jones (75) ■, 26 Robbie Garrett ■, 25 Scott Barron, 08 Danny Williams ■, 23 Neil Roberts (58), 09 Lee McEvilly.

Subs: 13 Michel Ingham (GK), 17 Josh Johnson (58), 20 Matty Done (43), 21 Marc Williams (75), 22 Cherno Samba.

Scott Barron makes his debut

Shots on Goal:	7	13
Shots on Target:	8	4
Shots off Target	3	4
Possession:	56%	44%
Fouls Conceded:	10	15
Corners:	4	1
Yellow Cards:	0	3
Red Cards:	0	0

Michael Carvill wrestles off Chester defender David Artell as he runs at goal

Coca Cola League 2: February 18th, 2007

Wrexham 0   Chester City 0

Referee: R.J.Beeby (Northampton)
Attendance (Away): 6,801 (1,775)

Wrexham climbed out of the relegation zone with a goalless draw at home to rivals **Chester in a midfield tussle that saw six yellow cards for the 'Cestrians' and one for the home side. Although, the score line was a fair reflection of the game, the 'Dragons' had dominated for long spells, but neither side displayed any real quality in front of goal.**

The first half was littered with free kicks and there were few chances for either side. Chris Llewellyn's early effort from

outside of the area, failed to find the target, while Robbie Garrett forced the first save of the game from John Danby midway through the first half. Making his home debut, John Ruddy was called into action, but comfortably held an effort from Simon Yeo after the striker had found space.

Mark Wright's side began to stretch the home defence, and a short back pass from Scott Barron almost caused problems, until Mike Williams managed to recover in time. Ruddy was then required to make two attempts to collect a Martinez corner, but overall both sides struggled to create any decent chances from open play.

There were no changes from either side at half-time, and so the stalemate continued after the break as neither side wanted to make the first mistake that could prove so costly, but it was Chester who won the first corner of the half on 55 minutes, and Ruddy claimed it well from Martinez's centre.

Another home debutant Andy Fleming was then replaced by Mike Carvill to try improve the home sides attacking options, but if anything, the change worked against Wrexham as Chester began to enjoy their best spell of the game, with Ruddy doing well to punch clear while under pressure from Kevin Sandwith's free-kick.

Mark Wright introduced Alex Meechan for Lee Steele, and their best opportunity of the game came soon after. Having forced a free-kick on the left, a quality cross found Sean Hessey who escaped his marker at the back post to see his header well saved by Ruddy as the 'Dragons' defence recovered to clear the danger.

Chris Llewellyn late on curled a right footed shot wide of the far post, but Marc Williams' left footed shot lacked the power to trouble Danby. A late free-kick was wasted by Wrexham as the three minutes of injury time concluded with the inevitable goalless draw.

Overall, a typical derby game with plenty of passion and endeavour in front of a good sized Sunday lunchtime crowd.

Wrexham:
33 John Ruddy, 14 Simon Spender, 05 Steve Evans, 24 Gareth Evans, 15 Mike Williams ■, 25 Scott Barron (85), 19 Andy Fleming (61), 08 Danny Williams, 26 Rob Garrett, 09 Lee McEvilly (85), 11 Chris Llewellyn.

Subs: 10 Michael Carvill (61), 13 Michael Ingham (GK), 20 Matty Done (85), 21 Marc Williams (85), 22 Cherno Samba.

Chester:
12 John Danby, 02 Simon Marples, 19 Paul Linwood ■, 05 Phil Bolland ■, 21 David Artell ■, 03 Kevin Sandwith, 16 Dean Bennett, 20 Roberto Martinez ■, 06 Sean Hessey (88) ■, 08 Simon Yeo (88) ■, 34 Lee Steele (67).

Subs: 11 Glenn Cronin, 14 Alex Meechan (67), 15 Graham Allen, 27 Chris Holroyd (88), 35 Alan Kearney (88).

Robbie Garrett shakes off Chester's Sean Hessey.

	Wrexham	Chester
Shots on Goal:	7	13
Shots on Target:	2	2
Shots off Target	7	1
Possession:	48%	52%
Fouls Conceded:	16	21
Corners:	4	5
Yellow Cards:	1	6
Red Cards:	0	0

Lee McEvilly opens the scoring for Wrexham at Blundell Park

Coca Cola League 2: February 20th, 2007

Grimsby Town 2   Wrexham 1

Paul Bolland 45   Lee McEvilly 28
Ciaran Toner 90

Referee: Andy Woolmer (Northamptonshire)
Attendance (Away): 5,850 (approx. 75)

Gutted! That's how the 'Dragons' felt after a valuable point was snatched away courtesy of Ciaran Toner's cruel winner deep into added time.

Having taken a 28th minute lead when McEvilly latched onto an under hit back pass - ironically by Toner - to score at the third attempt (having seen his first effort saved, and his second rebound off a post!) the 'Dragons' looked well set for a point

having conceded an equaliser deep into added-on time at the end of the first half.

But you have to ask if the defeat, coming so late in the game as it did, can really be classed as 'cruel'? Surely it can't be just coincidental - or damn right unfortunate - that we've conceded so many goals late on (both at the end of the first and second half) in recent weeks? Darlington, Stockport and now Grimsby (twice) have all scored goals in added time that have

---

cost us valuable points.

Given the situation we find ourselves in - in the relegation zone thanks to this defeat, and Boston's draw at Peterborough - maybe one of the problems is a tendency to drop back and look to hold onto what we've got, rather than look to push on and make things happen at the other end. Maybe then, we'd start turning one point into three points at the end of games rather than the other way round. That's how it looked at Blundell Park!

Both Mark Jones, and Mike Carvill, went close early on as Wrexham, looking to end the recent goal drought, started promisingly. But after the early enterprise didn't bring the much-needed goal, it was typical that when it did come, it came as a result of a defensive howler rather than from some deserving build-up play.

Wrexham deserved to be ahead, but were unable to increase their advantage, and as the half neared its end, it was Grimsby that began to dominate proceedings. Their pressure finally paying off when Paul Bolland, unmarked eighteen yards out, headed Danny Boshell's corner into the top corner.

The second half saw Grimsby generally

hold the upper hand, with several anxious moments around the Wrexham goal to keep the travelling fans biting their nails. It wasn't all one-way traffic though, and Mark Jones, Chris Llewellyn and Steve Evans all had chances to restore Wrexham's lead after the break.

But just when it looked that a hard-earned point had been secured, Matt Bloomer's cross was nodded down by substitute Gary Jones, and Toner smashed home the winner. Gutted!

Grimsby:
01 Phil Barnes, 29 Matthew Bloomer, 03 Tom Newey, 06 Justin Whittle, 05 Nick Fenton, 08 Paul Bolland, 16 Danny Boshell, 18 Peter Bore (77), 25 James Hunt (38), 10 Ciaran Toner, 14 Martin Patterson ■.

Subs: 02 John McDermott, 13 Robert Murray (GK), 19 Gary Jones (38), 22 Danny North (77), 24 Simon Grand.

Wrexham:
33 John Ruddy, 02 Lee Roche ■, 05 Steve Evans, 24 Gareth Evans, 03 Ryan Valentine, 07 Mark Jones ■, 08 Danny Williams, 26 Rob Garrett, 10 Mike Carvill, 09 Lee McEvilly (80) ■, 11 Chris Llewellyn ■.

Subs: 13 Michael Ingham (GK), 15 Mike Williams, 20 Matty Done, 21 Marc Williams, 22 Cherno Samba (80).

Mike Carvill tests the Grimsby keeper.

Shots on Goal:	7	15
Shots on Target:	3	6
Shots off Target:	4	9
Possession:	54%	46%
Fouls Conceded:	14	14
Corners:	3	4
Yellow Cards:	2	4
Red Cards:	0	0

Steve Evans receives his third red card of the season for a high elbow

Coca Cola League 2: February 25th, 2007

Wrexham 1   Shrewsbury Town 3

Danny Williams 55

Leo Fortune-West 8, 51
Derek Asamoah 38

Referee: Mike Dean (Wirral)
Attendance (Away): 5,605 (1,802)

Wrexham's season hit a new low following a comprehensive home defeat by local rivals Shrewsbury Town. This defeat left Wrexham in the relegation zone and without a win in 12 league games. Wrexham's problems were compounded when Steve Evans collected his third red card of the season.

With Jeff Whitely making his debut on loan from Cardiff City, Wrexham were still look-

ing for their first home victory of 2007.

It was the promotion chasing visitors who started strongly, forcing three corners in the opening minutes of the game. The lively Asamoah was a handful for the home defence and Shrewsbury took the lead after eight minutes as the former Chester City striker curled in a perfect ball to the far post for Leo Fortune-West to head past Ruddy.

Wrexham tried to muster a response and Garrett went close with a swerving shot that the Shrewsbury keeper failed to hold. Further pressure saw three corners in quick succession for the home side, with a Steve Evans header going narrowly over the bar. Shrewsbury looked threatening on the break and Asamoah doubled Shrewsbury's advantage seven minutes before half time as he raced clear to meet a ball played over the Wrexham defence, brushing aside Gareth Evans and Steve Evans before his low shot crept underneath keeper Ruddy.

Five minutes before half time Steve Evans challenged Fortune-West for a header and collected his third red card of the season for his high elbow, earning a five match ban.

Six minutes into the second half Shrewsbury put the game beyond doubt. David Edwards made a surging run down the left wing and his low cross found Asamoah, whose shot was spilled by Ruddy into the path of Fortune-West for an easy tap in at the far post.

Against the run of play, a stunning goal from Danny Williams gave Wrexham renewed confidence. Williams picked up the ball just outside the centre circle and

fired home from thirty yards into the top corner. Shrewsbury were clearly rocked and Wrexham increased the tempo with Mark Jones and Chris Llewellyn both going close to scoring.

Shrewsbury eventually regained their composure and went close to scoring a fourth late in the game when Fortune-West missed out on his chance of a hat trick when he headed wide at the far post.

Wrexham were well beaten by a lively and well organised Shrewsbury side and the home crowd left this local derby disappointed after a poor performance.

Wrexham:
33 John Ruddy, 02 Lee Roche, 05 Steve Evans ■, 08 Danny Williams ■, 24 Gareth Evans, 25 Scott Barron (52), 07 Mark Jones, 26 Robbie Garrett (61), 32 Jeff Whitley, 11 Chris Llewellyn ■, 23 Neil Roberts (74) ■.

Subs: 09 Lee McEvilly (74), 10 Mike Carvill (61), 13 Michael Jones (GK), 15 Mike Williams (52), 20 Matty Done.

Shrewsbury:
21 Chris Mackenzie, 12 Ben Herd, 05 Richard Hope (55), 28 Sagi Burton, 08 Kelvin Langmead, 23 Marc Tierney (46) ■, 19 Dave Edwards ■, 04 Stuart Drummond, 14 Ben Davies, 10 Derek Asamoah (83), 29 Leo Fortune-West.

Subs: 02 Daniel Hall (83), 03 Neil Ashton (46), 06 Lee Canoville, 07 Mike Jones (55), 31 Scott Shearer (GK).

Neil Roberts goes up for a header with Leo Fortune-West.

	Wrexham	Shrewsbury
Shots on Goal:	6	8
Shots on Target:	2	3
Shots off Target:	4	5
Possession:	49%	51%
Fouls Conceded:	8	13
Corners:	8	7
Yellow Cards:	4	2
Red Cards:	1	0

Mike Carvill takes a tumble against Newport County

Welsh Premier Cup Quarter Final: February 28th, 2007

Newport County 2   Wrexham 1

Jason Bowen 54p
Craig Hughes 57

Mike Carvill 52

Referee: Dean John (Swansea)
Attendance (Away): 733 (approx. 40)

Does it come much worse than this? Okay, so our recent record - no wins since before Christmas, a run stretching back 13 games - meant that we shouldn't have travelled to Spytty Park expecting an evening stroll and comfortable victory.

Given the predicament we find ourselves in the League, it was always likely that Brian Carey would ring the changes. But surely we'd still have enough about us to take another step towards another FAW Premier Cup Final appearance (and £100,000 first prize) against our Conference South opponents?

And just to rub it in even more, County even let us open the scoring early in the second half, before deciding to hit back with the two goals they needed to earn a home Semi-Final tie against Port Talbot Town. No, it really doesn't get much worse than this does it?

Indeed, when Carey was asked how this defeat would affect the players he said: "The players have been kicked and bruised in a mental sense a lot already. If you are asking me could it go any further? The answer to that is probably no." The thing is, if it's bad for the players, just think how bad it is for the fans!

Despite the negativity it would probably have all been so different had Mike Carvill, pouncing on uncertainty at the back, opened the scoring inside the first 30 seconds. Instead, his first effort was blocked and his second saved by the legs of keeper Marc Ovendale.

In difficult conditions and with the wind behind them, County rarely threatened in the opening period, though former Wales international Jason Bowen forced Michael Jones into a fingertip save just before the break.

Wrexham opened the scoring on 51 minutes. From a County free kick that struck the 'Dragons' wall, Levi Mackin picked out Carvill who brushed off a defender before composing himself and coolly slotting the ball to Ovendale's right and inside the far post.

Any thoughts that the hard work had now

been done were quickly dispelled, as virtually from the restart County attacked, Lee Roche bundled over Charlie Griffin inside the box and Bowen converted with the spot kick.

Five minutes later, embarrassment was a real possibility as Steve Jenkins crossed, Darren Garner nodded down, and Craig Hughes bundled the ball over the line from close range.

There was still plenty of time left in which to avoid humiliation, but in truth County looked the better side, and the more likely side to score again.

Newport:
01 Mark Ovendale, 02 Steve Jenkins, 03 Damon Searle, 04 Lee Collier, 05 John Brough, 06 Stewart Edwards, 07 Jason Bowen, 08 Darren Garner, 09 Charlie Griffiths, 10 Craig Hughes, 11 Richard Evans (90) ■.

Subs: 12 Ian Hillier (90), 13 Matthew Prosser, 14 Tyrone Toppar, 15 Kris Leek, 16 Jacob Giles (GK).

Wrexham:
13 Michael Jones, 02 Lee Roche, 04 Shaun Pejic, 15 Mike Williams, 03 Ryan Valentine, 07 Mark Jones (68), 16 Levi Mackin, 32 Jeff Whitley, 20 Matty Done, 09 Lee McEvilly, 10 Mike Carvill (90).

Subs: 05 Steve Evans, 14 Simon Spender, 17 Josh Johnson (90), 21 Marc Williams, 27 Jamie Reed (68).

Brian Carey reflects on another defeat.

Shots on Goal:	n/a	n/a
Shots on Target:	n/a	n/a
Shots off Target:	n/a	n/a
Possession:	n/a	n/a
Fouls Conceded:	n/a	n/a
Corners:	n/a	n/a
Yellow Cards:	1	1
Red Cards:	0	0

Neil Roberts out-jumps the Barnet defence and heads towards goal

Coca Cola League 2: March 3rd, 2007

Barnet 1   Wrexham 2

Oliver Allen 27   Lee McEvilly 57, 60

Referee: Ray Lee (Brentwood)
Attendance (Away): 2,180 (394)

In one afternoon in north London, **Wrexham fans experienced the full range of emotions possible for a follower of the 'beautiful game'.**

The first half, despite a display much improved from the dismal showing at Newport in midweek, ended with the 'Dragons' trailing to Oliver Allen's 27th minute goal.

That, coupled with the news that Boston had overturned a 1-0 deficit to lead 2-1 at MK Dons, left Wrexham followers sensing the worst at the interval. Let's face it, our away record didn't exactly hint at a stirring second half comeback, did it?

But come the end of the game, Lee McEvilly's superb double, and a couple of fantastic saves by Michael Ingham (back in the side in favour of loan signing John Ruddy after the latter's erratic display against Shrewsbury) had miraculously

---

given the 'Dragons' a vital victory - Brian Carey's first as manager.

The scenes of jubilation - on the pitch and on the terraces - at the final whistle, were totally understandable. To then hear over the tannoy that MK Dons had beaten Boston 3-2, as fans left the ground, made an already sweet moment even sweeter. It was a real roller coaster of emotions without a doubt. Such is life watching our beloved Wrexham FC!

Barnet had started well, and when Allen's shot proved too strong for Ingham to keep out, it was probably just about a deserved lead. Back came Wrexham, and McEvilly came near when he saw his free kick turned onto the bar by Ross Flitney. Dean Sinclair should have increased the 'Bees' lead on 38 minutes, but he headed Jason Puncheon's pinpoint cross over when it looked easier to score.

Sinclair's miss proved to be the turning point. With the slope to their advantage after the break Wrexham looked a totally different proposition, and equalised on 57 minutes. Chris Llewellyn did all the spadework, and fed McEvilly, who beat Flitney with a superb 25-yard shot that flew into the top corner. Three minutes

later and pandemonium ensued on the away terrace, as Llewellyn crossed from the left and McEvilly beat Flitney with a perfectly placed looping header.

Llewellyn could have wrapped up the points eight minutes from time, but his far post strike from McEvilly's teasing cross struck the upright and, as Wrexham once again started to fall deeper and deeper to protect the lead, the home side could have equalised on several occasions. Thankfully Ingham, in particular, stood firm and three very welcome points were heading back to north Wales.

Barnet:
01 Ross Flitney, 02 Nicky Bailey, 03 Simon King ■, 04 Ian Hendon (81), 05 Adam Gross, 07 Liam Hatch ■, 08 Dean Sinclair, 11 Richard Graham (75), 14 Ismail Yakubu, 20 Jason Puncheon, 28 Oliver Allen (79).

Subs: 09 Giuliano Grazioli, 15 Andy Hessenthaler (75), 16 Paul Warhurst, 21 Magno Vieira (79), 23 Barry Cogan (81).

Wrexham:
01 Michael Ingham, 15 Mike Williams, 04 Shaun Pejic, 08 Danny Williams (29), 02 Lee Roche, 11 Chris Llewellyn, 32 Jeff Whitley, 26 Robbie Garrett ■, 07 Mark Jones, 23 Neil Roberts, 09 Lee McEvilly.

Subs: 10 Mike Carvill, 33 John Ruddy (GK), 25 Scott Barron, 20 Matty Done, 24 Gareth Evans (29).

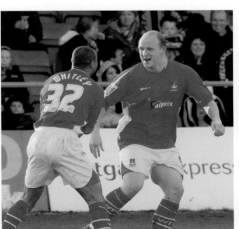

Lee McEvilly celebrates his two goals.

Shots on Goal:	12	10
Shots on Target:	8	6
Shots off Target	4	4
Possession:	35%	65%
Fouls Conceded:	19	14
Corners:	4	7
Yellow Cards:	2	1
Red Cards:	0	0

Ryan Valentine receives Wrexham's second red card following a lunging tackle

Coca Cola League 2: March 9th, 2007

Wrexham 1

Lee McEvilly 33

Bury 1

Glynn Hurst 90

Referee: Scott Mathieson
Attendance: 7,030 (544)

This heroic effort from a Wrexham team reduced to nine men following two red cards was warmly appreciated by the large Friday night crowd. 'The Red Dragons' came close to taking all three points, but were denied by an injury time equaliser from the 'Shakers' striker Glynn Hurst.

Wrexham started positively, but rarely threatened the visitors' goal. Bury looked dangerous from Dave Challinor's trade

mark long throws, but the home defence stood up well until the 'Shakers' increased the tempo after 20 minutes, with Glynn Hurst a constant threat and going close on several occasions.

It was Wrexham who opened the scoring against the run of play in the 32nd minute. Lee McEvilly started and finished the move, passing to Llewellyn on the left wing. Jones mis-controlled the ball into the path of McEvilly who fired low into the bottom corner from 10 yards. McEvilly almost doubled the lead before half-time when he combined well with Neil Roberts and flashed a superb twenty yard volley narrowly wide of the far post.

Bury should have equalised straight after the restart, but Andy Bishop fired over from the edge of the six-yard box after Ruddy failed to deal with a corner. The red mist then descended on Wrexham with Llewellyn receiving a red card for a two-footed lunge on Jason Kennedy. Nine minutes later Valentine received his marching orders following another lunging tackle.

The final half hour was a rearguard action, with Bury pressing forward and the 'Dragons' defence hanging on. Time after time the visitors missed golden chances, while the home side struggling to break forward, but youngster Robbie Garrett almost scored the goal of the season. The on-loan midfielder collected the ball just outside his own box, and ran 60-yards, skipping past challenges and going agonisingly close with a shot from the edge of the area that flew just over the bar.

The pressure continued on the Wrexham

goal with Ruddy making a brilliant save to deny Tony Bedeau. With four minutes of injury time signalled Bury scored the equaliser they deserved. From another one of Challinor's long throws, the ball rebounded into the path of Hurst who made no mistake by firing a shot past Ruddy at the near post.

It could have been worse for nine-man Wrexham, who were relieved to have gained another vital point in the fight to avoid relegation. The players received a standing ovation at the end from the 7,000 plus crowd who had appreciated the battling performance.

Wrexham:
33 John Ruddy, 02 Lee Roche, 04 Shaun Pejic, 24 Gareth Evans, 03 Ryan Valentine ■, 07 Mark Jones (64), 26 Robbie Garrett, 32 Jeff Whitley, 11 Chris Llewellyn ■, 23 Neil Roberts, 09 Lee McEvilly.

Subs: 10 Mike Carvill, 13 Michael Jones (GK), 15 Mike Williams (64), 16 Levi Mackin, 20 Matty Done.

Bury:
20 Andy Warrington, 02 Paul Scott ■, 05 Dave Challinor, 21 Darren Kempson, 03 Tom Kennedy, 18 Marc Pugh, 19 Jason Kennedy ■, 14 Richie Baker (84), 17 David Buchanan (64), 12 Andy Bishop, 28 Glynn Hurst.

Subs: 04 John Fitzgerald, 08 Nicky Wroe, 24 Jake Speight (84), 25 Tony Bedeau (64), 23 Andrew Parrish.

Chris Llewellyn sent off for a two-footed tackle.

Shots on Goal:	4	12
Shots on Target:	2	4
Shots off Target:	2	8
Possession:	53%	47%
Fouls Conceded:	11	17
Corners:	2	9
Yellow Cards:	0	2
Red Cards:	2	0

Lee Roche is sent off for handling the ball in the penality area.

Coca Cola League 2: March 17th, 2007

Milton Keynes Dons 2   Wrexham 1

Keith Andrews 38p   Lee McEvilly 12
Clive Platt 85

Referee: Keith Hill (Hertfordshire)
Attendance (Away): 5,712 (Approx 300)

I know it's easy to be diplomatic when you've been the beneficiary of some dodgy decisions, but MK Dons' manager Martin Allen's post-match comments certainly demonstrate why Wrexham fans were so irate with referee Keith Hill's performance at the National Hockey Stadium.

Talking about Lee Roche's handball that brought the 'Dons' their 38th minute equaliser from the penalty spot, and the defender's subsequent red card, Allen observed: "He handballed, and it was inside the box. But from where I was, one of our players kicked the ball, and at that moment in time it was probably going at about 177 miles an hour in about half a yard, and it hit the Wrexham player on the hand. How the bloke is supposed to get his hand out of the way of that I don't know, he'd have to be Steve Austin to do that." Enough said; and an honest assessment, though immaterial really as it didn't help our cause one bit!

Having taken a deserved 12th minute lead when Neil Roberts sprung the offside trap to run onto Jeff Whitley's through ball, and cross low for Lee McEvilly to steer the ball in at the far post, the 'Dragons' were making a mockery of the respective League positions.

But when you're on top to the extent that the 'Dragons' were, you need the second goal to rubberstamp your authority. It didn't come though, and thanks to the intervention of Mr Hill, Keith Andrews equalised from the spot, and Wrexham were left to play the final 52 minutes of the game with ten men - just a week having finished with nine men against Bury!

Level at half-time, it was always going to be an uphill struggle with a man short after the break, but despite not really threatening to regain the lead, the 'Dragons' battled away bravely against the in-form 'Dons', and deserved the luck that came their way on the odd occasion - notably when Gary Smith's spectacular effort crashed against the crossbar.

The non-stop pressure finally told five minutes from time - but again in contentious circumstances. Jon Hayes crossed and Clive Platt headed goalwards. Ingham appeared to have scooped the ball away before it crossed the line but, with the now customary celebratory music already blurting out over the speakers, Mr Hill awarded the goal. Did the music sway his decision? We'll never know!

Ingham then limped off injured, with Spender taking over in goal for the closing minutes as Wrexham finished with nine men for the second successive game.

Milton Keynes:
25 Lee Harper, 15 Gareth Edds (80), 04 Drissa Diallo, 06 Sean O'Hanlon, 03 Dean Lewington (75), 07 Jon-Paul McGovern (75), 14 Gary Smith, 13 Keith Andrews, 22 Lloyd Dyer ■, 09 Clive Platt, 10 Izale McLeod.

Subs: 12 Jude Stirling (80), 16 Leon Knight (75), 21 Jon Hayes (75), 31 Adolfo Baines (GK), 39 Sam Collins.

Wrexham:
01 Michael Ingham, 02 Lee Roche ■ ■, 04 Shaun Pejic, 08 Danny Williams (76), 15 Mike Williams, 14 Simon Spender, 26 Robbie Garrett (63) ■, 32 Jeff Whitley, 07 Mark Jones (87), 09 Lee McEvilly ■, 23 Neil Roberts,

Subs: 13 Michael Jones (GK), 16 Levi Mackin (63), 17 Josh Johnson (87), 20 Matty Done, 24 Gareth Evans (76).

Mark Jones races away from a Dons player.

	MK DONS	WREXHAM F.C.
Shots on Goal:	7	13
Shots on Target:	7	3
Shots off Target	8	3
Possession:	52%	48%
Fouls Conceded:	11	19
Corners:	5	3
Yellow Cards:	1	3
Red Cards:	0	1

Jeff Whitley is mobbed by his team mates after scoring the only goal of the game

Coca Cola League 2: March 24th, 2007

Bristol Rovers 0   Wrexham 1

Jeff Whitley 87

Referee: Ray Olivier (West Mids)
Attendance (Away): 5,209 (196)

The previous evening's results (Boston drawing at Wycombe, and Macclesfield's win at Mansfield) meant that those supporters that chose the delights of the Memorial Ground, rather than Croke Park for Wales' game against Ireland, travelled with a high degree of trepidation.

With a four-point gap having opened up between the 'Dragons' and the 'safety' of third-bottom in the League, this trip down the M5 really did take on the mantle of a 'must win' game.

That's why the celebrations that greeted both Jeff Whitley's 87th minute winner, and the final whistle, were so demonstrative. Even Brian Carey seemingly got carried away, running down the touchline towards the Wrexham fans a la Barry Fry and Jose Mourinho, the moment Whitley's header hit the back of the Rovers net.

You can bet the news of Whitley's decisive strike was also greeted in a rather different

---

manner by fans of those clubs also deep in relegation trouble - just as news of Boston and Macclesfield's results less than 24 hours earlier had with us!

All three of Carey's new signings - Anthony Williams, Richard Walker and Michael Proctor - were in the starting eleven, with Williams in particular standing out with a safe and assured display. It was a good game too, with chances at both ends, but it was the experienced Whitley that deservedly took the man of the match honours with an all-round display that would probably have won him the accolade even without his match-winning header.

With suspensions, injuries, and international call-up's depleting the ranks, and Rovers having had two wins in the previous week, the victory was even more impressive with Wrexham setting the tempo from the start. McEvilly headed a couple of corners over; and a Mark Jones shot was turned behind for a corner at the near post as the 'Dragons' probed for the crucial opening.

Anthony Williams safely handled everything that Rovers had to offer, and with the game goalless at the break there was still everything to play for.

The introduction of the lively Matty Done

proved a key moment, with the winger constantly proving a handful with his penetrating runs down the left. From one of his crosses McEvilly thumped a header against the bar, and Neil Roberts forced a decent save from Steve Phillips with an acrobatic shot from another.

Then came the moment all Wrexham fans had waited for. McEvilly's free kick wasn't the best, but Roberts kept the ball in play and found Shaun Pejic, who crossed for Whitley to stoop and head past Phillips from close range.

Bristol:
01 Steve Phillips, 32 Aaron Lescott, 05 Craig Hinton, 16 Samuel Oji, 11 Chris Carruthers, 26 Lewis Haldane, 07 Stuart Campbell, 20 Craig Disley, 04 Sammy Igoe (57), 19 Stuart Nicholson, 09 Richard Lambert (69).

Subs:03 Joe Jacobson, 27 Sean Rigg (57), 10 Richard Walker (69), 22 Chris Lines, 15 Byron Anthony.

Wrexham:
33 Anthony Williams, 14 Simon Spender, 22 Richard Walker, 04 Shaun Pejic, 15 Mike Williams, 07 Mark Jones (46), 08 Danny Williams, 32 Jeff Whitley, 22 Michael Proctor (69), 23 Neil Roberts, 09 Lee McEvilly.

Subs: 10 Michael Carvill (69), 13 Michael Jones, 16 Levi Mackin, 20 Matt Done (46), 24 Gareth Evans.

Brian Carey and Danny Williams celebrate victory.

	Bristol	Wrexham
Shots on Goal:	15	16
Shots on Target:	7	11
Shots off Target	8	5
Possession:	41%	59%
Fouls Conceded:	5	13
Corners:	10	5
Yellow Cards:	0	0
Red Cards:	0	0

Lee McEvilly fights off three Mansfield players for the ball

Coca Cola League 2: March 31st, 2007

Wrexham 0   Mansfield Town 0

Referee: Jarnail Singh (Middlesex)
Attendance (Away): 7,752 (266)

A single point from this dour encounter was sufficient to lift the 'Dragons' above Boston United on goal difference and out of the relegation zone. Defences dominated a game contested by two poor teams with few goalscoring opportunities.

Wrexham made two changes from the previous game with Jeff Whitley replaced by Robbie Garrett, Matty Done starting on the left wing and Mark Jones on the bench. Early in the game Neil Roberts

limped off to be replaced by Mike Carvill.

Done looked to have won a penalty as he burst past two Mansfield players on the edge of the area, but referee Singh waived play on. McEvilly did well to send Carvill clean through down the right channel, but the striker delayed his shot too long and was run out of play.

Mr Singh thankfully waived away Mansfield's penalty appeal when Brown went down following Mike Williams' challenge. Wrexham had another lucky escape on the half hour when goalkeeper Anthony Williams failed to clear the ball on the edge of the area, but Spender cleared a weak shot off the goal line. Done chased down a superb flick by Garrett following Spender's pass, and arrived at the ball to be fouled by goal-keeper Jason White. McEvilly took the resulting free kick and crashed a curling effort off the cross bar from a tight angle.

Wrexham started the second half well with Done supplying a good cross from the left but there was no 'Dragons' player able to get on the end of it. It was Mansfield who should have been cele-brating on the hour when Gritton missed an absolute sitter heading wide from six yards out, completely unmarked. This seemed to wake up the 'Dragons' fans who started to really get behind the team.

Mark Jones replaced Michael Proctor for the final twenty-five minutes as Wrexham pushed forward looking for the three points. Mike Williams delivered a low ball across the box and McEvilly went close to converting at the back post. During the four minutes of injury time, Mark Jones sent in a deep corner for McEvilly to head back towards goal and force an excellent save from White. In the dying seconds

Anthony Williams held a well struck shot from the edge of the area to keep another clean sheet.

The season's largest home crowd of almost 8,000 had responded in numbers to a discounted ticket offer, but they went home disappointed as Wrexham failed to capitalise.

Wrexham:
33 Anthony Williams, 14 Simon Spender (88), 04 Shaun Pejic, 22 Richard Walker, 15 Mike Williams, 18 Michael Proctor (65) ▪, 26 Robert Garrett, 08 Danny Williams ▪, 20 Matt Done, 09 Lee McEvilly, 23 Neil Roberts (05).

Subs: 02 Lee Roche (88), 07 Mark Jones (65), 10 Michael Carvill (05), 13 Michael Jones (GK), 24 Gareth Evans.

Mansfield:
01 Jason White ▪, 02 Johnny Mullins, 05 Jon Olav Hjelde (39), 06 Alex Baptiste, 03 Gareth Jelleyman ▪, 07 Matthew Hamshaw ▪, 14 Bryan Hodge, 08 Stephen Dawson (46), 11 Michael Boulding (78), 10 Simon Brown ▪, 20 Martin Gritton.

Subs: 09 Barry Conlon, 16 Nathan Arnold (78), 19 Carl Muggleton (GK), 21 Asa Charlton (39), 23 Danny Sleath (46).

Mike Carvill shoots at goal.

Shots on Goal:	7	13
Shots on Target:	1	1
Shots off Target	0	3
Possession:	52%	48%
Fouls Conceded:	10	10
Corners:	11	4
Yellow Cards:	2	4
Red Cards:	0	0

Mike Proctor is challenged on a depressing afternoon for the Dragons

Coca Cola League 2: April 7th, 2007

Macclesfield Town 2   Wrexham 0

Matt McNeil 34
John Murphy 62

Referee: Graham Salisbury (Lancashire)
Attendance (Away): 4,142 (1,786)

A sunny Easter Saturday, a large travelling support and something of a carnival-like atmosphere amongst Wrexham fans before the game, how typical then that the players spoilt everything with a dreadful performance?

The opening ten minutes or so were fairly encouraging. The remaining eighty minutes had us thinking that relegation to the Conference was more of a probability than a possibility.

Macclesfield may only have been two points ahead of us going into the game but their record since Paul Ince took over is more like that of play-off hopefuls, and they demonstrated how much they had improved under his leadership with a victory that was far more convincing than the 2-0 scoreline might suggest.

A defeat against one of our relegation rivals is never easy to take, especially so late in the campaign, but it was the manner of the defeat that made it worse. A win would have seen us take a massive step towards Football League safety. The defeat not only sees the relegation trap door lurk ominously behind us but also puts the home side five points clear and seemingly safe.

To put it simply, Wrexham were awful. "The fans were on our back and rightly so because they came here to watch a performance and we didn't deliver," was boss Brian Carey's verdict after the game. Over 1,700 travelling supporters - many taking advantage of the club's decision to put on around twenty free buses for the relatively short journey - will completely agree with his assessment!

Steve Evans, available again after completing his 5-match suspension, was kept on the bench with Carey keeping faith with on-loan Richard Walker. Whilst the decision may have looked merited beforehand, in hindsight it looked a costly one. That was proven when Evans replaced Walker on 67 minutes with Wrexham 2-0 down, a move that seemed more to do with keeping the score down and in so doing keeping us above Boston in the table on goal difference than it did an attempt to find a way back into the game.

It would probably have been too late any-

way. Matt McNeil played a one-two with John Mile on the edge of the area and rounded Anthony Williams to open the scoring on 34 minutes and John Murphy was unmarked at the far post to head in a Carl Regan cross for the second on 62 minutes. Simon Spender had Wrexham's only real chance of the afternoon when he latched onto a Lee McEvilly flick on to force a save from keeper Tommy Lee early in the second half. His reward was to be immediately substituted! It kind of summed up the afternoon!

Macclesfield:
13 Tommy Lee, 02 Carl Regan ■, 04 David Morley, 24 Robert Scott, 14 Kevin McIntyre, 17 Jordan Hadfield (83), 23 Adam Murray, 10 John Miles, 06 Martin Bullock (66), 09 Matty McNeil (71), 26 John Murphy,

Subs: 19 James Jennings, 27 Simon Wiles, 35 Ashan Holgate (83), 36 Isaiah Rankin (71), 37 Ronayne Benjamin (66),

Wrexham:
33 Anthony Williams, 14 Simon Spender (52), 15 Mike Williams, 67 Richard Walker (67), 04 Shaun Pejic, 02 Lee Roche, 32 Jeff Whitley, 20 Matt Done, 18 Michael Proctor (74), 09 Lee McEvilly, 07 Mark Jones.

Subs: 05 Steve Evans (67), 13 Michael Jones (GK), 16 Levi Mackin, 17 Josh Johnson, (74), 21 Marc Williams (52).

Lee McEvilly wins a header		
Shots on Goal:	7	12
Shots on Target:	7	4
Shots off Target:	6	8
Possession:	60%	40%
Fouls Conceded:	12	8
Corners:	9	3
Yellow Cards:	1	0
Red Cards:	0	0

The Wrexham players thank the fans for sticking by them

Coca Cola League 2: April 9th, 2007

Wrexham 0

Notts County 1

Spender 87 (og)

Referee: Darren Deadman (Cheshunt)
Attendance (Away): 4,557 (312)

Despite a more spirited performance, Wrexham slipped back into the relegation zone as a late own goal from the unfortunate Simon Spender allowed the play off chasing 'Magpies' to steal the points, leaving the 'Red Dragons' to curse their luck.

The home side made three defensive changes from the side that had underperformed against Macclesfield Town, with Lee Roche, Mike Williams and Richard Walker all dropped. Chris Llewellyn

returned up front, with Michael Proctor reverting to the right, and Simon Spender filling the position vacated by Roche.

Wrexham dominated the opening period without really threatening. The best chance of the game coming midway through the first half when Ryan Valentine delivered a deep cross from the left that Lee McEvilly headed back across goal for Llewellyn, who looped his header onto the top of the bar. The bad luck continued when an injury to Mark Jones saw him

---

replaced by Levi Mackin just before the break.

Following the interval, the 'Dragons' began playing with a lot more endeavour. McEvilly went close with a dipping right foot shot from the edge of the area. Valentine's composure saved a certain goal, when he headed out a deep cross from underneath the bar. Wrexham began to exert greater control following the intro-duction of Josh Johnson for Proctor, and looked dangerous from set plays. McEvilly went close with a free kick following a foul on Mackin, but his right-footed effort from the edge of the area curled harmlessly over the bar.

Jeff Whitley went even closer midway through the second half as a flowing move involving Matty Done down the left creat-ed the shooting opportunity for Whitley, but his shot from the edge of the area cannoned off the angle of the post and bar. A good penalty appeal was then turned down when Steve Evans appeared to be pushed in the box.

Despite the home sides valiant efforts, Notts County struck a cruel blow with just two minutes remaining. Evans looked to have been in control of the situation, but his misdirected clearance allowed Jay Smith to pick out James Walker, who fired the ball across goal for the in-running Simon Spender to inadvertently turn the ball into his own net. There was almost time for Evans to almost snatch a late equaliser as he almost turned in a way-ward McEvilly shot during injury time.

A stunned silence echoed around the Racecourse as the news of Boston's 4-1 lead over Macclesfield sank in, and the sound of the final whistle was greeted with disbelief as Wrexham slipped back into the relegation zone following two back to back defeats over the Easter weekend.

Wrexham:
33 Anthony Williams, 14 Simon Spender, 04 Shaun Pejic, 05 Steve Evans, 03 Ryan Valentine ■, 18 Michael Proctor (58), 32 Jeff Whitley, 07 Mark Jones (40), 20 Matt Done, 09 Lee McEvilly ■, 11 Chris Llewellyn (84).

Subs: 13 Michael Jones (GK), 15 Mike Williams, 16 Levi Mackin (40), 17 Josh Johnson (58), 21 Marc Williams (84)

Notts County:
01 Kevin Pilkington, 12 Gary Silk, 04 Mike Edwards, 18 Stephen Hunt, 03 Austin McCann, 27 Jay Smith ■, 06 Matthew Somner, 24 Ian Ross (54), 07 James Walker, 10 Lawrie Dudfield (72), 11 Andy Parkinson (52).

Subs: 23 Saul Deeney (GK), 09 Jason Lee (54), 21 Michael Byron, 17 Myles Weston (52), 15 Tcham N'Toya (72).

Chris Llewellyn chases the ball.

Shots on Goal:	8	3
Shots on Target:	0	0
Shots off Target	8	3
Possession:	53%	47%
Fouls Conceded:	14	13
Corners:	7	2
Yellow Cards:	2	1
Red Cards:	0	0

The Wrexham fans celebrate an emphatic victory over Lincoln City

Coca Cola League 2: April 14th, 2007

Lincoln City 0

Wrexham 3

Simon Spender 18
Scott Kerr 29 (og)
Lee McEvilly 52

Referee: Tony Bates (Staffordshire)
Attendance (Away): 4,279 (245)

Easter Monday's results had certainly put Boston in the driving seat in the race to avoid the second relegation spot. They'd also created a severe sense of doom and gloom amongst Wrexham fans in the five days leading up to this meeting with the fifth-placed Imps.

But the reaction of the players after Monday's game, when many slumped to the turf on hearing the final whistle, suggested that (finally) they'd realised the precarious situation we're in. We'll never know if that was the case but suffice to say this display at Sincil Bank was as far removed from the dismal display the previous Saturday at Macclesfield as it possibly could be.

From the opening kick-off when Jeff Whitley won possession and brought a save from Alan Marriott inside 12 seconds the

Dragons looked a side that wasn't going to accept anything other than victory. It was also a triumphant afternoon for Simon Spender, who scored the first and had a hand in the other two goals to help banish the memories of his unfortunate own goal against County.

Whitley's opening gambit led the way for a resurgent and confident display that was rewarded with an opening goal on 17 minutes. Matty Done swung over a corner from the right and Spender's looping header found the top left-hand corner of the net.

With Boston playing what many considered to be a very winnable game at Hereford this was just the start the Dragons needed. Almost immediately Michael Proctor was only denied by a last-ditch tackle, and headed over from the resulting corner, as Wrexham pressed again. And the enterprising start was rewarded for a second time on 20 minutes when Spender delivered a long-throw from the right towards the near post, Danny Williams flicked on, and Scott Kerr's head inadvertently diverted the ball into the net.

The home side responded, as you would expect by a side stung by the two-goal deficit, but the Wrexham rearguard were in an obstinate mood and showed a real determination not to let the Imps back into the game. The foundations laid by the defence enabled the attack to grow in confidence and the game was effectively killed off with a third goal in the 52nd minute. Chris Llewellyn returned a short throw to Spender's feet and Lee McEvilly met the full back's accurate cross with a clinical downward header into the bottom left-hand corner of Marriott's net.

The celebrations could begin in earnest, boosted by the news that Hereford were winning 3-0 and Boston's goal difference advantage from Monday had not only been wiped out but also overturned. Out of the relegation zone again. Phew!

Lincoln:
01 Alan Marriott, 12 Nicky Eaden, 02 Lee Beevers (46), 03 Paul Mayo ■, 06 Paul Green, 11 Scott Kerr ■, 14 Ryan Amoo, 17 Peter Holmes (46), 24 Jeff Hughes, 09 Mark Stallard, 22 Jamie Forrester (77).

Subs: 05 Paul Morgan (46), 08 Dany N'Guessan (46), 10 Junior Mendes (77), 20 Owain Warlow, 21 Robert Olejnik (GK).

Wrexham:
33 Anthony Williams, 14 Simon Spender, 05 Steve Evans, 04 Shaun Pejic, 03 Ryan Valentine, 11 Chris Llewellyn, 08 Danny Williams (81) ■, 32 Jeff Whitley, 20 Matty Done (82), 09 Lee McEvilly, 18 Michael Proctor (86) ■.

Subs: 13 Michael Jones (GK), 15 Mike Williams (82), 16 Levi Mackin (81), 17 Josh Johnson (86), 21 Marc Williams.

The players celebrate Simon Spender's opener.

	Lincoln	Wrexham
Shots on Goal:	7	13
Shots on Target:	1	7
Shots off Target	6	6
Possession:	50%	50%
Fouls Conceded:	12	17
Corners:	6	6
Yellow Cards:	3	2
Red Cards:	0	0

Matty Done fends off a challenge from Matt Hockley

Coca Cola League 2: April 21st, 2007

Wrexham 1   Torquay United 0

Neil Roberts 79

Referee: Russell Booth (Nottinghamshire)
Attendance (Away): 6,057 (74)

Wrexham recorded their first home league win of 2007 in a close encounter against a bottom placed Torquay side already relegated to the Conference. A late goal from Neil Roberts gave Wrexham their first back to back league wins of the season and kept alive our hopes of avoiding relegation.

Fielding an unchanged starting line up from the previous weeks emphatic win at Lincoln, the first half saw Wrexham enjoy plenty of possession but unable to convert their opportunities, with good early chances falling to Llewellyn, McEvilly and Danny Williams.

Playing a high tempo game, Williams and Whitley dominated the midfield with Done and Llewellyn providing width and Proctor enjoying another fine attacking display for the reds.   Done was unlucky not to win a penalty after 20 minutes when he appeared to be pulled back by Andrews, but the referee waved away the home side's protests.

Towards the end of the half, Wrexham began to tire and the visitors enjoyed more possession, with Hockley coming close with a shot fired wide of the Wrexham goal. In the closing minutes of the half further chances fell to Llewellyn, who came close to converting a deep cross from Proctor but was denied by an excellent save by Rayner pushing his effort around the post, and McEvilly who headed over from the resultant corner.

The second half was less entertaining, with Wrexham playing more directly but wasting possession with some wayward long balls. After an hour, Carey decided that changes were required and replaced the busy Proctor with club captain Neil Roberts, much to the distain of the home crowd, who clearly felt that the less effective McEvilly should have been sacrificed instead.

The presence of Roberts paid dividends almost straight away, as he set up McEvilly with a clever flick, only for the burly striker to shoot straight at the Torquay keeper. A spectacular 25 year

volley from Whitley then smashed against the Torquay crossbar with the keeper well beaten. Revitalised, Wrexham pushed forwards looking for the winning goal. Llewellyn set the much improved Spender free down the right wing and a measured cross to the near post was neatly turned in by substitute Neil Roberts, evading his marker.

Not an easy game by any stretch of the imagination, but a timely victory giving the reds 3 vital points in the hunt for league survival, particularly following the news that relegation rivals Bury and Boston had both won their games

Wrexham:
33 Anthony Williams, 14 Simon Spender, 05 Steve Evans, 04 Shaun Pejic, 03 Ryan Valentine, 18 Michael Proctor (60), 32 Jeff Whitley, 08 Danny Williams (90), 20 Matty Done, 09 Lee McEvilly, 11 Chris Llewellyn.

Subs: 13 Michael Jones (GK), 15 Mike Williams, 16 Levi Mackin (90), 17 Josh Johnson, 23 Neil Roberts (60).

Torquay:
01 Simon Rayner, 02 Lee Andrews, 18 Steve Woods, 23 Chris Robertson, 30 Mark Robinson, 26 David Graham, 04 Matt Hockley, 10 Lee Mansell, 15 Stephen Cooke, 09 Lee Thorpe ■, 19 Chris McPhee (85).

Subs: 11 Kevin Hill, 17 Stevland Angus, 20 Martin Horsell (GK), 27 Ryan Dickson (90), 28 Reuben Reid (85).

Steve Evans challenges Gulls keeper Simon Rayner.

	Wrexham	Torquay
Shots on Goal:	10	5
Shots on Target:	7	3
Shots off Target:	3	2
Possession:	55%	45%
Fouls Conceded:	14	13
Corners:	4	2
Yellow Cards:	0	1
Red Cards:	0	0

Simon Spender celebrates the cross that led to Proctor's goal

Coca Cola League 2: April 24th, 2007

Shrewsbury Town 0   Wrexham 1

Michael Proctor 79

Referee: A D'Urso (Essex).
Attendance (Away): 6,749 (1,418)

Our rivalry with Shrewsbury will never be as great as that with Chester, much to the annoyance of our rivals from over the Shropshire border. But even so, there can rarely have been a more important, or celebrated derby victory than this, whoever it was against.

With news filtering through from Moss Rose that Macclesfield were trailing at home to Bristol Rovers, and this game still locked in a goalless stalemate, the fans knew that a goal would see the 'Dragons' move three points clear of Boston, and a point ahead of both Macclesfield and Accrington. 20th place had never looked so good!

So the stakes were high. But, and it was a big but, a goal was still needed. That's where Michael Proctor came in. The on-loan striker's performances had improved game-by-game since his debut against Bristol Rovers, and with just over ten minutes remaining he popped up with the goal that sent the travelling fans into total delirium!

The play-off chasing 'Shrews' had looked the more controlled side in the first half, but with the Wrexham defence again outstanding, it's difficult to recall any occasion when they really threatened to break the deadlock, other than one moment when a Ryan Valentine clearance hit Steve Evans, and fortunately flew over his own bar.

Having weathered the predicted early storm, Wrexham gradually put more and more of a foothold on the game, and had strong appeals for a penalty turned down when Lee McEvilly looked to be held down by defender as he tried to attack a Simon Spender long throw.

Chris Llewellyn wasted a couple of good openings as the 'Dragons', and the boisterous travelling support, started believing that maybe, just maybe, it could just be our night, and that a crucial blow could be dealt our relegation rivals.

Then it came, our last ever goal at the Gay Meadow, and almost certainly our most important. Again the impressive Spender was the instigator with a pass to

Danny Williams. His cross was headed down by Proctor, and Spender, who'd continued his run into the box, took a couple of touches before returning the ball to the striker who smashed the ball into the net from about ten yards out.

Llewellyn could have made the game safe late on, but by then the celebrations were in full swing, and the 'Dragons' had taken an enormous stride towards safety. What a night! What a journey home!

Don't you just love football?

Shrewsbury:
31 Scott Shearer, 25 Luke Jones, 08 Kelvin Langmead, 05 Richard Hope (83), 23 Marc Tierney, 14 Ben Davies, 19 Dave Edwards, 04 Stuart Drummond, 03 Neil Ashton, 09 Andy Cooke (71), 10 Derek Asamoah.

Subs: 18 Steve Leslie, 21 Chris MacKenzie, 24 Michael Symes (71), 28 Sagi Burton, 29 Leo Fortune-West (83).

Wrexham:
33 Anthony Williams ,14 Simon Spender, 05 Steve Evans, 04 Shaun Pejic, 03 Ryan Valentine ■, 18 Michael Proctor ■, 08 Danny Williams, 32 Jeff Whitley, 11 Chris Llewellyn ■, 09 Lee McEvilly, 23 Neil Roberts.

Subs: 02 Lee Roche, 13 Michael Jones (GK), 15 Mike Williams, 20 Matty Done, 26 Robbie Garrett.

Mike Proctor goes in for a tackle.

Shots on Goal:	4	6
Shots on Target:	3	4
Shots off Target:	1	2
Possession:	53%	47%
Fouls Conceded:	13	19
Corners:	4	2
Yellow Cards:	0	3
Red Cards:	0	0

Ryan Valentine dances down the wing!

Coca Cola League 2: April 28th, 2007

Walsall 1   Wrexham 0

Ishmel Demontagnac 61

Referee: Clive Penton (Sussex)
Attendance (Away): 7,057 (1,369)

In a game of two contrasting halves, the 'Dragons' fought back against the league leaders to earn a deserved point after going a goal behind. Overall, there was little to choose between the two teams with Wrexham not looking out of their depth against a Walsall team five points clear at the top of League Two.

Injuries and suspension left Denis Smith needing to make three changes from the side beaten comprehensively at Boston.

With Steve Evans suspended after his sending off Mike Williams moved to centre back and Ryan Valentine replaced him at left back. Matty Done and Marc Williams came into the side replacing Levi Mackin and Kevin Smith.

Walsall started the game the brighter and set the tone for the first half. Ingham was a spectator as he watched Kris Taylor curl a free kick narrowly wide of the near post. Wrexham's best effort in the first half was from Matty Done who shot wide following a lay off by Chris Llewellyn.

The opening goal came from a corner that the Wrexham defence failed to deal with effectively. Gerrard won the initial header and Hector Sam, in the six-yard box, flicked this in. He kept a promise that he had made to supporters of his former club as he refused to celebrate his goal. He then came close to extending the 'Saddlers' lead, but he failed to connect with a corner at the back post.

The second half started in the same vein as the first until the introduction of Lee McEvilly. The burly striker began to terrorise the Walsall defence and it was no surprise when cracks started to appear. The equaliser came when Marc Williams skipped past his marker on the left touchline, and quickly raced to the edge of the area. He showed great composure in laying the ball back for Llewellyn to whip in a great finish from inside of the 'D', giving Clayton Ince no chance of saving at his near post.

Wrexham then dominated proceedings for the final twenty minutes, and almost took the lead when Pejic connected powerfully with a Ferguson corner.

The 'Saddlers' could have been celebrat-

ing an undeserved winner in the last minute when they broke quickly down the Wrexham right. A cross was swung into the far post, but Wright completely missed his header despite being unmarked.

The last chance of the match fell to Wrexham deep into injury time when McEvilly volleyed inches wide from Llewellyn's cross, but overall the score line was a fair reflection of a decent game of football.

Walsall:
01 Clayton Ince, 11 Tony Bedeau (51), 05 Chris Westwood, 04 Anthony Gerrard, 03 Daniel Fox, 20 Ishmel Demontagnac (70), 08 Martin Dobson, 12 Dean Keates, 14 Mark Wright, 09 Martin Butler, 30 Trevor Benjamin (64).

Subs: 02 Craig Pead (51), 07 Darren Wrack (70), 10 Hector Sam (64), 27 Emmanuele Smith, 41 Bertrand Bossu (GK).

Wrexham:
33 Anthony Williams, 14 Simon Spender, 04 Shaun Pejic, 05 Steve Evans, 03 Ryan Valentine, 18 Michael Proctor, 32 Jeff Whitley, 08 Danny Williams, 11 Chris Llewellyn, 23 Neil Roberts (89), 09 Lee McEvilly (68).

Subs: 10 Mike Carvill (89), 13 Michael Jones (GK), 15 Mike Williams, 20 Matt Done (68), 26 Robbie Garrett.

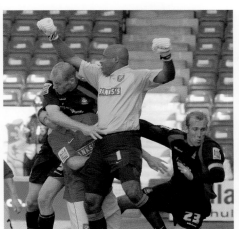

Steve Evans and Neil Roberts challenge Clayton Ince.

Shots on Goal:	10	12
Shots on Target:	2	3
Shots off Target:	8	9
Possession:	45%	55%
Fouls Conceded:	10	15
Corners:	4	3
Yellow Cards:	0	0
Red Cards:	0	0

Ryan Valentine's penalty sets Wrexham on the way to securing its Football League status

Coca Cola League 2: May 5th, 2007

Wrexham 3

Ryan Valentine 56p
Chris Llewellyn 87
Michael Proctor 90

Boston United 1

Francis Green 39

Referee: Mark Halsey (Lancashire)
Attendance (Away): 12,374 (684)

I n a game billed as the most important in the clubs history, the season's final fixture saw a nervous Wrexham needing a single point to secure their league status and condemn Boston United to relegation to the Conference. The biggest league crowd for over 25 years witnessed a tense encounter but the Racecourse faithful were eventually rewarded with a crucial and memorable victory.

The visitors enjoyed the better of a poor first half, creating several good chances and looking dangerous from set plays. Striker Drew Broughton, on loan from Chester, was a constant threat. The Wrexham midfield, weakened by the unexplained absence of Jeff Whitley, failed to impose themselves, with only the lively Matty Done and the combative Ryan Valentine emerging with credit. It was no surprise when Boston took the lead 6 minutes before the interval, a through ball caught out the static Wrexham defence and Francis Green raced clear to slot the ball home inside the far post.

This seemed to galvanise the home supporters, responding with increased noise levels and applauding the team off the pitch at half time. But as 500 Boston fans celebrated, there was no disguising the home fans concerns, with only 45 minutes remaining to ensure league survival.

Following Brian Carey's half time talk, a much livelier Wrexham team put Boston under sustained pressure. The home side won a penalty in the 57th minute as Danny Williams was pushed following a Matty Done corner. Ryan Valentine confidently placed the penalty to Marriott's left, with the ex Wrexham keeper diving the wrong way in front of the packed kop. The Racecourse erupted into a noisy celebration. With just 11 minutes remaining Ellender missed a golden opportunity to restore Boston's advantage following a goal mouth scramble, as he fired his shot high into the stand from just 6 yards.

With 3 minutes left, Chris Llewellyn made it 2-1. Cutting in from the right touchline

he hammered a low shot inside the near post, throwing his shirt into the crowd in celebration. Two minutes later, wearing a replacement shirt borrowed from a supporter, Llewellyn improvised a clever back heel cross for Proctor to seal the victory with a well placed header.

The ensuing pitch invasion and celebration showed how much this victory meant to Wrexham's supporters. As the Racecourse slowly emptied after another emotional day, this eventful season ended on a high note. Wrexham could look forward to another season in league football.

Wrexham:
33 Anthony Williams, 14 Simon Spender, 04 Shaun Pejic, 05 Steve Evans, 03 Ryan Valentine ■, 11 Chris Llewellyn ■, 07 Mark Jones, 08 Danny Williams, 20 Matty Done, 18 Michael Proctor, 23 Neil Roberts (84).

Subs: 02 Lee Roche, 09 Lee McEvilly (84), 13 Michael Jones (GK), 15 Mike Williams, 16 Levi Mackin.

Boston:
01 Andy Marriott, 20 Jamie Stevens ■, 24 Colin Cryan, 05 Mark Greaves, 16 Jamie Clarke, 04 Paul Ellender, 23 Ernie Cooksey, 15 David Farrell, 14 David Galbraith (75), 09 Drewe Broughton, 10 Francis Green.

Subs: 06 Mark Albrighton, 07 Brad Maylett (75), 22 Ben Nunn, 27 Adam Rowntree.

Chris Llewellyn celebrates Wrexham's second goal.

Shots on Goal:	11	5
Shots on Target:	4	3
Shots off Target	7	2
Possession:	52%	48%
Fouls Conceded:	11	15
Corners:	10	7
Yellow Cards:	2	1
Red Cards:	0	0

Players' Appearances & Goals

Player	Appearances in league and cup competitions					
	Lge	LC	FAC	JPT	PC	Tot
Barron, Scott	3					3
Carvill, Mike	1/6				1	2/6
Craddock, Tom	1					1
Crowell, Matt	10/5	2	1	1		10/5
Done, Matty	26/7	1	2	1	1	31/7
Evans, Gareth	9/3	0/2				9/5
Evans, Steve	34/1	1	3	1		39/1
Ferguson, Darren	19/1	1	3			23/1
Fleming, Andy	1/1					1/1
Garrett, Rob	10					10
Ingham, Mike	31	2	3	1		37
Johnson, Josh	10/12	1	1/1	1		13/13
Jones, Mark	30/1	2	2	1	1	36/1
Jones, Michael	1				1	2
Lawrence, Dennis	3					3
Llewellyn, Chris	39	2	2	1		44
Mackin, Levi	1/6	0/2	0/1		1	2/9
McAliskey, John	3	1				4
McEvilly, Lee	18/10		1/1		1	20/11
Mitchell, Paul	5					5
Molango, Maheta	3		1			4
Morgan, Craig	1			1		2
Newby, Jon	2/9	0/1		0/1		2/11
Pejic, Shaun	33	1	3		1	33
Proctor, Michael	9					9
Reed, Jamie	0/4				0/1	0/5
Roberts, Neil	17/2	1				18/2
Roche, Lee	26/2	1/1	2		1	30/3
Ruddy, John	5					5
Samba, Cherno	1/2					1/2
Smith, Kevin	5/3		2			7/3
Spender, Simon	23/2	1				24/2
Ugarte, Juan	0/2		0/1			0/3
Valentine, Ryan	32/2	1	1	1	1	36/2
Walker, Richard	3					3
Whitley, Jeff	11				1	12
Williams, Anthony	9					9
Williams, Danny	40	2	3	1		46
Williams, Marc	11/5		0/1			11/6
Williams, Mike	20/11	2	3	1	1	27/11

Goals in league and cup competitions					
Lge	LC	FAC	JPT	PC	Tot
					0
				1	1
1					1
			1		1
1	1				2
					0
2					2
					0
					0
					0
					0
1					1
5	1	1			7
					0
					0
9	2				11
					0
					0
7		1			8
					0
					0
					0
					0
					0
2					2
					0
3	1				4
					0
					0
					0
1		1			2
2					2
					0
2					2
					0
1					1
					0
3		1			4
1					1
					0

Player of the Season:
Steve Evans

Young Player of the Season:
Matt Done

Leading Goalscorer:
Chris Llewellyn (9)

Ever Present: 0

Coca Cola League 2 Results 2006/07

No	Date	Att	Pos Pl	F-A	H-T	Scorers, Times, and Referees
1	A WYCOMBE 5/8	4,763	- / -	1-1	1-1	Jones Ma 32 / Mooney 6 / Ref: P Miller
2	H GRIMSBY 8/8	5,180	W 6/13	3-0	2-0	Evans 16, Llewellyn 34, Done 68 / Ref: D Whitestone
3	H PETERBORO 12/8	4,706	D 10/3	0-0	0-0	Ref: A Taylor
4	A CHESTER 20/8	4,206	W 6/12	2-1	1-0	Roberts 42p, Jones Ma 52 / Hand 81 / Ref: U Rennie
5	H BARNET 26/8	4,304	D 7/17	1-1	1-0	Jones Ma 15 / Kandol 62 / Ref: A Woolmer
6	H SWINDON 9/9	5,257	W 6/1	2-1	0-1	Valentine 68p, Jones Ma 69 / Brown 28 / Ref: S Mathieson
7	A ACCRINGTON 13/9	2,689	L 9/16	0-5	0-1	[52, 67, Cavanagh 55] Mullin 41, Craney 49, Roberts / Ref: C Oliver
8	A STOCKPORT 16/9	4,884	L 12/20	2-5	1-2	[85, 87] Williams D 43, 61, Robinson 24p, Le Fondre 24, 54 Ruddy / Ref: R Olivier
9	H HEREFORD 24/9	4,705	W 10/12	1-0	1-0	Evans S 28 / Ref: P Joslin
10	H ROCHDALE 27/9	3,577	L 12/16	1-2	1-0	Llewellyn 12 / Dagnall 48, 77 / Ref: S Bratt
11	A HARTLEPOOL 30/9	4,452	L 15/7	0-3	0-2	Daly 20, 22, 68 / Ref: G Sutton

Match reports

1. Paul Lambert's side's dominant start saw Tommy Mooney slot in Chris Palmer's cross, but Ricardo Batista fluffed a clearance under Roberts' challenge, chased the ball to allow Jones to curl the ball 40-yds into an empty net. The Dragons had their share of possession.

2. Having seen a header cleared off the line early on Evans headed in Ferguson's cross. Ingham nearly gifted Grimsby an equaliser, but Llewellyn's long-range header from Ferguson's cross doubled the lead. A great run by Llewellyn led to Matty Done firing in.

3. Both sides kept their unbeaten records at a blustery Racecourse. The Dragons went closest when Llewellyn hit the bar & Roberts had a shot cleared off the line. Dean Holden & Richard Butcher went close for the Posh. Crowell almost won it late on when his free-kick hit the Posh bar

4. A lively game that saw Ravenhill sent off (25) for a rash challenge on Ingham. Wrexham were down to nine Welsh players led when Vaughan brought down Done for Roberts to net. Jones lobbed Danby; Steve Evans was dismissed for a 2nd caution (77); James Hand fired in as Chester rallied.

5. Tresor Kandol's close range header from Barry Cogan's cross saw the 'Bees' secure a point in an ill-tempered game that saw seven booked as the Dragons struggled to find any rhythm. Jones had Wrexham ahead with a 20-yard strike, but Kandol & Grazioli went close to winning it

6. Denis Wise's side looked set for their 7th straight win when Paul Evans's 35-yard free-kick found the net as Ingham was caught napping. The Dragons hit back when Llewellyn was floored by Brezovan & Valentine fired in the penalty. Mark Jones drilled home the winner from 12 yds.

7. Stanley inflicted Wrexham's first defeat, Paul Mullin began the rout stabbing in a rebound from Doherty's 15-yard strike. Ian Craney curled his corner directly in; Gary Roberts seized on a Pejic lapse to make it 3-0. Cavanagh hit in a 20-yard free-kick; Roberts broke through to slot in.

8. The floodgates opened with two goals within a minute. Gareth Evans fouled Adam Le Fondre & Mark Robinson hit home. Le Fondre scored from a poor back-pass. Two Danny Williams' pile-drivers, either side of Le Fondre's 2nd, kept Wrexham in touch but Le Fondre hit two more.

9. Steve Evans' goal ensured Wrexham ended a run of three defeats. He rose highest to head Ferguson's cross past Wayne Brown. On-loan John McAliskey had two goal-bound shots cleared off the line. Tamika Mkandawire should have levelled, prodding wide of an unguarded goal.

10. Dale ended the Dragons unbeaten home record after McAliskey's header saw Llewellyn fire in a left-footer. Gary Jones's mazy run & cross set up Chris Dagnall to fire in. Ingham spilled Alan Goodall's shot & Dagnall finished. Llewellyn went close but 'Dale' held on for a deserved win

11. The Dragons continued to press the self-destruct button. John Daly headed in John Brackstone's corner, and then unmarked, hit home a close-range shot from Willie Boland's low left-wing cross. He completed his hat-trick with a looping header from Brackstone's left-wing free-kick.

Line-ups (positions 1–11) and subs used

No	1	2	3	4	5	6	7	8	9	10	11	subs used
1	Ingham	Spender	Wlliams D	Evans S	Lawrence	Done		Jones Ma	Roberts	Llewellyn	Ferguson	Oakes/Dixon
2	Ingham	Barnes	Wlliams D	Evans S	Lawrence	Done		Jones Ma	Roberts	Llewellyn	Ferguson	Bore/Toner
3	Ingham	Spender^	Wlliams D^	Evans S	Lawrence	Done^		Jones Ma	Roberts	Llewellyn	Crowell	Richards/Stirling
4	Ingham	Spender^	Valentine	Wlliams D	Evans S!	Pejic	Done^	Jones Ma	Roberts	Llewellyn	Crowell	M'ples/Brou'ton/H'royd
5	Ingham	Spender^	Valentine	Wlliams D^	Evans S	Pejic	Done^	Jones Ma	Roberts	Llewellyn	Crowell	Warhurst/Norville
6	Ingham	Roche	Valentine	Wlliams D	Evans S	Pejic	Done	Jones Ma	Roberts^	Llewellyn	Crowell	Caton/Ince/Brownlie
7	Ingham	Spender^	Valentine	Wlliams D	Evans S	Pejic	Done^	Jones Ma / Newby^	Roberts	Llewellyn / Ferguson	Crowell	Boco/Mangan/Brown
8	Jones Mi	Wms Mi / Vale'tine^	Wlliams D	Evans S	Pejic	W'ms Ma^	Jones Ma / Newby^	Roberts	Llewellyn	Ferguson	Crowell/Spender/Reed	Griffin/Bramble/Pr'lock
9	Ingham	Roche	Valentine	Wlliams D	Evans S	Crowell	Done^	Jones Ma	McAliskey	Llewellyn	Ferguson / Johnson	Ferrell/Webb
10	Ingham	Roche	Valentine	Wlliams D	Evans S	Crowell	Done^	Jones Ma	McAlisk'y^	Llewellyn	Ferguson / Mi/Nby	Moyo-Modise/Cooksey
11	Ingham	Spender^	Valentine	Wlliams D	Evans S	Crowell	Done^	Jones Ma	McAliskey	Llewellyn / Roche	Williams Mi/Newby	Bul'ck/Brown/Wams E

Match results

No	Date	Venue / Opponent	Att	Pos	Opp Pos	Pt	F-A	H-T	Scorers, Times, and Referees
12	14/10	H MK DONS	3,828	19	5	15	L 1-2	1-0	Roberts 20 / McLeod 46, O'Hanlon 77. Ref: U Rennie
13	22/10	A MANSFIELD	2,971	20	15	15	L 0-3	0-2	Barker 21, 36, Reet 69. Ref: A Penn
14	29/10	H BRISTOL ROV	3,803	19	17	18	W 2-0	1-0	Llewellyn 22, Craddock 90. Ref: R Booth
15	4/11	H MACCLESFIELD	3,568	18	24	19	D 0-0	0-0	Ref: E Ilderton
16	7/11	A BURY	2,506	18	8	19	L 0-1	0-1	Mattis 7. Ref: R Shoebridge
17	18/11	A NOTTS CO	4,416	19	6	19	L 1-2	0-1	Llewellyn 65 / Parkinson 37, Lee 60. Ref: R Lee
18	25/11	H LINCOLN	3,619	15	3	22	W 2-1	2-0	Jones Ma 22, Llewellyn 44 / Stallard 64. Ref: T Kettle
19	5/12	A TORQUAY	1,588	17	22	23	D 1-1	1-0	Smith 7 / Robertson 51. Ref: S Tanner
20	9/12	A BOSTON	1,706	18	22	23	L 0-4	0-1	Elding 22, 83, Broughton 48. Ref: D Whitestone
21	16/12	H WALSALL	4,270	19	1	24	D 1-1	0-1	Llewellyn 68 / Sam 27. Ref: C Webster
22	23/12	H DARLINGTON	3,401	18	13	27	W 1-0	1-0	Holloway 19 og. Ref: R Oliver
23	26/12	A ROCHDALE	2,837	18	22	28	D 2-2	0-0	McEvilly 48, Llewellyn 55 / Murray 63, Doolan 78. Ref: J Moss

Match reports

12 — MK Dons (H): The Dragons led when Neil Roberts forced the ball home following two blocked efforts, but the turning point came with Izale McLeod came on and within 38 seconds of the restart he'd levelled with a low shot. McLeod then turned provider, setting up Sean O'Hanlon to sweep home.

13 — Mansfield (A): The Stags eased their way to a comfortable win over the struggling Dragons. Matt Hamshaw put Richie Barker through to round Ingham and coolly slot home. He raced on to an Alan Sheehan pass to fire in. Llewellyn had a shot blocked by Muggleton, before Danny Reet volleyed in.

14 — Bristol Rov (H): Wrexham ended a run of 9 defeats in 10 games. Walker & Rigg went close for Rovers, but Llewellyn hit in a 25-yds shot. Dan Williams hit a post, but a two-footed Llewellyn tackle on Elliott (65) led to a red card. On-loan Tom Craddock sealed it with a solo strike from a tight angle.

15 — Macclesfield (H): Paul Ince earned the first point of his managerial career, but it was amazing how the game stayed goalless. Steve Evans missed a free header & Maheta Molango spurned a sitter from Ferguson's pass. A last-ditch tackle denied John Murphy & Martin Bullock hit the post with 10 mins left.

16 — Bury (A): Dwayne Mattis extended Bury's winning run to six games before he fired in after Andy Bishop's shot ricocheted back to him. Floodlight failure twice delayed the game. The Shakers started off the better, but Wrexham fought back after the break with Molango's goal ruled out for offside.

17 — Notts Co (A): Wrexham played much of the early football at County favoured a high-tempo game, pumping the ball forward to Jason Lee & Junior Mendes, who set-up Parkinson to fire into the net. David Pipe set up Lee from close in. Llewellyn headed in a Josh Johnson cross, but it proved in vain.

18 — Lincoln (H): A well-fought game saw Lee Roche put in Mark Jones from 30-yds and his shot deflected in off Lee Beevers. Steve Evans headed down a corner for Llewellyn to turn and fire in. An attempted clearance rebounded to Mark Stallard who hammered home, as the Imps fought back.

19 — Torquay (A): Two loan players lit up a night of wind and rain at Plainmoor. Kevin Smith headed home a rebound from 10-yds. The Gulls equalised when on-loan Sheffield United striker Jordan Robertson blasted in a 25-yds free-kick. Ugarte almost stole a win with a free-kick that went just wide.

20 — Boston (A): Cash-strapped Boston put their woes behind them. Anthony Elding stroked in Lee Canoville's cross from 6-yds. Steve Evans was sent off (23) for kicking Drewe Broughton, who side-footed in Tim Ryan's cross from 8-yds & drilled in from 16-yds. Elding glanced in Rowson's cross.

21 — Walsall (H): Richard Money's league leaders lead when Anthony Gerrard flicked on a corner for ex-Dragon Hector Sam to nod in. Llewellyn should have equalised when he shot over from 6-yds following a sliced clearance, but the Wales forward made no mistake when he fired in from 25-yards.

22 — Darlington (H): Injury-hit Wrexham condemned David Penney's side to a 5th defeat in a row. The Dragons lead when Darren Holloway turned Llewellyn's cross into his own net. David Stockdale's fine save denied Marc Williams, while Simon Johnson & Clark Keltie both had chances to equalise.

23 — Rochdale (A): After a dull first half Llewellyn set up Lee McEvilly to fire in low. Matt Gilks parried McEvilly's drive into the path of Llewellyn, who fired in after good control. Ingham missed a corner cross, giving Glenn Murray an easy header in. Slack defending at a corner let John Doolan head in.

Coca Cola League 2 Results 2006/07

No	Date		Att	Pos	Pt	F-A	H-T	Scorers, Times, and Referees
1	A	WYCOMBE 5/8	4,763	-	-	1-1	1-1	Mooney 6 — Ref: P Miller
2	H	GRIMSBY 8/8	5,180	6	4	3-0	2-0	Evans 16, Llewellyn 34, Done 68 — Ref: D Whitestone
3	H	PETERBORO 12/8	4,706	10	5	0-0	0-0	Ref: A Taylor
4	A	CHESTER 20/8	4,206	6	8	2-1	1-0	Roberts 42p, Jones Ma 52, Hand 81 — Ref: U Rennie
5	H	BARNET 26/8	4,304	7	9	1-1	1-0	Jones Ma 15, Kandol 62 — Ref: A Woolmer
6	H	SWINDON 9/9	5,257	6	12	2-1	0-1	Valentine 68p, Jones Ma 69, Brown 28 — Ref: S Mathieson
7	A	ACCRINGTON 13/9	2,689	9	12	0-5	0-1	Mullin 41, Craney 49, Roberts [52, 67], Cavanagh 55 — Ref: C Oliver
8	A	STOCKPORT 16/9	4,884	12	12	2-5	1-2	Williams D 43, 61; Robinson 24p, Le Fondre 24, 54 [85, 87] — Ref: R Olivier
9	H	HEREFORD 24/9	4,705	10	15	1-0	1-0	Evans S 28 — Ref: P Joslin
10	H	ROCHDALE 27/9	3,577	12	15	1-2	1-0	Llewellyn 12, Dagnall 48, 77 — Ref: S Bratt
11	A	HARTLEPOOL 30/9	4,452	15	15	0-3	0-2	Daly 20, 22, 68 — Ref: G Sutton

Line-ups (positions 1–11 and subs used; Wrexham first, opposition in italics):

1. WYCOMBE
Wrexham: Ingham, Wiliams D, Evans S, Valentine, Spender, Lawrence, Done, Jones Ma 32, Roberts, Llewellyn, Ferguson — subs: Newby/Williams Mi
Opposition: *Batista, Stockley, Martin, Antwi, Wili'mson, Grant*, Palmer, Bl'omfield, Betsy, Mooney, Easter^* — subs: *Oakes/Dixon*
Paul Lambert's side's dominant start saw Tommy Mooney slot in Chris Palmer's cross, but Ricardo Batista fluffed a clearance under Roberts' challenge, chased the ball to allow Jones to curl the ball 40-yds into an empty net. The Dragons had their share of possession.

2. GRIMSBY
Wrexham: Ingham, Spender, Wiliams D, Valentine, Lawrence, Done, Jones Ma*, Roberts, Llewellyn, Fe'guson*, Crowell — subs: **Johnson**
Opposition: *Barnes, McD'rmott, Whittle, Futcher, Newey, Rankin, Harkins, Bolland, Beagrie*, Reddy/*, Jones* — subs: *Bore/Toner*
Having seen a header cleared off the line early on Evans headed in Ferguson's cross. Ingham nearly gifted Grimsby an equaliser, but Llewellyn's long-range header from Ferguson's cross doubled the lead. A great run by Llewellyn led to Done firing in.

3. PETERBORO
Wrexham: Ingham, Spender^, Valentine, Wiliams D^, Evans S, Lawrence, Done^, Jones Ma, Roberts, Llewellyn, Crowell — subs: Wiliams Mi/Mkin/J'nson
Opposition: *Tyler, Newton, Arber, Plummer, Branston, Day^, Holden, Butcher, Crow*, Benjamin, Yeo* — subs: *Richards/Stirling*
Both sides kept their unbeaten records at a blustery Racecourse. The Dragons went closest when Llewellyn hit the bar & Roberts had a shot cleared off the line. Dean Holden & Richard Butcher went close for the Posh. Crowell almost won it late on when his free-kick hit the Posh bar

4. CHESTER
Wrexham: Ingham, Spender^, Valentine, Wiliams D, Evans S!, Pejic, Done^, Jones Ma, Roberts, Llewellyn, Crowell — subs: Newby/Williams Mi
Opposition: *Danby, Ravenhill!, W'stwood, Vaughan, Artell, Linwood, Martinez, Hand, Wilson, Blundell, Walters* — subs: *M'ples/Brou'ton/H'royd*
A lively game that saw Ravenhill sent off (25) for a rash challenge on Ingham. Wrexham with nine Welsh players led when Vaughan brought down Done for Roberts to net. Jones lobbed Danby; Steve Evans was dismissed for a 2nd caution (77); James Hand fired in as Chester rallied.

5. BARNET
Wrexham: Ingham, Spender^, Valentine, W'ams D^, Evans S, Pejic, Done^, Jones Ma, Roberts, Llewellyn, Crowell — subs: M'kin/Newby/Wi'ms Mi
Opposition: *Harrison, Hendon^, Charles, King, Gross, Cogan, Bailey, Sinclair, Puncheon, Kandol, Grazioli^* — subs: *Warhurst/Norville*
Tresor Kandol's close range header from Barry Cogan's cross saw the 'Bees' secure a point in an ill-tempered game that saw seven booked as the Dragons struggled to find any rhythm. Jones had put Wrexham ahead with a 20-yard strike, but Kandol & Grazioli went close to winning it

6. SWINDON
Wrexham: Ingham, Roche, Valentine, Wiliams D, Evans S, Pejic, Done, Jones Ma, Roberts*, Llewellyn, F'guson^ — subs: Newby/Crowell
Opposition: *Brezovan, Smith J, Williams, Nicholas, Con-Platt, Shakes*, Weston^, Evans, Roberts, Peacock* — subs: *Caton/Ince/Brownlie*
Denis Wise's side looked set for their 7th straight win when Paul Evans' 35-yard free-kick found the net as Ingham was caught napping. The Dragons hit back when Llewellyn was floored by Brezovan & Valentine fired in the penalty. Mark Jones drilled home the winner from 12 yds.

7. ACCRINGTON
Wrexham: Ingham, Dunbavin, Cavanagh, Williams, Pejic, Done^, Craney, Proctor, Todd^, Llewellyn, Mullin* — subs: Newby/Crowell
Opposition: *Edwards, Rich'dson, Doherty^, Craney, Proctor, Todd*, Roberts, Mulin** — subs: *Peacock …*
Stanley inflicted Wrexham's first defeat. Paul Mullin began the rout stabbing in a rebound from Doherty's 15-yard strike. Ian Craney curled his corner directly in; Gary Roberts seized on a Pejic lapse to make it 3-0. Cavanagh hit in a 20-yard free-kick; Roberts broke through to slot in.

8. STOCKPORT
Wrexham: Jones Mi, W'ams Mi, Vale'line^, Wiliams D, Evans S, Pejic, W'ms Ma*, Jones Ma, Newby*, Llewellyn, Ferguson — subs: Crowell/Spender/Reed
Opposition: *Ruddy, Williams, Owen, Raynes, Robinson, Poole*, Taylor, Briggs, Malcolm*, Le Fondre, Murray^* — subs: *Griffin/Bramble/Pr'lock*
The floodgates opened with two goals within a minute. Gareth Evans fouled Adam Le Fondre & Mark Robinson hit home. Le Fondre scored from a poor back-pass. Two Danny Williams' pile-drivers, either side of Le Fondre's 2nd, kept Wrexham in touch but Le Fondre hit two more.

9. HEREFORD
Wrexham: Ingham, Roche, Valentine, Wiliams D, Evans S, Crowell, Done^, Jones Ma, M'cAliskey, Llewellyn, Ferguson — subs: Ferrell/Webb
Opposition: *Brown, Travis, Beckwith, Rose^, Mk'dawire, Purdie, Jeannin, Giles, Sills, Fle'twood, Connell** — subs: *Johnson*
Steve Evans' goal ensured Wrexham ended a run of three defeats. He rose highest to head Ferguson's cross past Wayne Brown. On-loan John McAliskey had two goal-bound shots cleared off the line. Tamika Mkandawire should have levelled, prodding wide of an unguarded goal.

10. ROCHDALE
Wrexham: Ingham, Roche, Valentine, Wiliams D, Evans S, Crowell^, Done^, Jones Ma, M'cAlisk'y^, Llewellyn, Ferguson — subs: Moyo-Modise/Cooksey
Opposition: *Gilks, Brown, Stanton, Sharp, Goodall, Doolan^, Crooks, Jones, Barker*, Sako, Dagnall* — subs: *Mi/Nby*
Dale ended the Dragons unbeaten home record after McAliskey's header saw Llewellyn fire in a left-footer. Gary Jones's mazy run & cross set up Chris Dagnall to fire in. Ingham spilled Alan Goodall's shot & Dagnall finished. Llewellyn went close but 'Dale' held on for a deserved win

11. HARTLEPOOL
Wrexham: Ingham, K'Poulous, W'iams D, Valentine, Wiliams D, Crowell, Done^, Jones Ma, Liddle*, Llewellyn, Daly^ — subs: Williams Mi/Newby
Opposition: *Nelson, Clark, Bracks'te, Gibb, Boland, Robson, Porter*, Roche* — subs: *Bul'ck/Brown/W'ams E*
The Dragons continued to press the self-destruct button. John Daly headed in John Brackstone's corner, and then unmarked, hit home a close-range shot from Willie Boland's low left-wing cross. He completed his hat-trick with a looping header from Brackstone's left-wing free-kick.

No	Date	Att	Pos	Opp	Pt	F-A	H-T	Scorers, Times, and Referees	1	2	3	4	5	6	7	8	9	10	11	subs used
35	A BARNET 3/3	2,180	22	18	34	W 2-1	0-1	McEvilly 57, 60; Allen 27; Ref: R Lee	Ingham	Roche	W'ms Mi	Garrett	W'ams A	D' Pejic	Jones Ma	Whitley	McEvilly	Llewellyn	Roberts	Evans G
									Filtney	Hendon*	King	Yakubu	Gross	Puncheon Bailey	Sinclair	Graham*	Hatch	Allen^		H'thaler/Cogan/Viera
36	H Bury 9/3	7,030	22	19	35	D 1-1	1-1	McEvilly 33; Hurst 90; Ref: S Mathieson	Ruddy	Roche	Valentine	Garrett	Evans G	Pejic	Jones M*	Whitley	McEvilly	Llewellyn	Roberts	Williams Mi
									Warr'ton Scott	Challinor	Kempson	K'nedy T	Pugh	Baker^	K'nedy J	Buch'nan	Bishop	Hurst		Bedeau/Speight
37	A MK DONS 17/3	5,712	23	3	35	L 1-2	1-1	McEvilly 12; Andrews 38p, Platt 85; Ref: K Hill	Ingham	Roche!	W'ms Mi	Garrett*	W'ams D*	Pejic	Jones M*	Whitley	McEvilly	Spender	Roberts	Mackin/Evans G/J'son
									Harper	Edds*	O'Hanlon Diallo	Lewi'ton* McGov'n*	Smith G	Andrews	Dyer	McLeod	Platt	Knight/Hayes/Stirling		
38	A Bristol R 24/3	5,209	23	11	38	W 1-0	0-0	Whitley 87; Ref: S Olivier	W'ams A	Spender	W'ms Mi	W'iams D	Walker	Pejic	Jones M*	Whitley	McEvilly	Proctor^	Roberts	Done/Carvill
									Phillips	Lescott	Hinton	Oji	Ca'uthers Haldane	Campbell Disley	Igoe*	Nicholson Lambert*	Rigg/Walker			
39	H Mansfield 31/3	7,752	22	14	39	D 0-0	0-0	Ref: J Singh	W'iams A	Spender*	W'ms Mi	W'iams D	Walker	Pejic	Garrett	McEvilly	Proctor^	Roberts*	Roberts	Crvill/Jones Ma/Roche
									White	Mullins	Hjelde*	Baptiste	Jelleyman Hamshaw Hodge	Dawson^	Boulding^ Brown	Bulluck^	Gritton	Charlton/Sleath/Arnold		
40	A Macclesfield 7/4	4,142	22	21	39	L 0-2	0-1	McNeil 34, Murphy 62; Ref: G Salisbury	W'ms Mi	Spender*	Walker^	Edwards Hunt	Evans S	Pejic	Jones Ma Proctor^	McEvilly	Proctor^	Llewellyn^ Done	Done	W'ms Ma/E'ns S/J'son
									Lee	Regan	Morley	Scott	McIntyre	Murray	Miles	Bulluck^	McNeil^	Murphy		B'amin/Rankin/Holgate
41	H Notts Co 9/4	4,557	23	10	39	L 0-1	0-0	Spender 88 og; Ref: D Deadman	W'iams A	Spender	Pilkington Silk	Whitley	Evans S	Pejic	Jones Ma Proctor^	Walker	McEvilly	Llewellyn^ Done	Done	Johnson/Williams Ma
										Edwards Hunt			McCann Smith	Sommer Ross^	Dudfield^ Park'son^	Weston/Lee/N'Toya				
42	A Lincoln 14/4	4,279	22	5	42	W 3-0	2-0	Spender 18, Kerr 29 og, [McEvilly 52]; Ref: T Bates	W'iams A	Spender	Valentine	W'ams D*	Evans S	Pejic	Done^	Garrett	McEvilly	Llewellyn	Proctor*	Roberts/Mackin
									Marriott	Eaden	Beevers^	Mayo	Green	Amoo	Kerr	Holmes^	Stallard	Forrester^		M'gan/N'Gu'n/Mendes
43	H Torquay 21/4	6,057	22	24	45	W 1-0	0-0	Roberts 79; Ref: R Booth	W'iams A	Spender	Valentine	W'ams D^	Evans S	Pejic	Done^	Whitley	McEvilly	Llewellyn Proctor*	Roberts*	Roberts/Mackin
									Rayner	Andrews	Woods	Rob'tson Robinson Graham^	Hockey	Mansell Thorpe	Cooke	McPhee^				Reid/Dickson
44	A Shrewsbury 24/4	6,749	20	6	48	W 1-0	0-0	Proctor 79; Ref: A D'Urso	W'iams A	Spender	Valentine	W'iams D	Evans S	Pejic	Proctor	Whitley	McEvilly	Llewellyn	Roberts	Roberts
									Shearer	Jones L	Langm'ad Hope^	Tierney	Davies	Edwards Dru'mond Ashton	Cooke^	Asamoah Symes/Fortune-West				
45	A Walsall 28/4	7,075	21	1	48	L 0-1	0-0	Demontagnac 61; Ref: C Penton	W'iams A	Spender	Valentine	W'iams D	Evans S	Pejic	Proctor	Whitley	McEvilly*	Llewellyn Proctor*	Roberts*	Done/Carvill
									Ince	Bedeau*	Gerrard	Westwo'd Fox	Wright	Dobson	Keates	Dtagnac*	Benj'min^	Pead/Sam/Wrack		
46	H BOSTON 5/5	12,374	19	23	51	W 3-1	0-1	Valentine 56p, Llewellyn 87, [Proctor 90]; Green 39; Ref: M Halsey	W'iams A	Spender	Valentine	W'iams D	Evans S	Pejic	Done	Jones Ma	McEvilly*	Llewellyn	Proctor	Done/Carvill
									Marriott	Stevens	Cryan	Greaves	Clarke	Ellender	Galbraith* Cooksey	Farrell	Green	Maylett		Broighton Green
	Home 5,030																				
	Away 4,127																				
	Average 4,127																				

Match notes:

35 — Brian Carey's first win as manager after 11 games in charge lifted Wrexham out of the relegation zone. Oliver Allen gave Barnet the lead when he ran on to Hatch's pass to finish. Llewellyn set up McEvilly for a fine 25-yard strike & then crossed for his strike partner to loop in a header.

36 — The Dragons led when McEvilly thundered in a shot from six yards, but were reduced to nine-men after Llewellyn (51) & Valentine (60) were dismissed for dangerous tackles. However, they were denied a crucial win when Glynn Hurst fired in Dave Challinor's long throw for Bury.

37 — McEvilly fired the Dragons ahead from Roberts' square pass. Keith Andrews levelled with a penalty after Roche was cruelly judged to have handled & sent off. Clive Platt's late header won the points despite doubts it had crossed the line. Simon Spender replaced Ingham in goal.

38 — Relegation-threatened Wrexham gained a vital win at the Memorial Stadium. New loan signings Anthony Williams & Richard Walker proved solid & with the game drifting towards a draw, on-loan Jeff Whitley powered in a short-range header from Pejic's cross to kill off the 'Pirates'.

39 — Wrexham moved out of the relegation zone, if only on goal difference, after this stalemate. The 'Dragons' were lucky to escape a penalty when Mike Williams appeared to bring down Simon Brown. However, Jason White only received a yellow card for hauling down Matt Done late on.

40 — The 'Silkmen' took a giant stride towards FL survival & piled the pressure on a disappointing Wrexham. McEvilly twice headed inches over & Macc twice hit the bar before Matt McNeil broke the deadlock from John Miles' pass & John Murphy converted Carl Regan's pin-point cross.

41 — Wrexham fell back into the relegation zone after Spender turned in James Walker's cross to give the 'Magpies' an undeserved win. After a poor first-half, McEvilly headed against the bar & saw a 25-yard free-kick fly inches wide & Whitley's thunderous shot rebounded off the post.

42 — A rampant performance saw the 'Dragons' climb of the drop zone. Spender headed in from Done's cross for the opener; their first in 4 games. Danny Williams' flicked on a long throw that turned into his own goal by Scott Kerr. Lee McEvilly headed in Spender's right-wing cross.

43 — The 'Dragons' dominated the game, but found 'keeper Simon Rayner on superb form, but Neil Roberts tucked away Simon Spender's right-wing cross against already relegated 'Gulls'. Boston's win over Chester meant Wrexham needed victory to stay ahead of their relegation rivals.

44 — Wrexham went three points clear of the relegation battle with this vital win. Having weathered the 'Shrews' assault, the 'Dragons' looked to hit on the break. Proctor emerged from a scrum of players in the box to lash in a right-footed shot following Spender's cross from the right.

45 — This result put the 'Saddlers' top, but leaves Wrexham in a relegation dogfight, needing to avoid a defeat v Boston to guarantee their FL status. Williams blocked Mark Wright's shot, but Ishmel Demontagnac pounced on the loose ball to net. McEvilly went close earlier, but headed wide

46 — A second-half fightback secured Wrexham's Football League status & condemning Boston to the drop. Francis Green gave the 'Pilgrims hope, but Drewe Broughton fouled Danny Williams & Valentine hit in the penalty. A Llewellyn left-foot shot & Proctor header set off wild scenes.

Carling Cup

#			Att	Pos	F-A	W/L	H-T	Scorers, Times, and Referees
1	A	SHEFF WED	8,047 C:16	6	4-1	W	2-0	Roberts 33, Llew'yn 39, Done / *Whelan 79* [63 Jones 84] Ref: N Swarbrick
		23/8						

The Dragons outplayed their Championship hosts & led when Roberts converted Jones' knock-down & Llewellyn dispossessed Tommy Spurr to net. Done bundled home Jones' cross for a third; Glenn Whelan's screamer gave the Owls hope, but Jones cut inside to curl home a beauty.

Wrexham: 1 Ingham, 2 Spender*, 3 Valentine, 4 W'liams D, 5 W'ams Mi, 6 Pejic^, 7 Done, 8 Jones Ma, 9 Roberts, 10 Llewellyn, 11 Crowell* — subs used: M'kin/Roche/Evans G
Sheff Wed: Adamson, Simek, Bo'gherra, Bullen, Hills, Lunt, Whelan, McAlister, Spurr, Boden^ — subs: McClements/Bowman*

#			Att	Pos	F-A	W/L	H-T	Scorers, Times, and Referees
2	A	BIRMINGHAM	10,491 C:2	12	1-4	L	1-1	Llewellyn 29 / *Jerome 41, McSh'ry 102, 113, [Bendtner 117] Doyle* Ref: P Armstrong (After Extra Time)
		19/9						

Llewellyn put Wrexham ahead from Ferguson's corner. Jerome netted McSheffrey's deep cross to level. Ingham brought down DJ Campbell (66), but he missed the spot-kick. Extra-time saw McSheffrey smash in from 20-yds & fire in again before Bendtner rounded Ingham for four.

Wrexham: 1 Ingham, 2 Roche, 3 W'ams Mi, 4 W'liams D, 5 Evans S, 6 Crowell, 7 Johnson*, 8 Jones M^, 9 McAllis'y*, 10 Llewellyn, 11 Ferguson — subs used: Newby/Mackin/Evans G
Birmingham: Doyle, Kelly, Taylor M, Painter, Larsson, Muamba", Kilkenny, Jerome, McSh'ry, Forssell*, Jerome^ — subs: Camp'l/Bendtner/Dunn*

Johnstons Paint Trophy

#			Att	Pos	F-A	W/L	H-T	Scorers, Times, and Referees
1	H	ROCHDALE	1,209 2:12	19	1-1	L	0-1	Crowell 80 / *Dagnall 40* Ref: M Haywood
		17/10						

Chris Llewellyn's missed penalty proved crucial. Dale lead when Chris Dagnall's shot deflected in off on-loan Craig Morgan. Matt Gilks was lucky when he clearly dropped a cross over the line before Crowell levelled with a deflected shot, but Dagnall hit in the winning penalty.

Wrexham: 1 Ingham, 2 Valentine, 3 W'ams Mi, 4 W'liams D, 5 Evans S, 6 Morgan, 7 Done, 8 Jones Ma, 9 Johnson*, 10 Llewellyn, 11 Crowell — subs used: Newby
Rochdale: Gilks, Ramsden, B'ardman, Sharp, Goodall, Doolan, Jones, Crooks, Modise^, Dagnall, Barker — subs: Cooksey/Sako*

FA Cup

#			Att	Pos	F-A	W/L	H-T	Scorers, Times, and Referees
1	H	STEVENAGE	2,863 N:13	18	1-0	W	1-0	Williams D 40 Ref: M Haywood
		11/11						

Steve Morison almost headed Stevenage into an early lead before Wrexham took control. Boro failed to clear a corner, and Evans' cross saw Danny Williams direct this header into the top corner. Evans & Smith both went close, while Boro's Morison & Dobson both missed chances.

Wrexham: 1 Ingham, 2 Roche, 3 W'ams Mi, 4 W'liams D, 5 Evans S, 6 Pejic, 7 Done, 8 Jones Ma, 9 Molango*, 10 Smith*, 11 Ferg'son^ — subs used: Williams Ma/Mackin
Stevenage: Julian, Fuller, Gaia, Henry, Nutter, Nurse, Miller, Beard, Binns*, Boyd, Morison — subs: Dobson/Oliver*

#			Att	Pos	F-A	W/L	H-T	Scorers, Times, and Referees
2	A	SCUNTHORPE	5,054 L1:2	15	2-0	W	0-0	Jones Ma 49, Smith 66 Ref: K Friend
		2/12						

Andy Keogh went closest before the Dragons took a deserved lead when Mark Jones drilled home from 30-yds, & set up Wrexham to become only the 2nd team to win at Glanford Park this season. Kevin Smith hooked in before Keogh's header was ruled out for offside.

Wrexham: 1 Ingham, 2 Roche, 3 W'ams Mi, 4 W'liams D, 5 Evans S, 6 Pejic, 7 Johnson^, 8 Jones Ma, 9 Smith*, 10 Llewellyn, 11 Ferguson — subs used: McEvilly/Ugarte
Scunthorpe: Murphy, Byrne, Crosby, Foster, Hinds^, Taylor, Sparrow, B'aclough, Morris, Sharp, Keogh — subs: Torpey/Williams*

#			Att	Pos	F-A	W/L	H-T	Scorers, Times, and Referees
3	A	DERBY	15,609 Ch:2	18	1-3	L	0-1	McEvilly 61 / *Lupoli 32, 56, 85* Ref: R Beeby
		6/1						

Arturo Lupoli's left foot shot from Morten Bisgaard's fine pass fired the Rams ahead. Bisgaard's inswinging corner saw Lupoli's bullet header double the lead. McEvilly seized on Rob Malcolm's dreadful backpass to net with ease. Lupoli reacted quickest to Howard's header off the bar

Wrexham: 1 Ingham, 2 Valentine, 3 W'ams Mi, 4 W'liams D, 5 Evans S, 6 Pejic, 7 Crowell*, 8 Done, 9 McEvilly, 10 Llewellyn, 11 Ferguson — subs used: Johnson
Derby: Bywater, Edworthy, Moore, J'hnson, M.Camara, Bisgaard, Malcolm^, Oakley*, Howard, Lupoli, Jones — subs: Smith*/Barnes/P.solido*

Welsh Premier Cup

#			Att	Pos	F-A	W/L	H-T	Scorers, Times, and Referees
Q	A	NEWPORT	733 CS:8	23	1-2	L	0-0	Carvill 51 / *Bowen 53p, Hughes 56*
		28/2						

Rain lashed Spytty Park saw Carvill race onto Mackin's long kick to fire past Ovendale. Roche pulled back Charlie Griffin & Jason Bowen hit in the penalty. Craig Hughes rose to head in a Steve Jenkins cross. Lee McEvilly mis-kicked to waste a chance to send the tie into extra time.

Wrexham: 1 Jones Mi, 2 Roche, 3 Valentine, 4 Mackin, 5 W'ams Mi, 6 Pejic, 7 Jones Ma, 8 Done, 9 McEvilly, 10 Carvill, 11 Whitley — subs used: Reed
Newport: Ovendale, Jenkins, Searle, Collier, Brough, Edwards, Bowen, Darner, Griffin, Hughes, Evans — subs: Hillier*

Key:

!	sent-off!
*	first substitution
^	second substitution
'	third substitution

Wrexham players in bold are making their debuts
Substitutes are made in order shown.
Scores in bold indicate Wrexham's biggest league win and heaviest defeat (both home and away)
Attendances in bold indicate Wrexham's biggest and smallest attendances (both home and away)

Reserves Review 2006-07
A Review of the Pontin's Holiday League Season 2006-07

A review of the 2006/07 Pontin's Holidays League season could almost begin with the same opening paragraph to that which appeared in last season's yearbook for 2005/06. For like twelve months previously the season can be split once again into three distinct parts - a good start, a miserable middle, and a good run-in at the end of the campaign.

The campaign began with a 2-0 defeat by a strong Manchester City side at Sport City, next door to their impressive City of Manchester Stadium at Eastlands. But two successive wins, followed by two successive draws, saw Joey Jones' side occupy a comfortable position in the top half of the table within striking distance of leaders Oldham Athletic, who were held to a goalless draw at Boundary Park in the first of the two drawn games.

With Jamie Reed once again amongst the goals with a brace in a 3-1 victory over Blackpool in the first Globe Way game of the season the 'Dragons' went into the first mini derby of the season against Chester City a week later in confident mood. And the confidence was justified as a solitary Levi Mackin strike earned the 'Dragons' a second successive home victory.

After the entertaining goalless draw at Oldham already mentioned, Accrington Stanley visited Globe Way, the home of Buckley Town, and showed why they are fast becoming our 'bogey' side by coming back from two goals down at half time to salvage a point in a 2-2 draw. The game saw Jon Newby's only goal in a Wrexham shirt - though he did manage to find the Globe Way net later in the season... in a 3-1 victory for Rochdale!

Then came the miserable middle part of the season as six successive defeats followed, including a painful defeat at Deepdale when the 'Dragons' led until the final minute of the game before two quick-fire goals gave Preston North End all three points in dramatic fashion.

The turning point was the return derby at the Deva Stadium on the last day of January, when Andy Fleming's second half goal clinched a memorable double, although the broken leg suffered by young striker Alex Darlington late in the game overshadowed the victory.

Defeat followed in the next game at Accrington despite Jamie Reed's goal after just 67 seconds, but that was the springboard for a run of four wins and two draws in the next six games. Bury were beaten 2-1 at Radcliffe Borough's Stainton Park ground, Oldham were held to a goalless draw for the second time at Globe Way, before a scintillating second half display turned a 1-1 half time score against Preston into a 4-2 victory aided by three spectacular goals scored by Matty Done, Levi Mackin and Josh Johnson. The performances of Johnson were a feature of the second half of the season, the

Trinidadian winger starting to look like he'd finally come to terms with the playing styles and conditions, and looked a real threat down the right hand side.

Jamie Reed notched his sixth and seventh goals of the season in a hard-fought 2-1 win at Rochdale that saw the return to action of Ryan Valentine and Steve Evans after their lengthy suspensions, and young defender Gareth Evans receiving several stitches to a nasty facial injury that ended his season prematurely.

A rare victory at this level over Tranmere Rovers followed thanks to another Reed goal before the season came to its conclusion with home and away games against Carlisle United, Mike Carvill netting in both, though the 'Dragons' only had one point from a 1-1 home draw to show for his efforts.

Results-wise the season saw a vast improvement on 2005/06 and the likes of John Hunt, Lee Jones, Chris Marriott, Wes Baynes and Andy Fleming will all have benefited greatly from their increased exposure at this level, Fleming even earning his Football League debut as an early substitute in the 1-1 draw at Darlington in January. So, as well as the obvious highlight of a double over arch rivals Chester City, there are many other positives to be taken out of the campaign. Hopefully there will be more in 2007/08!

Pontins League Division One West

		P	W	D	L	F	A	W	Pts
1	Oldham Athletic	20	10	7	3	39	18	+21	37
2	Preston NE	20	11	2	7	48	32	+16	35
3	Bury	20	10	5	5	43	32	+11	35
4	Accrington Stanley	20	9	3	8	38	36	+2	30
5	Tranmere Rovrs	20	9	2	9	30	31	-1	29
6	Blackpool	20	9	1	10	32	34	-2	28
7	Manchester City	20	7	5	8	26	32	-6	26
8	Rochdale	20	8	1	11	32	39	-7	25
9	**Wrexham**	**20**	**7**	**4**	**9**	**21**	**33**	**-12**	**25**
10	Carlisle United	20	6	4	10	28	38	-10	22
11	Chester City	20	6	2	12	21	33	-12	20

Pontin's Holidays League Division One (West) 2006-2007

Date	Opponent	V	Res	1	2	3	4	5	6	7	8	9	10	11	Sub	Sub	Sub	Sub	Sub
AUGUST																			
15	Manchester City	A	0-2	Mi Jones	Roche	Marriott	Pejic	G Evans	Mackin	Johnson	Baynes	Newby	Reed	Taylor	Braisdell(3)	Whelan	Darlington(10)	L Jones	Stew...
21	Blackpool	H	3-1	Mi Jones	Roche	Taylor	G Evans	Ml Williams	Mackin	Johnson	Ma Williams[1]	Reed[1]	Newby	Braisdell	Fleming(8)	Whelan	Marriott(5)	Baynes(10)	L Jon...
28	Chester City	H	1-0	Mi Jones	Roche	Taylor	L Jones	G Evans	Mackin[1]	Johnson	Ma Williams	Newby	Reed	Braisdell	Fleming	Maxwell	Darlington	P Williams	Matisc...
SEPTEMBER																			
6	Oldham Athletic	A	0-0	Mi Jones	Roche	Marriott	Ml Williams	G Evans	Mackin	Johnson	Ferguson	Reed	Newby	Taylor	Stewart(9)	Whelan	Brady(8)	L Jones	Flemin...
20	Accrington Stanley	H	2-2	D Evans	Spender	Marriott	L Jones	G Evans	Mackin	Newby[1]	Fleming	Reed[1]	Ma Williams	Taylor	Braisdell(3)	Matischok	A Hughes	Brady	
OCTOBER																			
9	Bury	H	0-3	Whelan	Spender	Marriott	G Evans	D Williams	Hughes	Johnson	Fleming	Newby	Ma Williams	Taylor	Baynes	Maxwell	L Jones	Brady	Darlingto...
18	Preston North End	A	1-2	Whelan	Spender	Marriott	L Jones	G Evans	Mackin[1]	Newby	Ma Williams	Reed	Darlington	Hughes	Brady	Baynes	Stewart(11)	Price	P Willi...
NOVEMBER																			
DECEMBER																			
15	Tranmere Rovers	A	0-2	Mi Jones	Spender	Taylor	Marriott	L Jones	Fleming	Mackin	Crowell	Ma Williams	Ugarte	Johnson	Baynes	Maxwell	Hughes	Darlington(10)	Price...
19	Manchester City	H	0-2	Mi Jones	Spender	Marriott	G Evans	L Jones	Fleming	Baynes	Crowell	McEvilly	Darlington	Taylor	P Williams(9)	Maxwell	Vickers(3)	Hunt(11)	Pric...
JANUARY																			
17	Rochdale	H	1-3	Mi Jones	Price	Hunt	Vickers	L Jones	Mackin	Baynes	Fleming	Reed	P Williams	Johnson[1]	Backhouse(10)	Whelan	Matischok		
24	Blackpool	A	0-4	Mi Jones	Price	Hunt	L Jones	Ml Williams	Mackin	Baynes	Fleming	Reed	Darlington	Johnson	P Williams	Maxwell	Backhouse	Matischok	Vicke...
31	Chester City	A	1-0	Mi Jones	Spender	Hunt	L Jones	G Evans	Mackin	Johnson	Fleming[1]	Roberts	Reed	Ml Williams	Baynes(14)	Whelan	Darlington(9)	P Williams(8)	Vicke...
FEBRUARY																			
21	Accrington Stanley	A	1-3	Mi Jones	Baynes	Hunt	L Jones	Marriott	Whitley	Johnson	Cummins	Ma Williams	Reed[1]	Done	Mead(6)	Whelan	P Williams	Stewart(10)	Smit...
MARCH																			
7	Bury	A	2-1	Mi Jones	Price	Marriott	Spender	Taylor	Mackin	Johnson[1]	Ma Williams	Reed[1]	Carvill	Done	Fleming(10)	Whelan	Baynes(9)	Hunt(11)	Stew...
12	Oldham Athletic	H	0-0	Mi Jones	Price	Taylor	Spender	Ml Williams	Mackin	Fleming	Baynes	Ma Williams	Johnsn	Done	Reed(8)	Maxwell	Hunt	Marriott	P Willi...
19	Preston North End	H	4-2	Mi Jones	Baynes	Taylor	Marriott	G Evans	Mackin[1]	Carvill[1]	Fleming	Ma Williams	Johnson[1]	Done[1]	Reed	Whelan	P Williams	Stewart	Hun...
APRIL																			
4	Rochdale	A	2-1	Maxwell	Valentine	Marriott	G Evans	S Evans	Fleming	Johnson	Mackin	Reed[2]	Ma Williams	Taylor	Stewart	L Jones(4)	Price		
11	Tranmere Rovers	H	1-0	Mi Jones	Price	Taylor	Baynes	Ml Williams	Fleming	Johnson	D Williams	Reed[1]	Ma Williams	Carvill	Marriott(8)	Whelan	Stewart(10)	L Jones(3)	Prio...
16	Carlisle United	H	1-1	Mi Jones	Price	Taylor	Roche	Ml Williams	Mackin	Johnson	Garrett	Reed	Ma Williams	Carvill[1]	Fleming(8)	Whelan(1)	Baynes	Marriott	Stewa...
25	Carlisle United	A	1-4	Mi Jones	Price	Taylor	Roche	Ml Williams	Garrett	Johnson	Mackin	Reed	Ma Williams	Carvill[1]	Fleming(9)	Baynes(2)	Maxwell	Marriott	Stewa...

-DENOTES OWN GOAL

Youth Review 2006-07

A Review of the Puma Youth Alliance North West Conference: Group B 2006-07

It's been a season of change at youth level with the sacking of Denis Smith back in January seeing Steve Weaver move up from Centre of Excellence Manager to assist new boss Brian Carey with first team affairs. Brian's subsequent confirmation as manager at the end of the season also saw Steve's position reaffirmed.

This all meant that back in January Steve Cooper, who had been Assistant to Steve, stepped into the vacated shoes to oversee youth development at the club. While this carries responsibility for all the age levels in the Centre of Excellence system it also meant looking after the Under-18 side in Puma Youth Alliance matches alongside Joey Jones and George McGowan.

The under-18s experienced an up-and-down season results-wise. Having started the campaign with a four-game unbeaten run, which included a 2-1 home victory over reigning champions Oldham Athletic, they then embarked on a five-game winless run. This run included emphatic home defeats by Walsall (0-5) and Tranmere Rovers (0-3) on successive September weekends.

A 2-2 draw with Stockport County at Colliers Park stopped the rot, and began a three-game unbeaten run that included impressive wins at Mansfield Town (3-2) in the first round of the Puma League Cup and Port Vale (2-1). Those wins came in November and the young Dragons had to wait until 10th March 10 to next taste success due to an eight game sequence that yielded just two draws against rivals Chester City. Progress in the two cup competitions also ended during this spell, with Port Vale gaining revenge for their 2-1 League defeat a month earlier with a 1-0 home success in the second round of the Puma League Cup, and Carlisle United winning a stormy FA Youth Cup-tie at the Racecourse with the only goal of the game.

But once that poor sequence was broken - with a superb 3-0 victory against Walsall in an 'away' game played at Colliers Park - the final six games of the season brought four wins, one draw, and just one defeat. Wigan Athletic were beaten 3-1, Accrington Stanley 4-0 (our only success against them at any level during the season!) and Preston North End 2-1 in the final game.

Progress on the pitch is difficult to gauge from one season to the next at Youth level because of the movement of players through the age groups. But the incredible success of the club's younger age groups - week after week it seems they enjoy a successful series of games against their opponents - and the number of players that has gained international recognition over the course of the season certainly bodes for good times ahead.

Defender Kai Edwards and striker Matthew Hurdman began the season by representing Wales Schoolboys in the autumn series of SKY-televised Victory Shield internationals against England, Northern Ireland and Scotland, with Kai captaining the squad. And they both progressed to be included in Brian Flynn's Wales U17 squad for the Elite Round stage of qualifying for the 6th UEFA Under-17 Championships that were held in Belgium in the summer. Goalkeeper Chris Maxwell and defender Jamie Price were also in the squad for a series of matches against hosts Turkey, The Netherlands and Belarus in March, but three defeats meant elimination at the final hurdle and no place in the finals.

Chris also represented Wales at Under-19 level alongside Neil Taylor, Alex Darlington and Marc Williams in a UEFA Under-19 Championships qualifying tournament in Luxembourg against the hosts, the Czech Republic and Turkey. Marc netted in the defeat by Turkey as qualification again evaded Brian Flynn's side.

And whilst most of our international recognition is inevitably focussed on Wales we mustn't forget that Vince Whelan also made the Republic of Ireland squad for an Under-18 international against The Netherlands in Dublin in February.

Puma Youth Alliance North West Conference - Group B

		P	W	D	L	F	A	W	Pts
1	Walsall U18	23	13	4	6	40	24	+16	43
2	Chester City U18	23	12	6	5	40	17	+23	42
3	Tranmere Rovers U18	23	13	3	7	35	25	+10	42
4	Stockport County U18	23	12	4	7	50	38	+12	40
5	Port Vale U18	23	11	2	10	40	35	+5	35
6	Shrewsbury Town U18	23	8	4	11	29	43	-14	28
7	**Wrexham U18**	**22**	**6**	**5**	**11**	**27**	**42**	**-15**	**23**
8	Macclesfield Town U18	23	6	4	13	25	40	-15	22

Puma Youth Alliance - North West B 2006-2007

Date / Opponent		Res	1	2	3	4	5	6	7	8	9	10	11	Sub	Sub	Sub	Sub	Sub
AUGUST																		
12 Rochdale	H	1-0	Maxwell	Baynes	Hunt	L Jones	Marriott	Backhouse	P Williams	Fleming	Darlington¹	M Stewart¹	Taylor	S Smith(3)	Cronshaw(7)	Aby(6)		
19 Blackpool	A	1-1	Whelan	Smith	Hunt	L Jones	Marriott	Baynes	Aby	Fleming	Darlington	M Stewart¹	Taylor¹	J Jones(7)	Matischok(3)			
SEPTEMBER																		
2 Oldham Athletic	H	2-1	Maxwell	Smith	Hunt	L Jones	Marriott	Matischok	Cronshaw	Fleming	M Stewart¹	Darlington	Taylor¹	Aby(7)	Whelan	Price(2)		
9 Carlisle United	A	1-1	Whelan	Price	Hunt	L Jones	Marriott	Matischok	P Williams	Fleming	M Stewart¹	Darlington	Taylor	Aby(11)	S Smith(7)	Backhouse(6)		
16 Bury	A	1-3	Whelan	Smith	Hunt	L Jones	Marriott	Backhouse	P Williams¹	Fleming	M Stewart	Darlington	Matischok	Hughes(3)	Aby(6)			
23 Walsall	H	0-5	Whelan	Smith	Marriott	Vickers	L Jones	Matischok	P Williams	Fleming	M Stewart	Darlington	Taylor	Hunt(5)	Maxwell(1)			
30 Tranmere Rovers	H	0-3	Maxwell	Price	Marriott	L Jones	Vickers	Baynes	P Williams	Fleming	M Stewart	Darlington	Taylor	Matischok(5)	Aby(6)			
OCTOBER																		
21 Macclesfield Town	A	0-1	Maxwell	Baynes	Hunt	Vickers	Price	Backhouse	M Stewart	Fleming	P Williams	Boswell	Darlington	Marriott(10)	L Jones(9)	Matischok(6)		
28 Stockport County	H	2-2	Whelan	Price	Hunt	Marriott	L Jones	Fleming	Baynes	Matischok	Darlington²	M Stewart	Taylor	P Williams	Maxwell	Backhouse	Smith(2)	Aby
NOVEMBER																		
1 Carlisle United (FAYC1)	H	0-1	Whelan	Price	Hunt	L Jones	Marriott	Matischok	Baynes¹	P Williams	Cronshaw	M Stewart	Smith	Backhouse(11)	S Williams	Vickers	Aby(3)	Llwyd
4 Port Vale	A	2-1	Whelan	Price	Hunt	L Jones	Marriott	P Williams	Baynes¹	Fleming	M Stewart	Cronshaw	Smith¹	Backhouse(6)	Aby(11)			
10 Mansfield Town (PC1)	A	3-2	Whelan	Price	Hunt	L Jones	Marriott	Backhouse	Baynes¹	Matischok	Darlington¹	Fleming	Taylor¹	P Williams(8)	Maxwell(1)	Vickers(2)		
18 Shrewsbury Town	H	0-2	Maxwell	Price	Hunt	L Jones	Marriott	P Williams	Baynes	Fleming	Darlington	M Stewart	Taylor	Matischok(6)	Vickers(4)	Cronshaw(10)		
DECEMBER																		
2 Port Vale (PC2)	H	0-1	Maxwell	Price	Hunt	Vickers	Marriott	Matischok	Baynes	Backhouse	Darlington	Fleming	Taylor	M Stewart(3)	Cronshaw(6)			
16 Tranmere Rovers	A	1-3	Maxwell	Price	Marriott	Vickers	L Jones	P Williams	Baynes	Matischok	Darlington¹	Fleming	Taylor	Hunt(11)	Whelan	Backhouse(8)	Aby	Smith
JANUARY																		
6 Port Vale	H	2-4	Maxwell	Edwards	Hunt	Vickers	L Jones	Cronshaw¹	P Williams	Fleming	Baynes	M Stewart¹	Darlington	Price(3)	Whelan	Backhouse(8)		
20 Stockport County	A	1-4	Whelan	Price	Hunt	Edwards	L Jones	Matischok	P Williams	Fleming	Smith	Baynes	Cronshaw¹	Backhouse(7)	Aby(9)			
27 Chester City	H	0-0	Maxwell	Edwards	Hunt	L Jones	Vickers	P Williams	Smith	Baynes	Darlington	Cronshaw	Taylor	Aby(10)	Matischok(11)	Whelan	Price	
FEBRUARY																		
3 Chester City	A	1-1	Whelan	Price	Marriott	L Jones	Vickers	Hunt	Smith	P Williams	Baynes	Cronshaw	Matischok¹	Aby(2)	Edwards(7)	Hurdman(11)		
24 Shrewsbury Town	A	1-3	Whelan	Price	Marriott	L Jones	Vickers	Hunt	Smith	P Williams	Baynes	M Stewart	Hurdman¹	Edwards(2)	Cronshaw(6)	Maxwell		
MARCH																		
10 Walsall	A	3-0#	Maxwell	Price¹	Hunt	Edwards	Marriott¹	P Williams	G Stewart	Baynes	Cronshaw	M Stewart²	Taylor¹	Backhouse(6)	Smith(6)	Hurdman(9)		
31 Wigan Athletic	A	3-1	Whelan	Price	Hunt	L Jones	Marriott	P Williams	Baynes	Fleming	Cronshaw	M Stewart¹	Taylor¹	Matischok(8)	Head(10)	Backhouse	Hurdman	Edwards
APRIL																		
7 Accrington Stanley	H	4-0	Whelan	Price	Marriott	L Jones	Edwards¹	Hunt	Baynes	Cronshaw	Head¹	M Stewart¹	Taylor¹	Matischok(3)	Backhouse(11	Hurdman(10)	Smith	Maxwell
14 Burnley	A	1-4	Maxwell	Price	Marriott	L Jones	Edwards	P Williams	Baynes	Fleming	Cronshaw	M Stewart¹	Taylor¹	Hunt(4)	Matischok(6)	Backhouse(6)	Hunt	Whelan
21 Macclesfield Town	H	0-2	Whelan	Stroylous	Hunt	Marriott	Edwards	Matischok	Baynes	Fleming	Cronshaw	M Stewart	Taylor	Backhouse	Maxwell	P Williams	L Jones	Head
MAY																		
2 Preston North End	H	2-1	Maxwell	Price	Hunt	L Jones	Marriott	Backhouse	Baynes	P Williams	Fleming	Stewart	Taylor	Head(3)	Matischok(9)	Whelan		

# denotes game played at Colliers Park

Wrexham FC Youth Team Squad 2007-08

Back row L-R: Mark Morris (Centre of Excellence Coach), Jack Jones, Jamie Price, Kai Edwards, Chris Maxwell, Vinny Whelan, Luke Carden, Lee Jones, Dan Hughes, Stuart Webber (Centre of Excellence Head of Recruitment).

Middle row L-R: Michael Cronshaw, Obi Anoruo, Paul Williams, Joey Jones (Centre of Excellence Coach), Steve Cooper (Centre of Excellence Head of Youth), Maty Hurdman, Rob Pearson, Mark Head.

Front row L-R: Johnny Hunt, George Stewart, Mark Stuart, Tom Matischok, Chris Marriott.

A Warm Welcome to Silvio Spann

Having won over 30 caps for Trinidad & Tobago, Silvio Spann has earned a reputation for his hard work and stamina, and is said to: 'Ooze charisma, is calm on the ball, and is precise and unfussy in his movements, while blessed with a strong right foot'. Despite having had trials with both Sheffield United and Sunderland during the summer, he was finally snapped up by Wrexham FC in August 2007.

Silvio is a regular international player for Trinidad & Tobago, having won over thirty caps, including both legs against Bahrain that saw the Soca Warriors reach the World Cup finals for the first time ever. However, he was to miss out on the finals in Germany when, during the clubs preparations at Carden Park, he suffered a hamstring injury. However, Silvio hit the headlines for T&T in June 2007 in a Gold Cup match against El Salvador, when he scored a memorable 40-yard free kick. Trials with Sheffield United and Sunderland followed, before he finally found a club in the UK to show his wares at Wrexham. Let's hope we witness more goals like the one against El Salvador!

Silvio is the son of former Trinidad and Tobago midfield stand-out Leroy Spann, who currently coaches a youth football team, Roma, in the MAPLE league in Massachussetts. Described as being 'a good defensive midfielder, having a good first touch, and being able to shoot the ball very well', Spann had an unsuccessful trial with Sheffield Wednesday in 2006, before playing last season for W Connection in Trinidad with whom he won the league title.

Of his move to the Racecourse, Silvio stated: "I have to say W Connection are the best team in the whole of the Caribbean. It's only been together for only nine years and I have had a very good five years with the club, because I have travelled across the world playing football. But I want a move to Britain, because that's where it all happens. Any kid growing up wants and dreams of playing football in Britain, and I just want to start as soon as I can. I considered the move with my wife and we decided I should take my chances at Wrexham". At the moment it looks a good decision!

Name: Silvio Reinaldo Spann
Position: Midfielder
Birthplace: Couvo, Trinidad
Date of Birth: 21/08/81
Height: 5ft 9in
Weight: 10st 10lbs

Previous Clubs:
St Benedict's College; Vibe CT 105; W Connection; Doc's Khelwalaas (Trinidad) 2000; W Connection (Trinidad) 2001; A.C. Perugia (Italy) 2001; San Benedettesse Calcio (Italy) Jan 2002; W Connection (Trinidad) 2002; Dinamo Zagreb (Croatia) Apr 2004; Yokohama FC (Japan) Jan 2005; W Connection (Trinidad) 2006.

Honours:
33 Trinidad & Tobago international caps; CFU Club Champions 2007; First Citizens Cup winners medal 2004.